Colonial Records

of

Southern Maryland

*Trinity Parish and Court Records,
Charles County;*

*Christ Church Parish and Marriage Records,
Calvert County;*

*St. Andrew's and All Faith's Parishes,
St. Mary's County*

Compiled by
Elise Greenup Jourdan

HERITAGE BOOKS
2008

HERITAGE BOOKS
AN IMPRINT OF HERITAGE BOOKS, INC.

Books, CDs, and more—Worldwide

For our listing of thousands of titles see our website at
www.HeritageBooks.com

Published 2008 by
HERITAGE BOOKS, INC.
Publishing Division
100 Railroad Ave. #104
Westminster, Maryland 21157

Copyright © 1997 Elise Greenup Jourdan

All rights reserved. No part of this book may be reproduced or transmitted in any form or by any means, electronic or mechanical, including photocopying, recording or by any information storage and retrieval system without written permission from the author, except for the inclusion of brief quotations in a review.

International Standard Book Numbers
Paperbound: 978-1-58549-428-6
Clothbound: 978-0-7884-7680-8

Other Heritage Books by Elise Greenup Jourdan:

The Greenup Family

Abstracts of Charles County, Maryland Court and Land Records:
Volume 1: 1658-1666
Volume 2: 1665-1695
Volume 3: 1694-1722

Colonial Records of Southern Maryland:
Trinity Parish & Court Records, Charles County; Christ Church Parish & Marriage Records, Calvert County; St. Andrew's & All Faith's Parishes, St. Mary's County

Colonial Settlers of Prince George's County, Maryland

Early Families of Southern Maryland:
Volume 1 (Revised) and Volumes 2-10

Settlers of Colonial Calvert County, Maryland

Settlers of Colonial St. Mary's County, Maryland

The Land Records of Prince George's County, Maryland:
1702-1709
1710-1717
1717-1726
1733-1739
1739-1743

with Francis W. McIntosh

1840 to 1850 Federal Census: Tazewell County, Virginia

1860 Federal Census: Tazewell County, Virginia

1870 Federal Census: Tazewell County, Virginia

FOREWORD

This volume was done to consolidate the remaining records I was able to locate of Colonial births, marriages and deaths in Southern Maryland. Anne Arundel and Prince George's Counties' records have been published in *Prince George's County Index of Church Records 1686-1885, Volumes I & II,* and *Anne Arundel County Church Records of the 17th and 18th Centuries.*

The very early Charles County records included here were previously published in *Charles County Court and Land Records, Volumes I & II,* and are believed to be the records of Durham Parish. Records of St. Andrew's Parish have also been published in Volumes V-VII of the *Chronicles of St. Mary's* and the Catholic records of St. Mary's County in *Catholic Families of Southern Maryland,* Timothy J. O'Rourke. *Calvert County, Maryland, Family Records,* Mildred B. O'Brien, includes the Calvert County vital statistics.

I would like to thank Robert W. Barnes for checking original records of Trinity Parish and copying the Scharf Collection at the Maryland Historical Society. Two pages (113-B and 114-A) are missing from the original records of Trinity Parish.

Elise Greenup Jourdan
Knoxville, Tennessee
February 1997

CONTENTS

Trinity Parish, Charles County — Page 1
Special Collections, 1729-1797, Trinity Church Collection
Vestry Minutes and Accounts; microfilm MSA M258
[Checked with original records]

Charles County Court and Land Records — Page 22
From Libers C to I and P & Q 1665 - 1688

Christ Church Parish, Calvert County — Page 48
From Microfilm of Index to Registers of Births,
1688 -1847 Marriages and Deaths
Filmed at the Maryland Historical Society
Baltimore, MD

Calvert County Marriages — Page 85
From the Scharf Collection
Maryland Historical Society, Baltimore, MD

St. Andrew's Parish, St. Mary's County — Page 88
Births, Marriages and Deaths 1736 -1886
Copied 1907 by Miss L. H. Harrison
Filmed at the Maryland Historical Society
Baltimore, MD

All Faith's Parish, St. Mary's County — Page 140
Marriages and Births
Copied 1894 by L. H. Harrison
Microfilm WK.1342, Genealogical Society
Salt Lake City, Utah

Index — Page 142

Births, Marriages, and Deaths
of
TRINITY PARISH
Charles County, Maryland
1729 - 1797

Page 105-B
Brent, Robert and Mary Wharton; m. 6 May 1729
Brent, Mary; d/o Robert and Mary, b. 2 Sep 1731
Brent, Robert, s/o Robert and Mary, b. 6 May 1734
Brent, Jane, d/o Robert and Mary, b. 2 Jan 1736
Brent, George, s/o Robert and Mary, b. 3 May 1737
Brent, Susanna, d/o Robert and Mary, b. 2 Jan 1739
Brent, Elizabeth, d/o Robert and Mary, b. 4 Mar 1740
Brent, Nicholas, s/o Robert and Mary, b. 1 Nov 1741?
Brent, Francis, s/o Robert and Mary, b. 7 Jul 1745
Brent, George, d. 16 Dec 1745
Brent, Francis, d. 17 Dec 1745
Brent, Susanna, d. 4 Mar 1749
Brent, Elizabeth, d. 17 Oct 1740
Brent, Nicholas, d. 1 Aug 1741
Duffey, Patrick and Martha McHon, m. 27 Feb 1737
Duffey, Elizabeth, d/o Patrick and Martha, b. 23 Sep 1738
Duffey, Leonard, s/o Patrick and Martha, 3 Dec 1740
Duffey, Anne, d/o Patrick and Martha, b. 28 Dec 1742
Page 106-A
Duffey, Cassandra, d/o Patrick and Martha, b. 4 Aug 1744
Biggs, Sarah, d/o John and Ruth, b. 14 May 1735
Biggs, Elizabeth, d/o John and Ruth, b. 12 Jul 1737
Biggs, Priscilla, d/o John and Ruth, b. 18 Feb 1738
Biggs, Charity, d/o John and Ruth, b. 9 Jun 1741
Biggs, Elinor, d/o John and Ruth, b. 24 Jan 1745
Amory, John, s/o Sam'l and Mary, b. 21 Mar 1745/6
Hearben, Allen, s/o Elisha and Elizabeth, 5 Jan 1746
Hearben, Rachel, d/o Elisha and Elizabeth, 5 Mar 1747
Coale, James (waterman), d. 6 Oct 1748
Chunn, Chloe, d/o Benjamin and Rebekah, b. 4 Jan 1744

Chunn, Levi, s/o Benjamin and Rebekah, b. 23 Feb 1746
Dooley, John, s/o James and Elizabeth, b. 8 Jan 1739
Dooley, Thomas Read, s/o James and Elizabeth, b. 25 Nov 1740
Dooley, James, s/o James and Elizabeth, b. 20 Jan 1742
Dooley, Elizabeth, d/o James and Elizabeth, b. 4 Jul 1745
Page 106-B
Dooley, Elinor, d/o James and Elizabeth, b. 25 Dec 1747
Phillips, Zephaniah and Catherine Scott m. 8 Jan 1744
Phillips, Zephaniah, s/o Zephaniah and Catherine, b. 4 Dec 1745
Phillips, Elizabeth, d/o Zephaniah and Catherine, b. 8 Feb 1747
Higdon, Benjamin, s/o William and Jane, b. 11 Dec 4 Dec 1733
Higdon, William, s/o William and Jane, b. 21 Feb 1735
Higdon, Benedict Leonard, s/o William and Jane, b. 6 Aug 1738
Higdon, Ignatious, s/o William and Jane, b. 12 Aug 1740
Higdon, Susanna, d/o William and Jane, b. 25 Jun 1743
Higdon, Martha, d/o William and Jane, b 10 Nov 1745
Higdon, Clair, d/o William and Jane, b. 2 Feb 1748
Turner, Zephaniah, s/o Sam'l and Virlinda, b. 19 Sep 1737
Turner, Hezekiah, s/o Sam'l and Virlinda, b. 23 Jul 1739
Turner, Dorcas, d/o Sam'l and Virlinda, b. 21 Nov 1741
Turner, Deborah, d/o Sam'l and Virlinda, b. 25 Jan 1743/4
Turner, Martha, d/o Sam'l and Virlinda, b. 21 May 1748
Briscoe, Philip and Cassandra Chunn, m. 1 Nov 1748
Bryan, William, s/o William and Mary, b. 10 Jun 1749
Page 107-A
Dement, Elizabeth, d/o William and Mary, b. 20 May 1731
Dement, Mary, d/o William and Mary, b. 7 May 1733
Dement, Anne, d/o William and Mary, b. 15 Nov 1735
Dement, Benajah, s/o William and Mary, b. 17 Aug 1738
Dement, Jesse, s/o William and Mary, b. 10 Oct 1740
Dement, George, s/o William and Mary, b. 10 Jan 1742
Dement, Susanna, d/o William and Mary, b. 29 Mar 1745
Dement, Dorcus, d/o William and Mary, b. 1 Apr 1747
McHon, Virlinda, d/o William and Priscilla, b. 21 Mar 1740
McHon, Priscilla, d/o William and Priscilla, b. 12 Jan 1742
McHon, Elizabeth, d/o William and Priscilla, b. 17 Mar 1745
McHon, Lorana, d/o William and Priscilla, b. 9 Nov 1748

McHon, Chloe, d/o William and Priscilla, b. 9 Nov 1748
McHon, Robert, s/o William and Priscilla, d. 3 Sep 1745
Allen, Joseph and Susanna Davis, m. 2 Nov 1743
Allen, Pentheceelia, d/o Joseph and Susanna, b. 28 Apr 1745
Allen, Bartholomew, s/o Joseph and Susanna, b. 25 Jul 1747
Page 107-B
Davis, Joseph and Mary Barker, m. 2 Oct 1744
Davis, Solome, d/o Joseph and Mary, b. 28 Mar 1746
Davis, Notley, s/o Joseph and Mary, b. 9 Feb 1747
Smoot, Mary, d/o Thomas and Abigal, b. 17 May 1739
Smoot, Arthur, s/o Thomas and Abigal, 16 Aug 1742
Lewis, Henrietta Lewis Williams, d/o Thomas and Mary, b. 8 Jan 1743
Lewis, George Rogers Williams, s/o Thomas and Mary, b. 5 Jan 1746
McBride, John Duncan, s/o Mary McBride, b. 30 Mar 1745
McBride, Lazerus, s/o Mary McBride, b. 5 Aug 1748
Maddox, John, s/o James and Elizabeth, b. 29 May 1748
Leech, Rebekah, d/o Nefel? and Elizabeth, b. 26 Jul 1746
Murphey, Zephaniah, s/o Daniel and Mary, b. 20 Jan 1745
Saintclair, Thomas and Mary Huntington, m. 9 Jan 1748
Smoot, Margarite, d/o Thomas and Abigal, b. 13 Dec 1748
Page 108-A
Dent, John, s/o Hatch and Ann, b. 3 Dec 1729
Dent, Mary, d/o Hatch and Ann, b. 13 Apr 1732
Dent, Catherine, d/o Hatch and Ann, b. 4 Nov 1734
Dent, Ann, d/o Hatch and Ann, b. 7 May 1737
Dent, Lydia, d/o Hatch and Ann, b. 22 Dec 1739
Dent, Esther, d/o Hatch and Ann, b. 10 May 1742
Dent, Rhoda, d/o Hatch and Ann, b. 4 Nov 1744
Dent, Hezekiah, s/o Hatch and Ann, b. 2 Aug 1747
Dent, Hatch, s/o ?Hatch, b. 20 May 1751
Hall, Thomas Lant, s/o Ignatious and Mary, b. 12 Mar 1741/2
Hall, Rebekah, d/o Ignatious and Mary, b. 31 Jul 1746
Hall, Elinor, d/o Ignatious and Mary, b. 18 Sep 1748
Love, William and Elizabeth Scott, m. 17 Nov 1747
Love, Ann, d/o William and Elizabeth, 29 Nov 1748

Carico, Mary Ann, d/o Abel and Elisabeth, b. 4 Nov 1748
Carico, Abel, s/o Abel and Elisabeth, b. 21 Jan 1744
Page 108-B
Cooksey, Christian, d/o Justinian and Sarah, b. 9 Feb 1728
Cooksey, Justinian, s/o Justinian and Sarah, b. 8 May 1731
Cooksey, Samuel, s/o Justinian and Sarah, b. 16 Jul 1733
Cooksey, Mary, d/o Justinian and Sarah, b. 25 Sep 1735
Cooksey, John, s/o Justinian and Sarah, b. 21 Mar 1738
Cooksey, Sarah, d/o Justinian and Sarah, b. 21 Mar 1740
Cooksey, Elizabeth, d/o Justinian and Sarah, b. 8 Feb 1744
Cooksey, Susanna, d/o Justinian and Sarah, b. 2 Mar 1746
Waters, James, s/o James and Susanna, b. 8 Dec 1737
Waters, Ann, d/o James and Susanna, b. 6 Nov 1741
Waters, William, s/o James and Susanna, b. 15 Aug 1745
Cockram, Edward, s/o Nathan, Jr. and Sarah, b. 7 Jun 1748
Turner, Lydia, d/o Edward and Elinor, b. 13 Dec 1731
Turner, Samuel, s/o Edward and Elinor, b. 7 Oct 1733
Turner, William, s/o Edward and Elinor, b. 14 Dec 1737
Page 109-A
Turner, Randal, s/o Edward and Elinor, b. 20 Sep 1739
Turner, Joshua, s/o Edward and Elinor, b. 14 Jul 1741
Turner, Mary, d/o Edward and Elinor, b. 9 May 1743
Turner, Charles, s/o Edward and Elinor, b. 21 Apr 1745
Turner, Joseph, s/o Edward and Elinor, b. 1 Mar 1746/7
Turner, Elizabeth, d/o Edward and Elinor, b. 7 Nov 1748
Turner, John, s/o Edward and Elinor, b. 11 Feb 1729; d. 5 Sep 1743
Turner, Edward, s/o Edward and Elinor, b. 24 Aug 1735; d. 5 Sep 1743
Seems, Francis and Lucretia Chapman, m. 14 Jan 1733
Seems, Elizabeth, d/o Francis and Lucretia, b. 24 Oct 1734
Seems, Jane, d/o Francis and Lucretia, b. 28 Jun 1736
Seems, Joseph, s/o Francis and Lucretia, b. 3 Mar 1738/9
Seems, Marmaduke, s/o Francis and Lucretia, 23 May 1741
Seems, Chloe, d/o Francis and Lucretia, b. 2 Oct 1743
Seems, Ignatius, s/o Francis and Lucretia, b. 5 Sep 1745
Seems, Francis, s/o Francis and Lucretia, b. 28 Oct 1747

Page 109-B
Davis, Luke and Ann Hunt, m. 26 Feb 1737/8
Davis, Mary, d/o Luke and Ann, b. 25 Nov 1738
Davis, Elizabeth, d/o Luke and Ann, b. 26 Oct 1740
Davis, Priscilla, d/o Luke and Ann, b. 20 Dec 1742
Davis, Cornelious, s/o Luke and Ann, b. 7 Dec 1744
Davis, Barton, s/o Luke and Ann, b. 6 Dec 1746
Farrand, John and Mary Stonestreet, m. 2 May 1743
Farrand, Thomas, s/o John and Mary, b. 12 Jun 1744
Farrand, Catherine, d/o John and Mary, b. 8 Oct 1746
Farrand, John, d/o John and Mary, b. 6 Mar 1748
Stonestreet, Thomasen, d/o Thomas and Mary, b. 2 Jun 1741
Ching, John and Mary Farr, m. 9 Jul 1738
Ching, Elinor, d/o John and Mary, b. 15 May 1739
Ching, John, s/o John and Mary, b. 12 Oct 1745
Ching, Mary, d/o John and Mary, b. 24 Jun 1748
Lewis, Joseph, s/o Thomas and Mary, b. 3 Dec 1748

Page 110-A
Chunn, Samuel and Susanna Love, m. 20 Jan 1731
Chunn, Cassandra, d/o Samuel and Susanna, b. 26 Nov 1732
Chunn, Aquila, s/o Samuel and Susanna, b. 15 Mar 1734
Chunn, Mary, d/o Samuel and Susanna, b. 11 May 1737
Chunn, Mersilva, d/o Samuel and Susanna, b. 8 Jul 1739
Chunn, Elizabeth, d/o Samuel and Susanna, b. 26 Jul 1741
Chunn, Mersilva, d/o Samuel and Susanna, d. 18 May 1743
Chunn, Samuel, s/o Samuel and Susanna, b. 29 Jun 1744
Chunn, Elizabeth, d/o Samuel and Susanna, d. 2 Sep 1744
Chunn, Samuel, s/o Samuel and Susanna, d. 1 Jan 1744
Chunn, Elizabeth, d/o Samuel and Susanna, b. 11 Aug 1746
Chunn, Walter, s/o Samuel and Susanna, b. 14 Jan 1748
Dyson, Bennet, s/o John Bapt. and Ann, b. 13 Aug 1745
Reeves, Samuel, s/o Thomas and Mary, b. 9 Apr 1749
Williams, Justinian, s/o James and Esther, b. 19? Jan 1745/6

Page 110-B
Cooksey, Elinor, d/o Justinian and Sarah, b. 9 Apr 1749
Dyson, Maddox, s/o Thomas, Jr. and Mary, b. 25 Nov 1743
Dyson, Philip, s/o Thomas and Mary, b. 9 May 1746

Dyson, Zepheniah, s/o Thomas and Mary, b. 15 Nov 1748
Williams, Elizabeth and Thomas, twin children of Thomas and
   Ann, b. 2 Aug 1745
Davis, Chloe, d/o Luke and Ann, b. __ May 1749
Davis, Randolph, s/o Peter and Charity, b. 20 Feb 1747
Davis, Susanna, d/o Peter and Charity, b. 13 Jul 1749
Burch, Orpah, d/o John and Mary, b. 16 Jan 1746/7
Mackhon, Robert and Ann Amery, m. 27 Aug 1749
Dement, Lydia, d/o William and Mary, b. 20 May 1749
Wathen, Martin, s/o Hudson and Sarah, b. 2 Feb 1739
Wathen, Bennet, s/o Hudson and Sarah, b. __ Nov 17__
Wathen, Elinor, d/o Hudson and Sarah, b. __ __ 1744
Wathen, Sarah, d/o Hudson and Sarah, b. 27 Mar 1747?

Page 111-A

Dyson, [Ja]mes and Abigale Swann, m. 17 Jan 1744
Dyson, [Sar]ah, d/o James and Abigale, b. 15 Oct 1745
Dyson, [Re]bekah, d/o James and Abigal, b. 3 Nov 1747
Stonstreet, Butler, s/o Butler and Elizabeth, b. 20 Oct 1748
Stonstreet, Edward, d. 3 Nov 1749
Turlon, Mary Ann, d/o John and Catherine, b. 26 Apr 1745
Turlon, John, s/o John and Catherine, b. 9 Jul 1747
Turlon, William, s/o John and Catherine, b. 27 Oct 1749
Gill, Robert, Jr. and Lydia Musgrave, m. 19 Nov 1749
Winter, John, s/o Walter Winter, and Elizabeth Bruce, m. 6 Dec
   1736 by Rev. John Donaldson
Winter, Judith Townley, d/o John and Elizabeth, b. 4 Nov 1743
Winter, [Wa]lter, s/o John and Elizabeth, b. 7 Nov 1747
Winter, ___lish?, s/o John and Elizabeth, b. __ Oct 1749
Chunn, Susanna, wife of Capt. Sam'l Chunn d. 27 Feb 1749 abt. 12
   o'clock at night
Chunn, Capt. Sam'l, d. 2 Mar 1749/50 abt. 6 o'clock in the morning

Page 111-B

Waters, Ann, d/o Ja's? and Mary, b. 27 Aug 1735
Waters, Ja's and Mary Waters, twins of Ja's and Mary, b. 10 Mar
   1737/8
Waters, Sarah, d/o Ja's and Mary, b. 10 Sep 1740
Waters, Jno., s/o Ja's and Mary, b. 8 Mar 1742/3

Waters, Tho's, s/o Ja's and Mary, b. 11 Aug 1745
Waters, Elizabeth, d/o Ja's and Mary, b. 11 Jun 1747/8
Wathen, Ann, d/o Hudson and Sarah, b. 19 Mar 1749/50
Briscoe, Susannah, d/o Philip and Casandra, b. 17 Mar 1749/50 abt. 1/2 hr. after 4
Allen, Susannah, d/o Ja's and Susannah, b. 4 Jan 1749/50
Ramsey, Sarah, d/o Sarah Ramsey, b. 18 Jan 1749/50
Love, Sam'l, Jr. and Mary Haw, m. 5 Dec 1742
Love, Elinor, d/o Sam'l and Mary, b. 18 Sep 1743
Love, Samuel, s/o Sam'l and Mary, b. 20 Feb 1745/6
Love, Martha, d/o Sam'l and Mary, b. 24 Dec 1747
Love, Mary, wife of Sam'l Love, d. 30 Dec 1747/8
Love, Elinor, d/o Sam'l and Mary, d. 1_ April 1748

Page 112-A
Briscoe, John and Anne Wood, m. 27 Nov 1746
Briscoe, Ralph, s/o John and Anne, b. 24 Nov 1747
King, Chloe, d/o Benjamin and Elizabeth, b. 4 Jul 1750
Reeves, Mary Ann, d/o Tho's and Mary, b. 23 Jun 1751
Dyson, Barton, s/o James and Abigail, b. 24 Jul 1750
Amery, Lydia, d/o Samuel and Mary, b. 11 Oct 1738
Amery, Eleanor, d/o Samuel and Mary, b. 20 Feb 1740
Mackhon, Dorcas, d/o Robert and Ann, b. 20 Nov 1750
Winter, Elisabeth Bruce, d/o John and Elizabeth, b. Sunday 31 Mar 1754
Mackhon, Mary, d/o Robert and Ann, b. 5 Apr 1752
Amery, Sam'll, s/o Sam'll and Mary, b. 23 Dec 1752
Gray, James, s/o William and Ann, b. 8 Dec 1750
Gray, George, s/o William and Ann, b. 15 Oct 1752
Allen, Joseph Davis, s/o Joseph and Susannah, b. 29 Jun 1752
Goodrum, James and Susanna Pye Stonestreet, m. 20 Dec 1748
Goodrum, William, s/o James and Susannah, b. __ Feb 1749

Page 112-B
Love, Pentheselia, d/o Charles and Mary, b. 21 Dec 1742
Love, Thomas, s/o Charles and Mary, b. 29 Nov 1745
Love, Jane, d/o Charles and Mary, b. 26 Jan 1748
Love, Pamela, d/o Charles and Mary, b. 14 Jul 1751
Love, Mary, d/o Charles and Mary, b. 14 Dec 1753; d. Dec 30?

Love, Ann, d/o Charles and Mary, d. 6 Nov 1754
Love, Samuel Abbot William Augustine, s/o Charles and Mary, b. 17 Dec 1755
Love, Martha, d/o Charles and Mary, d. 27 Jul 1757
Love, Ann, d/o Charles and Mary, b. 19 Mar 1759
Hawkins, John and Dorothy Wood, m. 19 Jul 1761
Sympson, John Francis Royes, s/o Andrew and Mary, b. 10 Jul 1761
Grey, Katharine, d/o William and Ann, b. __ May 1760
Winter, John, s/o John Winter and Elisabeth, b. 4 Dec 1761
Scott, Thomas, s/o William and Christian, b. 14 Jan 1764
Page 113-A
Scott, Richard, s/o John Scott and Sarah Edgar, b. Sat 16 Jan 1762
Reeves, Ann, d/o Thomas and Mary, b. 25 Apr 1758
Reeves, Josias, s/o Thomas and Mary, b. 28 Oct 1761
Campbell, Gustavus Brown, s/o Rev. Isaac and Jane, b. 22 Aug 1759
Campbell, Isaac, s/o Isaac and Jane, b. 3 Jan 1761
Nalley, Rodolphea Gustavus, s/o Tho's and Anne, b. 4 Jan 1755
Nalley, _ary, d/o Tho's and Ann, b. 16 Jan 1757
Nalley, Thomas Cooksey, s/o Tho's and Ann, b. 11 Apr 1759
Nalley, Elisabeth, d/o Tho's and Ann, b. 27? Oct 1761
Matthews, Catherine, d/o William and Elisabeth, b. 16 Jul 1750
Matthews, Mary, d/o William and Elisabeth, b. 18 Oct 1752
Matthews, [Th]omas, s/o William and Elisabeth, b. 3 Jun 1755
Cooksey, [Tho]mas Reed, m. Elisabeth Matthews 12 Mar 1757
Cooksey, [Hen]ry, s/o Thomas Reed and Elisabeth, b. 8 Jun 1758
Cooksey, ___tny, d/o Tho's Reed and Elisabeth, b. 8 Jan 1761
Cooksey, _____, s/o Tho's Reed and Elisabeth, b. _____
Page 113-B - Missing
Page 144-A - Missing
Page 114-B
Farrand, Hezekiah, s/o John and Mary, b. 13 May 1752
Briscoe, Eleanor Wilson, d/o Hezeiah and Susanna, b. 21 Sep 1750
Briscoe, Margaret, d/o Hezekiah and Susannah, b. 30 Nov 1752
Winter, Ignatius, s/o John and Elizabeth, b. 4 Apr 1753

Trinity Parish

Cartwright, Jesse and Margaret Amery, m. 13 Dec 1753
Moor, James and Elizabeth Dement, m. 8 Dec 1747
Moor, Sarah, d/o James and Elizabeth, b. 6 Mar 17__ (torn)
Moor, James, s/o James and Elizabeth, b. 27 Aug 1752
Following very dim; right side of page partially crumbled:
Goodrum, Mary, d/o James Goodrum and Susanna Pye, 2 Jan 1754
Mackhon, Walter, s/o Robert Mackhon and Ann, b. 3 Nov 1753
Stonestreet, Edward, s/o Butler and Elizabeth, b. __ Jan ____
Compton, Elizabeth, d/o Matthew and Rachel, b. 21 May 1742
Compton, Matthew, s/o Matthew and Rachel, b. __ Dec 174_
Compton, John, s/o Matthew and Rachel, b. 28 Feb 1749?
Compton, Susanna, d/o Matthew and Rachel, b. __ Feb ____
Compton, Barton, s/o Matthew and Rachel, b. 3 Dec ____
Farrand, Mark, s/o John and Mary, b. 29 Sep 1744
Following on page partially crumbled on left:

Page 115-A
Winter, Eleanor, d/o John and Elisabeth, b. 8 Mar 1755
Holt, John, s/o William and Milicent, b. 17 Sep 1745
Holt, Mary, d/o William and Milicent, b. 17 Sep 1748
Holt, Ann, d/o William and Milicent, b. 15 Jan 1753
Slye, Robert, s/o John and Eleanor, b. 15 Nov 1745
Slye, Susanna, d/o John and Eleanor, b. 1? Sep 1749
Compton, Alexander, s/o Matthew and Rachel, b. Tues. 16 Sep 1755
Campbell, Jane, d/o Rev. Isaac an Jane, b. Mon. 3 Mar 1755
Davis, James, s/o Thomas and Elisabeth, b. 2 Aug 1751
Mackon, Elizabeth, d/o Robert and Ann, b. 1? Oct 1755
Cartwright, Mary, d/o Jesse and Margaret, b. 1? Nov 1755
Gray, Joseph, s/o William and Ann, b. 14 Feb 1755
Briscoe, Mary, d/o Hezekiah and Susannah b. 15 Mar 1755
Chunn, Andrew, d. 21 Oct 1756, age 54 years 6 mos. lacking _ days
Campbell, William, s/o Rev. Isaac and Jane, b. 28 Aug 1756
Turner, Mary, d/o Sam'll and Verlinder, b. 4 May 1750
Turner, Sam'll, s/o Sam'll and Verlinder, b. 9 Jun 1752

Page 115-B
Turner, Anna, d/o Sam'll and Ann his wife
Verlinder his wife was dec.? 29 Dec

Chunn, Lancelot and Judith Cartwright, m. 11 May 1753
Chunn, Jonathan, s/o Lancelot and Judith, b. 7 Nov 1754
Chunn, Thomas, s/o Lancelot and Judith, b. 10 Dec 1758
Mackcon, Ann, wife of Robert Mackcon and d/o Samuel Amery and Mary his wife, d. Sat. 2 Apr 1757, age 20 years _____ and 15 days
Farrand, Mary, d/o John and Mary, b. 9 Jun 1747
Gray, Willliam and Eleanor Gray, twins, son and dau. of William and Ann, b. 18 May 1757
Davis, George, s/o Peter and Charity, b. 22 Aug 1751
Davis, Joshua, s/o Peter and Charity, b. 22 Feb 1754
Davis, Hope, d/o Peter and Charity, b. 11 Mar 17__
Dement, William, s/o Will'm and Mary, b. 3 Apr 1753
Dement, Walter, s/o William and Mary, b. 1 May 1755
Somerset, Martha, d/o William and Mary and granddau. of William Dement and Mary, b. 1 Sep 175_
Dyson, Joseph and Elisabeth Chunn, m. 17 Apr 1752
Dyson, Winnefrid, d/o Joseph and Elisabeth, b. 23 Feb 175_
Dyson, Thomas Andrew, s/o Joseph and Elisabeth, b. 28 Oct 1754

Page 116-A

____[faded and missing]_____ 21 Feb 1757
3 May 1760
Waters, James, Jr. and Ann Dement m. 29 Dec 1754
Waters, Milicent, d/o James and Ann, b. __ Nov 1755
Waters, Asenath, d/o James and Ann, b. 22 Jul 1757
Mastin, Mary, d/o Richard and Ann, b. 25 Jun 1757
Stonestreet, Elisabeth, d/o Richard and Elisabeth, b. 9 Mar 1757
Cartwright, Hezekiah, s/o Jesse and Margaret, b. 3 Oct 1757
Reeves, Elizabeth, d/o Thomas and Mary, b. 18 Nov 1753
Reeves, Lydia, d/o Thomas and Mary, b. 25 Aug 1755
Mackmelon, Zechariah, s/o Hugh and Tabitha, b. 11 May 1748
Mackmelon, Compton, s/o Tabitha Mackmelon, b. 12 Nov 1757
King, Barton, s/o Benjamin and Elisabeth, b. 24 Jan 1753
King, Cornelius, s/o Benjamin and Elisabeth, b. 21 Sep 1755
King, Dorcas, d/o Benjamin and Elisabeth, b. 20 Feb 1758
Campbell, Frances, s/o Rev. Isaac and Jane, b. Tues. 14 Feb 1760
Swann, Thomas and Ann Dent m. 11 Jan 1757

Swann, Martha, d/o Thomas and Ann, b. 8 Feb 1758
Scott, John and Sarah Edgar, m. 14 Nov 1754 by Rev. Isaac
   Campbell
Scott, Elisa. Edgar, d/o John and Sarah, b. 25 Nov 1755; d. 19 Oct
   1756
Scott, John, d. 4 Feb 1763
Page 116-B
Murphy, William, s/o Daniel and Ann, b. 19 May 1762
Scott, Gustavus, s/o William and Christian, b. 11 Nov 1763
McPherson, William and Eliner Wilkinson, m. 13 Aug 1737
McPherson, Kerenhappuck, d/o William and wife, b. 19 Dec 1739
McPherson, John, s/o William and Elenor, b. 5 Apr 1742
McPherson, Alexander Wilkinson, s/o William and wife, b. 25
   Feb 1743
McPherson, Elizabeth, d/o William and Elinor, b. 15 Dec 1747
McPherson, William, s/o William and Elinor, b. 22 Dec 1751
McPherson, Elinor, d/o William and Elinor, b. 7 Feb 1753
McPherson, Mary, d/o William and Elinor, b. 16 May 1755
McPherson, Ann, d/o William and Elinor, b. 1 Nov 1757
McPherson, Helen, d/o William and Elinor, b. 2 Feb 1760
McPherson, Theophilus, s/o William and Elinor, b. 12 Nov 1762
Waters, Anna, d/o James and Ann, b. 24 Jul 1763
Simms, Joseph and Elizabeth Dent, m. 8 Sep 1760
_____ and Dorcas _____ [can't read]
Page 117-A
Mackey, ___ck and Ann White, m. 10 Dec 1763
Jameson, Sarah, d/o Benjamin and Sarah, b. 27 May 1763
Perry, __arity, d/o Francis and Elizabeth, b. 12 May 1760
Dyson, _ary, d/o Ja's and ____cas, b. 28 Jul 1763
Campbell, __mes, s/o Isaac and Jean, b. 28 Mar 1763
Croson, Zepheniah, s/o Tho's and Lydia, b. 23 Mar 1764
Turner, _____ and Heneritta Chunn, m. 29 Apr 1764
Chunn, Zachariah and Charity Courts, m. 23 Dec 1762
Chunn, Charles Courts, s/o Zach. and Charity, b. 17 Jul 1763
Chunn, Zachariah m. Deborah Turner, m. 30 May 1764
McPherson, Eliner, d/o William and Eli____, b. ____
Page 117-B

Stonestreet, Mary?, d/o Butler and Elizabeth, b. __ __ 1763
[Some vestry notes X'd]
Page 118-A
Turner, Elizabeth, d/o Hezekiah and Heneritta, b. 28 Mar 1765
Dyson, Bennit and Winifred Chunn, m. 27 Jan 1765
Davis, Charles and Sarah Moreland, m. 11 May 1762
Davis, Moses, s/o Charles and Sarah, b. 29 Mar 1763
Davis, Rachel, d/o Charles and Sarah, b. 30 Sep 1764
Turner, William and Rhoda Dent, m. 1 Jul 1764
Turner, John, s/o William and Rhoda, b. 13 Apr 1765
Dyson, Anna, d/o Bennet and Winnifred, b. 21 Nov 1765
Wood, Walter, s/o James and Sarah, b. 28 May 1765
Farrand, Zephaniah, s/o John and Mary, b. 18 Apr 1761
McPherson, Charles, s/o William and Elinor, b. 29 Sep 1765
Cooksey, Sarah, d/o Thomas Reed and Elizabeth, b. 8 Dec 1765
Turner, Samuel, s/o Hezekiah and Henrietta, b. 13 Sep 1766
Page 118-B
Dent, John and Margaret Dyson, m. 3 Feb? 1757
Dent, Thomas Hatch, s/o John and Margaret, b. 28 Jul 1760
Dent, Anne, d/o John and Margaret, b. [ink blot]
Dent, Rebeckah, d/o John and Margaret, b. 2 Dec 1764
Dent, James, s/o John and Margaret, b. 15 Jan 1767
Dyson, Samuel Turner, s/o Joseph and Dorcas, b. 29 Jul 1766
Dyson, John Baptist, d. 2 Jun 1760
Burch, Justinian, d. 10 Sep 1767
Murphey, Zephaniah and Margit Hill, m. 29 Dec 1765
Dyson, John, s/o Bennett and Winifred, b. 17 Jan 1768
Chunn, John Thomas and Martha Turner, m. 13 Oct 1767
Swann, Zedakiah, s/o Thomas and Ann, b. 16 Apr 1760
Swann, Hatch, s/o Thomas and Ann, b. 1 Feb 17[62?]
Swann, Asa, s/o Thomas and Ann, b. 8 Jul 1764
Swann, Ann Chapman, d/o Thomas and Ann, b. 21 May 1767
Waters, Orpha, d/o James, Jr. and Ann, b. 26 Nov 1766
Waters, Helin, d/o James, Jr. and Ann, b. 26 Nov 1766
Page 119-A
Davis, Zacchius, and Marget Stone, m. 15 Apr 1759
Davis, Henrietta, d/o Zacchius and Magret, b. 16 Feb 1760

Davis, Violetta, d/o above, b. 27 Dec 1764
Davis, Marget, d/o above, b. 10 Jan 1766
Reeves, Dorcas, d/o Thomas and Mary, b. 8 Jan 1764
Reeves, Bennett, s/o Thomas and Mary, b. 13 Mar 1766
Murphey, Abraham and Elizabeth Boswell, m. 10 Jan 1758
Murphey, Sarah, s/o Abraham and Elizabeth, b. 5 Jan 1759
Murphey, Mary, d/o above, b. 29 Oct 1761
Murphey, Martha, d/o above, b. 25 Sep 1764
Murphey, Dorithy, d/o above, b. 20 Apr 1767
Murphey, Daniel, s/o Zephaniah and Margaret, b. 10 Apr 1768
Murphey, Edward Hill, s/o Hezakiah and Elizabeth, b. 21 Apr 1768
Dyson, Thomas and Esther Dent, m. 17 Feb 1760
Dyson, Amelia, d/o Thomas and Esther (sic), b. 29 Jan 1761
Dyson, John, s/o Thomas and Eshter, b. 10 Feb 1763
Dyson, Ann'a, d/o Thomas and Eshter, b. 6 Oct 1765
Cooksey, Jane, d/o Thomas Reed and Elizabeth, b. 20 Mar 1769

Page 119-B

Scott, Samuel, s/o William and Christian, b. 10 Oct 1764
Scott, Sarah, d/o William and Christian, b. 22 Dec 1766
Dyson, Joseph, d. 20 Aug 1769
Wilder, Edward and Marget Compton, m. 31 Jan 1769
Waters, Shelah, d/o Bennett and Winifred, b. 20 Oct 1769
Dyson, Walter, s/o Bennett and Winifred, b. 24 Oct 1769
Murphey, Rebekah, d/o Zephaniah and Mary, b. 17 Oct 1769
Davis, Ann, d/o Zacchius and Marget, b. 1 Mar 1769
Reeves, William, s/o Thomas and Mary, b. 9 Feb 1770
Chunn, Zachariah and Deborah Turner, m. 31 May 1764
Chunn, Virlinder, d/o Zachariah and Deborah, b. 28 Apr 1765
Chunn, Winifred, d/o above, b. 30 Feb 1767
Chunn, Andrew, s/o above, b. 17 Dec 1768
Davis, Isaac, s/o Charles and Sarah, b. __ Apr 1766
Davis, Lydia, d/o Charles and Sarah, b. 14 Mar 1768
Davis, Joshua, s/o Charles and Sarah, b. 28? Apr 1770
Murphey, John Boswell, s/o Abraham and Elizabeth, b. 2 Sep 1769
Gill, Elizabeth, d/o John and Susanah, b. 1 Oct 1768

Gill, Joseph Allen, s/o John and Susanah, b. 4 Apr 1770
Davis, William, s/o William, Jr. and Rebecca?, b. 17 Jul 1769
Phillips, Hezakiah, s/o Zephaniah and Catherine, b. 1 Aug 1749
Page 120-A
Davis, Lydia, d/o Zaccheus and Margaret, b. 12 Feb 1771
Davis, Benjamin and Mary Cawood, m. 26 May 1757
Davis, Benjamin, s/o Benjamin and Mary, b. 13 Apr 1758
Davis, Mary, wife of Benjamin, d. 6 Oct 1761
Swann, Mary Amery, d/o Jonathan and Eliner, b. 28 Oct 1768
Swann, Samuel Amery, s/o Jonathin and Eleaner, b. 22 Jan 1771
Murphey, Mary, d/o Zeph. and Margaret, b. 24 Aug 1771
Dyson, Andrew, s/o Bennett and Wineford, b. 13 Oct 1771
Chunn, Samuel, s/o Zachariah and Deborah, b. 18 Mar 1771
Moreton, Anne, d/o William and Marget, b. 31 Feb 1740
Murphey, Dan'l, Jr., and Anne Moreton, m. 17 Feb 1757
Murphey, Samuel, s/o Dan'l and Anne, b. 15 Oct 1758
Murphey, Dan'l, s/o above, b. 13 Jun 1760; d. 7 Mar 1768
Murphey, William, s/o above, b. 13 May 1762
Murphey, Walter, s/o above, b. 25 May 1764
Murphey, Elizabeth Moreton, d/o above, b. 16 Aug 1766
Murphey, Nathaniel, s/o above, b. 31 Sep 1768
Murphey, Kenelm, s/o above, b. 23 Jun 1771
Page 120-B
Clarkson, Henry and Dorcas Dyson, m. 11 Feb 1772
Wilder, Susannah, d/o Edward and Margaret, b. 6 Nov 1769
Wilder, Mary, d/o Edward and Margaret, b. 31 Mar 1771
Wilder, Elizabeth, d/o Edward and Margaret, b. 16 Jan 1773
Davis, Francis and Lydia Dent, m. 3 Dec 1764
Davis, Rhoda, d/o Francis and Lydia, b. 3 Feb 1766
Davis, Winifred, d/o above, b. 2 Dec 1767
Davis, Lydia, d/o above, b. 6 Oct 177_
Davis, Essac Young, s/o above, b. 28 Feb 1773
Briscoe, Elizabeth, d/o Hezakiah and Susanah, b. 1? Dec 1756
Compton, William and Susannah Brisoce, widow of Hez'h?
  Briscoe, m. 18 Nov 1758
Compton, William, s/o William and Susannah, b. 23 Aug 1761
Briscoe, Walter and Elizabeth Compton, m. 13 May 1762

Trinity Parish

Page 121-A
Dent, Catherine, d/o John and Margaret, b. 15 Mar 1769
Dent, John Baptist, s/o John and Margaret, b. 1 Jun 1771
Dent, Esther, d/o John and Margaret, b. 6 Nov 1773
Trinity, Providence, b. 10 Jul 1772
Poston, Jeremiah, s/o William and Priscilla, b. 26 Aug 1745
Poston, Elias, s/o William and Priscilla, b. 14 Nov 1747
Poston, Alexander, s/o William and Priscilla, b. 21 Mar 1750
Poston, Richard, s/o Wm. and Priscilla, b. 24 Sep 1752
Poston, Catherine, d/o William and Priscilla, b. 24 Jun 1775 (sic)
Poston, Judith, d/o Wm. and Priscilla, b. 10 Jan 1758
Poston, Anne, and William, son and d/o William and Priscilla, b. 6 Oct 1760
Dent, Hezekiah and Catherine Poston, m. 2 Nov 1769
Dent, Mrs. Ca[therine], d. 6 Apr 1773
Dent, Alexan[der], s/o Hezekiah and Catherine, b. 22 Mar 1773
Canter, Truman and Elizabeth Hechky, m. 24 Nov 1774
Venables, Margaret, d/o Theodore and Mary, b. 9 Dec 1769
Venables, Dorcas Wright, d/o above, b. 17 Oct 1774
Good, Elizabeth, d/o William and Ann, b. 7 Nov 1781
Good, Ann, d/o above, b. 11 Feb 1763
Good, Cloe and Thomas, dau. and s/o above, b. 15 Feb 1768
Good, William, s/o above, 11 Apr 1770

Page 121-B
Good, Catherine, b. 26 Feb 1772
Davis, Mary R__my, d/o William and Rebecca, b. 29 Sep 1774
Davis, Rebecah, d. 6 Oct 1774
Davis, Philip and Chloe Poston, m. 10 Feb 1770
Davis, Elizabeth, d/o above, b. 9 Jan 1771
Burch, Benjamin and Mary Mathes, m. 9 Dec 1773
Davis, Catherine, d/o George and Jane, b. 7 Jun 1774
Johnson, Eleanor, d/o Jemima Johnson, b. 15 Sep 1764
Herman, Jediah, s/o John and Rhoda, b. 4 Aug 1767
Herman, Rhoda, d/o above, b. 7 Oct 1771 [or 1772]
Parker, Elizabeth, d/o Elizabeth Parker, b. 2 Dec 1774
Davis, Alexander, s/o Randolph and Elizabeth, b. 12 Sep 1771
King, Joseph and Dradon Johnson, m. 7 Jun 1756

King, Aquilla, s/o above, b. 9? Apr 1757
King, Zephaniah, s/o above, b. 1 Jul 1759
King, Basil, s/o above, b. 17 Oct 1761
King, Cornelius, s/o above, b. 6? Mar 1763
Page 122-A
King, Elias, s/o above, b. 17? Oct 1765
King, Walter, s/o above, b. 16 Nov 1768
King, Vinson, s/o above, b. 10 Jun 1769
King, James Carrol, s/o above, b. 30 Aug 1771
King, Ann, d/o above, b. 10 Mar 1773
King, Millicent, d/o above, b. 2 Nov 1774
Waters, Enos, s/o James and Ann, b. 26 Nov 1772
Waters, Rezin, s/o above, b. 31 Dec 1775
Waters, James, Sr., d. 11 Oct 1771
Waters, John, Sr., d. 20 Jun 1775
Poston, Anne, d/o Leonard and Ann, b. 9 Jul 1771
Tub, William and Martha Summerset, m. 1 Jan 1774
Tub, Mary Anne, d/o William and Martha, b. 7 Sep 1775
Chunn, Elizabeth W__n, d/o Aquilla and Mary, b. 12 Dec 1768
Chunn, Samuel, s/o Aquilla and Mary, b. 20 Mar 1773
King, Joseph, d. 8 Aug 1775
Swann, Esther, d/o Thomas and Anne, b. 2 Apr 1772
Swann, Ezra, s/o Thomas and Anne, b. 3 Jun 1774
Dent, Hatch, s/o Hezekiah and Martha, b. 6 Feb 1775
Glasgow, Hezekiah, s/o Elizabeth, b. 1 Oct 1756
Hutchings, Susannah, d/o Thomas and Elizabeth, b. 17 Dec 1759
Page 122-B
Davis, Elizabeth Reeder, d/o Zachius and Margaret, b. 22 May 1775
Waters, William and Elisabeth Welch, m. 4 Nov 1762
Waters, Edward, s/o William and Elisabeth, b. 15 Aug 1763
Waters, Susannah, d/o William and Elisabeth, b. 27 Dec 1765
Waters, Jonathan, s/o above, b. 6 Dec 1768
Waters, Hanson, s/o above, b. 1 Feb 1771
Waters, Josias, s/o above, b. 16 Sep 1774
Waters, Sarah, d/o above, b. 9 Feb 1776
Waters, Joseph, d. 25 Jan 1777

Henning, John, s/o John and Rhoda, b. 2 Feb 1760
Farrand, Elisabeth, d. 30 Jan 1777
Gill, Barton, s/o John and Susannah, b. 11 May 1773
Gill, Lydia, d/o John and Susannah, b. 25 Sep 1775
Waters, Joseph of James, and Katherine Carrico, m. 6 Aug 17_4
Waters, Katherine, wife of Joseph, d. 3 Sep 1766

Page 123-A

Waters, Priscilla, d/o Joseph and Katherine, b. 26 Nov 1754
Waters, Zephaniah, s/o above, b. 7 Feb 1757
Waters, James, s/o above, b. 13 May 1759
Waters, Lydia, d/o above, b. 18 Apr 1761
Waters, Jedidiah, s/o above, b. 9 Jul 1763
Waters, Jane, d/o above, b. 20 Feb 1766; d. 20 Mar 1768
Waters, Joseph, of James, and Chloe Dent, m. 17 Feb 1767
Waters, Dent, s/o Joseph and Chloe, b. 24 Feb 1768; d. 9 Apr 1768
Waters, Kezia, d/o above, b. 2 Aug 1769
Waters, Susannah, d/o above, b. 8 Mar 1771
Waters, Benjamin, s/o above, b. 22 Mar 1773
Waters, Joseph, s/o above, b. 16 Mar 1775
Waters, Phebe, d/o above, b. 1 Aug 1777 (twin)
Waters, Eda, d/o above, b. 1 Aug 1777 (twin)
Poston, William, d. 9 Mar 1777
Poston, Alexander, d. [no date]
Dement, William, s/o John, and Elisabeth Bryan, m. 27 Aug 1775
Dement, John Fenley, s/o William and Elisabeth, b. 2 Mar 1777

Page 123-B

Downing, Abednago and Milesent Waters, m. 30 Jun 1776
Downing, Eleanor, d/o above, b. 31 Mar 1777
Waters, Joseph Manning Dent, s/o Prisilla Waters, b. 2 Aug 1776
Murphey, Joseph, s/o Daniel and Anne, b. 15 Jun 1773
Waters, George Dement, s/o James and Anne, b. 16 Oct 1778
Dement, Eleanor, d/o William and Elisabeth, b. 27 Dec 1778?
Dement, Anne, d/o John and Mary, b. 29 Mar 1763
Gill, Charles, s/o John and Susannah, b. 5 Feb 1778
Davis, Benjamin, s/o Charles and Anne, b. 9 Sep 1778
Davis, Eleanor, d/o Charles and Anne, b. 4 Apr 1777

Waters, Anne, consort of James Waters, d. Saturday 22 Apr 1780 at half past 3 o'clock after
Waters, James and Draden King, m. Sunday 12 Sep 1780
Page 124-A
Waters, Kitty, d/o James and Draden, b. 31 Jul 1781
Waters, Rezin, s/o James and Anna, d. 11 Oct 1781
Gill, John, s/o John and Susannah, b. 13 Jul 1781
Downing, Anne, d/o Abednago and Milicent, b. 24 Jan 1780
Downing, Lydia, d/o Abednago and Milicent, b. 1 Jan 1782
Slye, Robert and Elizabeth Haddert, m. 3 Jun 1773
Slye, Thomas Gerrard, s/o Robert and Elisabeth, b. 29 Apr 1775
Slye, John, s/o Robert and Elisabeth, b. 27 Nov 1777
Dent, Hatch, s/o Hatch, and Judith Poston, m. 17 Dec 1778
Dent, Lucinda, d/o Hatch and Judith, b. 22 Jan 1780
Dent, Drusilla, d/o above, b. 1 Nov 1781; d. 15 Dec 1781
Dent, Mary, d/o above, b. 5 Oct 1782
Dent, Hezekiah and Martha Burch, m. 10 Feb 1774
Dent, Hatch, s/o above Hezh and Martha, b. 30? May 1777
Dent, John Chapman, s/o Hezh and Martha, b. 24 Feb 1778
Dent, ____, d/o Hezh and Martha, b. 26? Feb? 1782; d. 28 __

Page 124-B
Dyson, William, s/o Thomas and Esther, b. 17 mar 1768
Waters, Drusilla, d/o James and Draden, b. 1 Feb 1783
Davis, Thomas Blackman, s/o Charles and Anne, b. 23 Aug 1782
Matthews, Thomas and Anne Poston, m. 24 Dec 1780
Matthews, Billy, s/o Thomas and Ann, b. 2 Dec 1781
Roby, William, of Richard, and Susannah Dement, d/o Wm., m. 12 Dec 1762
Roby, George Dement, s/o William and Susannah, b. 22 Dec 1763
Roby, Charles, s/o above, b. 14 May 1766
Roby, Elisabeth, d/o above, b. __ Jan 176_
Roby, Townley, s/o above, b. 1 Jan 1770
Roby, Katherine, d/o above, b. 10 Dec 1771
Roby, Truman, s/o above, b. 24 Aug 1773
Roby, Cornelius, s/o above, b. 26 Jan 1775
Roby, Aquilla, s/o above, b. 4 Dec 1777

Roby, Hezekiah, s/o above, b. 18 Dec 1779
Roby, Mary, d/o above, b. 29 Oct 1781
Murphey, Anne, d/o Daniel and Anne, b. 31 Aug 1779
Murphey, Susannah, d/o above, b. 16 Feb 1782
Page 125-A
Roby, Deborah, d/o William and Susannah, b. 16 Aug 1783
Gill, Susannah, d/o John and Susannah, b. 21 Dec 1782
Roby, Susannah, consort of William, d. 17 Aug 1784
Murphey, Jane, d/o Zephaniah and Margaret, b. 11 Sep 1773
Murphey, Thomas, s/o Zephaniah and Marget, b. 20 Nov 1776
Murphey, Zephaniah and Eleanor Gray, m. 4 Jan 1778
Murphey, Townley, s/o Zephaniah and Eleanor, b. 25 Jul 1780
Murphey, Marget Hill, d/o above, b. 11 Jun 1782
Waters, Susannah, relict of James [formerly dec'd], d. 6 Jun 1785
Waters, Zephaniah and Elizabeth Morton Murphy, m. by Rev. Hatch Dent, Tuesday, 1 Jan 1786
King, Basil and Deborah Waters, m. by Rev. Isaac Campbell, Sunday 28 Sep 1783
King, Orpha, d/o Basil and Eeborah, b. 26 Jul 1784
King Deborah, d. 16 Oct 1785
Page 125-B
Ferrand, John, s/o John, and Elisabeth Broady, m. 13 Dec 1772
Farrand, William, s/o John and Elisabeth, b. 12 Nov 1773
Farrand, Catherine, d/o John and Elisabeth, b. 21 Apr 1776
Farrand, Susannah, d/o John and Elisabeth, b. 11 Jun 1778
Farrand, Mary, d/o John and Elisabeth, b. 20 May 1780
Farrand, Marget, d/o John and Elisabeth, b. 30 Mar 1782
Farrand, John, s/o John and Elisabeth, b. 18 Jan 1785
Gill, Mary Anne, d/o John and Elisabeth, b. 1 Jan 1786
Davis, Peter, s/o Charles and Anne, b. 13 Aug 1786
Farrand, Thomas, s/o John and Elisabeth, b. 26 Jun 1787
Waters, Jane, s/o Zephaniah and Elisabeth, b. 9 Feb 1787
Farrand, John, d. __ Jan 1788
Page 126-A
Davis, Benjamin, s/o Benjamin, and Mary Wood, d/o Peter and Elisabeth, m. by Rev. Hatch Dent, 1 Oct 1787

Davis, Mary was delivered of a son 12 Jul 1788 who d. 13 Jul 1788 and Mary Davis, wife of abv. Benjamin, d. 15 Jul 1788
Gill, Ursilla, d/o John and Elisabeth, b. 2 Mar 1790
King, Anna, d/o Basil King and Sarah, b. 4 Dec 1788
King, Elisabeth, d/o Basil and Sarah, b. 26 Aug 1790
Davis, Philip, s/o Philip and Chloe, b. 6 Aug 1782
Davis, Pamela, d/o Philip and Chloe, b. 4. Mar 1784
Gill, Druscilla, d/o John and Elisabeth, b. 19 Dec 1791
Amery, Samuel and Catherine Matthews, m. 14 Feb 1773
Amery, William, s/o Samuel and Catherine, b. Friday 17 Dec 1773
Amery, Mary, d/o Samuel and Catherine, b. Sunday 27 Aug 1775
Amery, Samuel John, s/o Samuel and Catherine, b. 29 Jun 1777
Amery, Thomas, s/o Samuel and Catherine, b. Friday 2 Mar 1780

Page 126-B

Amery, Samuel, s/o Samuel and Catherine, b. Wednesday 22 May 1782
Amery, Catherine, wife of Samuel, d. 13 Feb 1784?
Amery, Samuel, Sr., d. Friday 13 May 1777
Amery, John, d. Tuesday 24 Mar 1778
Amery, Mary, Sr., d. Friday 31 Aug 1787
Chunn, Charles Courts and Sarah Cooksey, m. 11 Dec 1788
Peake, William, s/o William and Elizabeth of Fairfax Co., Virginia, b. in the house of William Compton of this parish on 14 Sep 1793 at 8 o'clock in the evening; _____ and William Peake were present; immediately after the birth Margaret _____ and Henrietta Farr, the midwife, came in.....; on the second day of the m_____ instant, the child was baptized by Rev. J___ Wilson Compton
Gill, George, s/o John and Elizabeth, b. 21 May 1787
Murphey, William, s/o Zephaniah & Eleanor, b. 18 May 1787
Murphey, Josias, s/o Zephaniah and Eleanor, b. 8 Jan 1792

Page 127-A

Dent, John Shelton, s/o John and Mary, b. 12 Oct 1792
Turner, Samuel and Margaret Montgomery, m. by Rev. Isaac Campbell, 18 Nov 1762
Turner, William, s/o Samuel and Margaret, b. 3 Sep 1763

Turner, Alexander, s/o Samuel and Margaret, 10 Jul 1765
Turner, Eleanor, d/o Samuel and Margaret, 9 Mar 1768
Turner, Samuel, s/o Samuel and Margaret, 19 Dec 1769
Turner, Charles, s/o Samuel and Margaret, b. 20 May 1771
Turner, Elizabeth, d/o Samuel and Margaret, b. 20 Mar 1773
Turner, Margaret, d/o Samuel and Margaret, b. 10 Apr 1775
Turner, Deborah, d/o Samuel and Margaret, b. 12 Mar 1777
Turner, Anne Mary, d/o Samuel and Margaret, b. 5 Jul 1778
Colley, William, s/o James and Mary, b. 6 Sep 1791
Page 127-B
Matthews, Thomas, d. 24 Dec 1796
Matthews, Billy, s/o Thomas and Anne, b. 2 Dec 1781
Matthews, John, s/o Thomas and Anne, b. 14 Dec 1783
Matthews, Catherine, d/o Thomas and Anne, b. 19 Nov 1786
Matthews, Alexander, s/o Thomas and Anne, b. 25 Apr 1788
Matthews, Elizabeth Barnes, d/o Thomas and Anne, b. 24 Feb 1790
Matthews, Thomas, s/o Thomas and Anne, b. 3 Feb 1792
Matthews, Elias Poston, s/o Thomas and Anne, b. 3 Feb 1785
Matthews, Henry Cooksey, s/o Thomas and Anne, b. 29 Jul 1797
Gill, _____, d/o John and Elizabeth, b. 19 Sep 1797
Dyson, Adeline, d/o Richard and Ann E., b. 7 Jan 1826

Births, Marriages and Deaths
from
CHARLES COUNTY COURT and LAND RECORDS

Allen, Anne, d/o John and Elinor Allen of Portobacco, b. 28 Jan 1694 (Q.25)
Allward, John, s/o John and Anne Allward of the head of Portobacco Creek, b. 18 Dec 1678 (P.206) (Q.6)
Allward, Margarett, d/o John & Mary of head of Portobacco Creek, b. 4 Mar 1680 (P.207) (Q.7)
Allward, Mary, d/o John and Anne Allward of head of Portobacco Creek, b. 20 Dec 1676 (P.206) (Q.5)
Anderson, Edward, s/o John and Mary Anderson of Portobacco, b. 13 Aug 1691 (Q.20)
Anderson, George, s/o John and Mary Anderson of Portobacco, b. 22 Mar 1694 (Q.25)
Anderson, John, s/o John and Mary Anderson of Portobacco, b. 14 Apr 1693 (Q.22)
Asborough, Thomas, serv't of Alexander Sympson, d. 10 Aug 1667 (P.205)
Ashbrooke, John m. 1687 [1667; C.222] (P.204)
Ashman, Allward Hardy, s/o Richard and Anne Ashman of head of Wicomico River, b. 12 Jun 1691 (Q.17) (P.209)
Ashman, Elizabeth, d/o Richard and Anne Ashman of the head of Wicomico River, b. 29 Jun 1680 (P.209) (Q.7)
Ashman, Mary, d/o Richard and Anne Ashman of the head of Wicomico, b. 3 Aug 1685 (P.209) (Q.11)
Ashman, Richard, s/o Richard and Anne Ashman of the head of Wicomico River, b. 4 Feb 1682 (P.209) (Q.8)
Ashman, Standidge, s/o Richard and Anne Ashman of the head of Wicomico River, b. 1 Oct 1687 (P.209) (Q.13)
Baker, Andrew, s/o Thomas and Martha Baker of Potomac River side, b. 29 Mar 1679 (P.206) (Q.6)
Baker, Martha, d/o Thomas and Martha Baker of Potomac River, b. last day of March 1675 (P.205) (Q.5)
Barker, John, s/o John and ____ Barker of Nanjemy, b. 3 Apr 1691; bapt. 17 day of sd. month (P.211) (Q.17)

Barnes, Godshall, s/o Matthew and Elizabeth Barnes of Portobacco, b. 20 Dec 1692 (P.212) (Q.19)

Barnes, Jane, d/o Matthew and Elizabeth Barnes b. 19 Dec 1694 (Q.24)

Baron [or Barrow], Richard, servant to Humphrey Warren, d. 27 Jul 1666 (P.204) (Q.2)

Baron, Martha, d/o John and Mary Baron of Portobacco, b. 15 Jan 1694 (Q.24)

Barton, child of William Barton, Jr., b. 25 Mar 1667 (C.251)

Barton, David, s/o William and Elizabeth Barton of Mattawoman, b. 25 Jun 1695 (Q.26) (Q.123)

Barton, Elizabeth, d/o William Barton, Jr., b. 27 Feb 1671 (P.205) (Q.4)

Barton, Grace, d/o William Barton, Jr., b. 26 Aug 1659; d. last day of August (P.204) (Q.1)

Barton, Thomas, s/o William Barton and Elizabeth Barton of Mattawoman, b. 17 Jul 1689 (Q.14)

Barton, William, s/o Nathan Barton, b. 19 Feb 1667 (P.204) (Q.3)

Barton, William, s/o William Barton and Elizabeth Barton of Mattawoman, 11 Nov 1690 (Q.14)

Barton, William, s/o William Barton Jr., b. 27 Feb 1667 (C.260)

Barton, William, s/o William Barton, Jr., b. 29 Jun 1662 (P.204) (Q.1)

Bateman, George, s/o George & Elizabeth of Pickawaxen, b. 7 Dec 1692 (P.211) (Q.19)

Bayly, James, s/o John and Mary Bayly near Pope's Creek, b. 10 Jan 1683 (P.207) (Q.9)

Bayly, John, s/o John and Mary Bayly near Pope's Creek, b. 20 Jan 1680 (P.207) (Q.7)

Beade, Mary; d/o Nicholas (H.252)

Beade, Sarah; d/o Nicholas (H.252)

Beck, Elizabeth, d/o Richard and Elizabeth Beck, b. 2 Oct 1689 (P.206) (Q.3)

Beck, Margarett, d/o Richard and Elizabeth Beck, b. 1 May 1674 (P.206) (Q.5)

Beck, Mary, d/o Richard and Elizabeth Beck, b. 15 Nov 1673 (Q.4) [1672; G.166] (P.206)

Belaine [or Belayne], Elizabeth, d/o Nicholas and Mary Belaine of the head of Wicomico River, b. 25 Feb 1688 (P.211) (Q.14)
Belaine, Grace; orphan of John Blaiine (F.199)
Belaine, Nicholas, s/o John; chooses his bro.-in-law, John Posie, guardian (F.199)
Belayne, Jemima, d/o Nicholas and Mary Belayne of head of Wicomico River, b. 25 Mar 1686 (P.211) (Q.12)
Bonner, Henry, m. Eliz. Story, relict of Walter Story by 15 Nov 1665 (D.134)
Bowld, Elizabeth, d/o John and Jane Bowld of Pickawaxon, b. 27 Dec 1690 (Q.16)
Bowld, John, s/o John and Jane Bowld of Pickawaxon, b. 25 Jun 1686 (Q.12)
Bowld, Mary Anne, d/o John and Jane Bowld of Pickawaxon, b. 3 Apr 1694 (Q.23)
Boyse, William; s/o John and Elenor Boyse; 1680 (H.329)
Brawner, John, s/o Henry and Mary Brawner of Mattawoman, b. 2 Apr 1693 (Q.19)
Brayne, Jane; d/o John Caine 1680 (H.292)
Brown, Gerrard m. to the relict of William Allen 1674 (F.10)
Browne, Elizabeth m. John Robinson 21 Mar 1666 (C.253)
Browne, John, d. 7 Nov 1666 (P.204) (Q.2)
Browne, John, s/o Elizabeth Browne, b. 5 Jul 1666 (P.204) (Q.2)
Browne, Thomas, planter, m. Alise Horton, 26 Jul 1692 (P.210) (Q.18)
Browne, Thomas, s/o Thomas and Alice Browne of Pickawaxon Parish, b. 21 Dec 1693 (Q.21)
Bullott, Benjamin, s/o Joseph and Elizabeth Bullott of Mattawoman, b. 28 Apr 1693 (P.212) (Q.21)
Bullott, Joseph, s/o Joseph and Elizabeth Bullott of Mattawoman, b. 8 Feb 1688 (P.212) (Q.14)
Burdit, Elizabeth; d/o Thomas and Verlinda [reg. 1668] (C.271)
Burdit, Francis; d/o Thomas and Verlinda [reg. 1668] (C.271)
Burdit, Parthenia; d/o Thomas and Verlinda [reg. 1668] (C.271)
Burdit, Sarah; d/o Thomas and Verlinda [reg. 1668] (C.271)
Carr, Grace m. Geo. Mackmillion Jan 1669 (D.108)

Causin, Ignatius, s/o Ignatius and Jane Causin of Portobacco, b. 10 Sep 1685 (Q.11)

Causin, Jane, d/o Ignatius and Jane Caussin of Portobacco, b. 11 Jul 1682 (Q.9)

Causin, William, s/o Ignatius and Jane Causin of Portobacco, b. 20 Feb 1692 (Q.20)

Chandler, William, s/o William & Jane of Portobacco, b. 13 Oct 1678 (P.206)

Chandler, William, s/o William and Mary Chandler of Portobacco, b. 13 Oct 1678 (Q.6)

Chapman, Mary, d/o Thomas and Elizabeth Chapman of Nanjemy, b. 19 Aug 1693 (Q.21)

Chapman, Thomas, s/o Thomas and Elizabeth Chapman of Nanjemy, b. 26 Mar 1690 (Q.16)

CHARLES COUNTY COURT RECORDS

Charleson, Charles, m. Dorothy Mulgraves, widow, 14 Nov 1689 (P.208) (Q.15)

Cherrybub, Elizabeth, d/o John and Mary Cherrybub of Pickawaxon, b. 28 Mar 1687 (P.212) (Q.13)

Cherrybub, John (twin), s/o John and Mary Cherrybub of Pickawaxon, b. 20 Mar 1690 (P.212) (Q.16)

Cherrybub, Walter, s/o John and Mary Cherrybub of Pickawaxon, b. 25 Feb 1693 (Q.22)

Cherrybub, William (twin), s/o John and Mary Cherrybub of Pickawaxon, b. 20 Mar 1690 (Q.16)

Clarke, Ambros, s/o John Clarke, b. 13 Sep 1666; buried on 18 Feb following (P.204) (Q.2)

Clash, John, s/o Nicholas and Mary Clash of Portobacco, b. 20 Sep 1693 (Q.21)

Cofer, John, s/o John and Elizabeth Cofer of Portobacco, b. 5 Mar 1694 (Q.25)

Cofer, Sarah, d/o Thomas and Mary Cofer of Portobacco, b. 28 Oct 1694 (Q.24)

Cofer, Thomas, s/o John Cofer, b. 25 Nov 1667 [15 Aug; C.253] (P.204) (Q.3)

Coghill, James, s/o William & Christian of Portobacco, b. 10 Jan 1692 (P.212)

Cogwell, James, s/o James and Anne Cogwell of Nanjemy, b. 11 Jul 1693 (Q.21)
Cogwell, James, s/o William Cogwell and Christian Cogwell of Portobacco, b. 10 Jan 1692 (Q.19)
Cole, John, s/o Philip and Mary Cole of head of Wicomico River, 10 Jan 1678 (P.206) (Q.6)
Cole, Philip, s/o Philip and Mary Cole of head of Wicomico River, b. 4 Dec 1680 (P.206) (Q.7)
Cooper, Anne, d/o Nicholas and Penelope Cooper, b. 15 Mar 1688 (P.208) (Q.14)
Cooper, John, s/o Nicholas and Penelope Cooper, b. 14 Dec 1686 (P.208) (Q.12)
Cooper, Prudence, d/o Nicholas and Penelope Cooper of the River side, b. 11 Apr 1692 (Q.20)
Corner; child of Gilbert Corner, b. 4 Jun 1667 (C.251)
Cornish, Edward, s/o John and Martha Cornish of Mattawoman, b. 10 Oct 1682 (P.209) (Q.8)
Cornish, Elizabeth, d/o John and Martha Cornish of Mattawoman, b. 18 Aug 1678 (P.209) (Q.6)
Cornish, John, s/o John and Martha Cornish of Mattawoman, b. 27 May 1693 (Q.21)
Cornish, Margarett, d/o John and Martha Cornish of Mattawoman, b. last day of Nov 1690 (P.209) (Q.16)
Cornish, Martha, d/o John and Martha Cornish of Mattawoman, b. 4 May 1687 (P.209) (Q.13)
Cornish, Richard, s/o John and Martha Cornish of Mattawoman, b. 11 Dec 1679 (P.209) (Q.6)
Cosleton, Marie, d/o Robert Cosleton, b. 6 Feb 1667 (C.260)
Cotterell, Elizabeth, d/o James and Elizabeth Cotterell of head of Wicomico River, b. last day of Apr 1689 (Q.15)
Cotterell, James, s/o James and Elizabeth Cotterell of head of Wicomico River, b. 7 Sep 1694 (Q.23)
Cotterell, Jane, d/o James and Elizabeth Cotterell of head of Wicomico River, b. 15 Aug 1690 (Q.17)
Courts, Anne, d/o John and Charity Courts of Pickawaxon, b. 29 Aug 1693 (Q.22)

Courts, Charity, d/o John and Charity Courts of Pickawaxon, b. 4 Oct 1680 (P.210) (Q.7)
Courts, Elizabeth, d/o John and Margaret Courts, b. 15 May 1663 (P.205) (Q.1)
Courts, John, s/o John and Charity Courts of Pickawaxon, b. 3 Mar 1691 (P.210) (Q.17)
Courts, John, s/o John and Margarett Courts, b. 19 Feb 1655 (P.205) (Q.1)
Courts, Margarett, d/o John and Margaret Courts, b. 15 Jan 1665 (P.205) (Q.2)
Cox, Margarett, d/o James and Margarett Cox of Pickawaxon, b. 2 Nov 1680 (Q.7)
Cox, Thomasine, d/o James and Anne Cox of Pickawaxon, b. 27 Dec 1690 (Q.16)
Davis, Elizabeth, d/o John and Elizabeth Davis of Pickawaxon, b. 15 Jan 1688 (Q.14)
Davis, Mary, d/o John and Elizabeth Davis of Pickawaxon, b. 25 Dec 1685 (Q.11)
Davis, Thomas, tailor, m. Elizabeth Clouder, d/o Richard and Temperance Clouder of Nanjemy in 1693 (Q.21)
Dawson, John & Elizabeth Thirst, m. 16 Sep 1690 (P.210) (Q.18)
Dawson, John m. Elizabeth Thirst, 16 Sep 1692
Dawson, Mary, d/o John and Elizabeth Dawson, b. 22 Sep 1692 (P.210) (Q.18)
Dent, Anne, d/o William & Elizabeth of Nanjemy, b. __ Mar 1692 (P.212)
Dent, Anne, d/o William and Elizabeth Dent of Nanjemy, b. __ Mar 1692; bapt. 16 Mar 1692 (Q.19)
Dent, George, s/o William & Elizabeth Dent of Nanjemy, b. 27 Sep 1690; bapt. Christ Church 16 Apr following (P.209) (Q.16)
Dent, Gerard, bapt. 3 Feb 1688, s/o William & Elizabeth; these 3 children bapt. at their home at Portobacco by John Turlinge; document dated 25 May 1689 (P.208) (Q.14)
Dent, Peter, s/o William and Elizabeth Dent of Nanjemy b. __; bapt. 13 Jan 1694 (Q.24)

Dent, Thomas, s/o William and Elizabeth Dent near Portobacco, b. 15 Nov 1685; bapt. 19 Dec 1685 (P.208) (Q.11)

Dent, William and Elizabeth Fowke, d/o Mrs. Anne Fowke of Portobacco m. by Mr. John Turling on 8 Feb 1684 (Q.10)

Dent, William s/o William and Elizabeth Dent of Portobacco, .b. 1687; bapt. 25 Dec 1687 (P.208) (Q.13)

Deverell, Elizabeth, d/o Thomas and Anne Deverell, b. 1 Jan 1679 (P.207) (Q.6)

Dickason, Thomas, s/o Jeremy; chooses John Cable as guardian; Aug 1678 (H.1)

Dixon, Thomas, s/o Thomas Dixon of Pickawaxen, b. 8 Jun 1692 (P.210) (Q.18)

Dod, Anne, d/o Richard and Jane Dod at head of Baker's Creek, b. 24 Sep 1692 (P.210) (Q.18)

Dod, John, s/o Richard and Mary Dod, b. 2 Jul 1666 (P.206) (Q.2)

Dod, Mary, d/o Richard and Mary Dod, b. 25 Feb 1666 (P.204) (Q.2)

Dod, Richard, s/o Richard and Mary Dod of Potomac River, b. 13 Jan 1670 (P.206) (Q.4)

Dod, Richard, s/o Richard Dod, b. 4 Jan 1662 (P.204) (Q.1)

Downes, Robert, s/o Robert Downes, b. 4 Feb 1670 (P.207) (Q.4)

Duglas, Elizabeth, d/o John Duglas, b. 26 Apr 1673 (E.126) (P.205) (Q.4)

Duglas, John, s/o John and Catherine (sic) Duglas of Pickawaxon, cooper, b. 29 Oct 1686 (Q.12)

Duglas, John, s/o John Duglas, cooper, & Mary (sic) of Pickawaxen, b. 29 Oct 1686 (P.210)

Dutton, Matthew, s/o Thomas and Elizabeth Dutton of Wicomico, b. 28 Sep 1692 (P.211) (Q.18)

Dutton, Notley, s/o Thomas and Elizabeth Dutton of Wicomico, b. 19 Dec 1694 (Q.24)

Edgar, John, 3rd son of Richard and Joanna Edgar b. 30 Aug 1699 (Q.19)

Edgar, Sarah and Elizabeth, twin daughters of Richard & Joanna Edgar, were born 28 Oct 1706 (Q.123) (Q.26)

Edgar, William, s/o Richard and Johannah Edgar, b. 24 Jun 1693 (Q.19)

Elliott, William, s/o William and Joan Elliott of head of
Wicomico River (Q.9)

Emerson, William, s/o Nicholas Emmerson, b. 17 Nov 1666
(P.204) (Q.2)

Ettye, Rachell, d/o Arthur and Elizabeth Ettye of Wicomico, b. 30
Jul 1694 (Q.23)

Farlowe [or Farlor], William, s/o Ambros Farlowe, b. 15 Feb
1671; [15 Feb 1672 (E.166)] (P.205) (Q.4)

Fendall, Samuel; brother of Josias Fendall 1676 (F.194)

Ford, Edward of Chingamuxon, d. 6 Jan 1693 (Q.22)

Ford, Posthuma, d/o Edward and Elizabeth Ford of Chingamuxon,
b. 29 Jul 1694 (Q.25)

Fordinandoe, Agatha, d/o Peter and Elinor Fordinandoe of
Portobacco, b. 8 Nov 1694 (Q.24)

Fowke, Anne, d/o Gerrard and Sarah Fowke of Nanjemy, b. 13
Jan 1689 (Q.15)

Fowke, Frances, d/o Gerrard and Sarah Fowke of Nanjemy, b. 2
Feb 1691 (Q.17)

Fowke, Gerrard of Portobacco; m. Sarah Burdett the youngest d/o
Thomas Burdett late of this co., 31 Dec 1687 (Q.12)

Fowke, Gerrard, s/o Gerrard and Sarah Fowke of Nanjemy, b. 16
Oct 1687 (Q.13)

Fowke, Katherine, d/o Gerrard and Sarah Fowke of Nanjemy, b. 8
Apr 694 (Q.23)

Fowke, Mrs. Anne, at Portobacco 8 Feb 1684 joined together Wm.
Dent & Elizabeth Fowke, d/o Anne, in the holy estate of
matrimony; wit. Mrs. Anne Fowke, Col. Wm. Chandler,
Madm. Mary Chandler, Mr. Gerard Fowke, Mrs. Mary
Fowke, Owen Newen & diverse others; license from Hon.
Wm. Diggs, Esq. (P.208)

Franklin, Jane, d/o Henry and Mary Franklin of Wicomico, b. 31
Jan 1692 (P.212) (Q.19)

Franklin, Mary, d/o Henry and Mary Franklin of Wicomico, b. 12
Oct 1689 (P.212) (Q.15)

Garrett, Charles, s/o Charles and Joyce Garrett of head of
Wicomico River, b. 7 May 1684 (P.208) (Q.10)

Geer, George, s/o George and Anne Geer of head of Wicomico, b. 13 Jul 1689 (Q.15)
Geer, Mary, d/o George and Anne Geer of head of Wicomico [black]smith, b. 12 Jun 1683 (Q.9)
Geer, Sarah, s/o George and Anne Geer of head of Wicomico River, b. 1 May 1686 (Q.12)
Gibson, Thomas, s/o Thomas and Elizabeth Gibson of Pickawaxon, b. 30 May 1694 (Q.23)
Godfrey, Thomas; s/o George and Mary; 1680 (H.292)
Godfrey, William; s/o George and Mary 1680 (H.292)
Goodrick, Mary, d/o Robert Goodrick, b. 13 Mar 1673 (P.205) (Q.4)
Goos, George, s/o George & Anne, b. 13 Jul 1689 (P.209)
Goos, Mary, d/o George & Anne of head of Wicomico River, b. 12 Jun 1683 (P.209)
Goos, Sarah, d/o George & Anne, b. 1 May 1686 (P.209)
Goureley, Elizabeth, d/o John and Barbary Goureley, b. 20 Oct 1690 (Q.17)
Goureley, John, s/o John and Barbary Gourely of Cedar Point Neck, b. 23 Apr 1693 (P.212) (Q.21)
Goureley, Thomas, s/o John and Barbary Goureley of Cedar Point Neck, b. 4 Apr 1686 (Q.12)
Graves, George, s/o George and Alice Graves of head of Wicomico River, b. 2 Jun 1687 (Q.13)
Graves, John, s/o George and Alice Graves of head of Wicomico River, b. 9 Feb 1694 (Q.25)
Greene, Francis, s/o Francis and Elizabeth Greene of Portobacco, b. 23 Apr 1694 (Q.25)
Greene, Leonard, s/o Francis and Elizabeth Greene of Portobacco, b. 30 May 1691 (Q.20)
Greene, Verlinda, d/o Francis and Elizabeth Greene of Portobacco, b. 16 Aug 1692 (Q.20)
Greene, William, s/o Robert and Mary Greene of Portobacco, b. 28 Dec 1694 (Q.25)
Groves, Elizabeth, d/o George and Alice Groves of head of Wicomico River, b. 1 Feb 1692 (P.211) (Q.19)

Groves, William, s/o George and Alice Groves of head of
Wicomico River, b. 24 May 1690 (Q.16)
Guy, Elizabeth, d/o Charles and Elizabeth Guy of Wicomico, b. 1
Jul 1693 (Q.21)
Gwynn, Anne, d/o Christopher and Susanna Gwynn, b. 27 Jul 1692
(P.210) (Q.18)
Hall, John, s/o William and Mary Hall of Portobacco, Doctor, b.
4 Nov 1692 (P.211) (Q.18)
Hall, Richard, s/o Richard and Mary Hall of Portobacco, b. 28 Jul
1679 (P.207) (Q.6)
Hanson, Anne, d/o John and Mary Hanson of Portobacco, b. 18 Jan
1692 (P.212) (Q.19)
Hardy, Henry, of Pickawaxon, m. Elinor Compton, d/o John
Compton of St. Mary's Co., 25 Aug 1694 (Q.23)
Harris, John, s/o Thomas and Mary Harris of Pickawaxon, b. 5
Mar 1684 (P.212) (Q.10)
Harris, Mary, d/o Thomas and Mary Harris of Pickawaxon, b. 16
Nov 1680 (P.212) (Q.7)
Harris, Richard; orphan of Richard Harris (H.330)
Harris, Susanna; orphan of Richard Harris chooses William
Brown and Mary as guardians; 10 Aug 1680 (H.330)
Harris, Thomas, s/o Thomas and Mary Harris of Pickawaxon, b. 6
Feb 1682 (P.212) (Q.8)
Harris, ____; orphan of Richard Harris (H.330)
Harrisson, Catherine, d/o Joseph Harrisson, b. 4 Jan 1666 (P.204)
(Q.2)
Harrisson, Elizabeth, d/o Joseph Harrisson, b. 11 Mar 1663
(P.204) (Q.1)
Harrisson, Elizabeth, d/o Richard and Jane Harrisson of Nanjemy,
b. 24 Jul 1685 (Q.11)
Harrisson, Joseph, s/o Richard and Jane Harrisson of Nanjemy, b.
27 Oct 1687 (Q.13)
Harrisson, Mary, d/o Joseph Harrison, b. 21 Dec 1661 (P.204)
(Q.1)
Harrisson, Richard, s/o Joseph Harrison, b. 12 Oct 1659 (P.204)
(Q.1)

Harrisson, Richard, s/o Richard and Jane Harrisson of Nanjemy, b. 31 Jan 1689 (Q.15)
Harrisson, Tabitha, d/o Richard and Jane Harrisson of Nanjemy b. 23 Jun 1693 (Q.22)
Hawking [or Howling], Mary, d/o William and Mary Hawking of Portobacco, b. 29 Jun 1687 (Q.13)
Hawking, Mary, d/o William & Mary, b. 20 Jun 1687 (P.208)
Hawking, William, s/o William & Mary Hawking of Portobacco, b. 18 Mar 1689 (P.208) (Q.15)
Hawkins, Alexander Smith, s/o Henry and Sarah Hawkins, Jr. of head of Wicomico River, b. 20 Jan 1691 (Q.17)
Hawkins, Henry, s/o Henry, Jr. and Sarah Hawkins of head of Wicomicoof Zachia Hundred, b. 5 Jan 1689 (P.208) (Q.15)
Herberd, William, s/o John and Elizabeth Herberd of head of Wicomico River, b. 6 Jul 1688 (Q.14)
Herbert, Catherine, d/o William and Mary Herbert of Pickawaxon, b. 6 Dec 1692 (P.211) (Q.19)
Herbert, William, s/o John & Elizabeth of Zachia Hundred, b. 6 Jul 1688 (P.208)
Hill, Onsley, s/o Thomas and Mary Hill, servants to Benjamin Rozer of Portobacco, b. 5 May 1677 [bapt. 3 Jun 1677; F.244] (P.206) (Q.5)
Hills, daughter of William Hills, b. 7 Aug 1667 (C.253)
Hills, William, m. Edith Headlow __ Jun 1667 [at Mr. Montague's; C.253] (P.204) (Q.3)
Holt, Jane, d/o James and Margarett Holt of Pickawaxon Parish, b. 19 Nov 1693 (Q.21)
Holt, Robert, s/o William and Mary Holt of Portobacco, b. 15 Feb 1694 (Q.25)
Hoskins, Benedistal, d/o Philip Hoskings and Elizabeth Hoskings of Portobacco, b. 18 Dec 1685 (Q.11)
Hoskins, Elizabeth, d/o Philip Hoskins and Elizabeth Hoskins of Portobacco, b. 9 Feb 1687 (Q.13)
Hoskins, Jane, d/o Philip and Elizabeth Hawkins of Portobacco, b. 1 Mar 1681 (Q.8)
Hoskins, Margarett, d/o Philip Hoskins and Elizabeth Hoskins of Portobacco, b. 15 Aug 1694 (Q.23)

Hoskins, Mary, d/o Philip and Elizabeth Hoskins of Portobacco, b. 24 Mar 1692 (Q.20)
Hoskins, William, s/o Philip Hoskings and Elizabeth Hoskings of Portobacco, b. 18 Mar 1690 (Q.17)
Hungerford, Elizabeth, d/o William and Margarett Hungerford of Portobacco, b. 14 Feb 1691 (Q.20)
Hungerford, William, s/o William and Margarett Hungerford of Portobacco, b. 12 Jun 1694 (Q.23)
Hunt, Alice m. Garret Synnet 21 Nov 1666 (C.253)
Hunt, Mary, "ye daughter of Law of Garrett Sinnett", b. 2 days before Easter 1665 (P.204) (Q.2)
Hus, Robert, living at Edward Tells at Mattawoman, formerly belonging to Robert Smallpage, d. 24 Jul 1694 (Q.23)
Hussey, Thomas m. relict of John Nevill by 15 Nov 1665 (D.134)
Izall, servant of William Marshall, bur. 31 Aug 1667 (C.251)
Jenkins, Enock, s/o Daniel and Elizabeth Jenkins of Pickawaxon, b. last day of Jul 1694 (Q.23)
Jenkinson, Ignatius, s/o William Jenkinson and Mary Jenkinson of Wicomico, b. 2 May 1693 (Q.22)
Jones, Anne, d/o Richard and Jane Jones of Cedar Point Neck, b. Christmas 1684 (P.208) (Q.10)
Jones, Elizabeth, d/o Richard and Elizabeth Jones of Mattawoman, b. 27 Apr 1679 (P.206) (Q.6)
Jones, Jane, d/o Moses and ____ Jones of Portobacco, b. 4 Jan 1692 (P.211) (Q.19)
Jones, Margarett, d/o Richard Jones and Elizabeth Jones of Mattawoman, b. 6 May 1673 (P.206) (Q.4)
Jones, Mary, d/o Richard and Elizabeth Jones, b. 27 May 1677 (P.206) (Q.5)
Jones, Richard, s/o Richard and Jane Jones of Cedar Point Neck, b. 1 Apr 1680 (P.208) (Q.7)
Jones, Thomas, s/o Moses and Elizabeth Jones of Portobacco, b. 2 Mar 1694 (Q.24)
Karnes, Henry, s/o Robert and Mary Karnes of Portobacco, b. 3 Sep 1688 (P.209) (Q.14)
Karnes, William, s/o Robert Karnes, tailor, and Mary of Portobacco, b. 3 Apr 1691 (P.210) (Q.17)

Kingersley, Elizabeth, d/o George and Elizabeth Kingersley of Portobacco, b. 25 Mar 1694 (Q.25)
Kingersley, Mary, d/o George and Elizabeth Kingersley of Portobacco, b. 15 Feb 1692 (Q.20)
Kirkley, Christopher, s/o Christopher and Catherine Kirkley of head of Wicomico, b. 3 Feb 1684 (P.211) (Q.10)
Kirkley, Susanna, d/o Christopher and Catherine Kirkley of head of Wicomico River, b. 17 Mar 1681 (P.211) (Q.8)
Knight, Anne, d/o John and Jennett Knight of Cedar Point Neck, b. last Thursday in March 1688 (Q.14)
Knight, John, s/o John and Jennett Knight of Cedar Point Neck, b. last day of Sep 1691 (Q.17)
Knight, Mary, d/o John and Jennett Knight of Cedar Point Neck, b. 27 Mar 1694 (Q.23)
Kylborne, Francis, wife Eliza, court record 14 Mar 1670 (F.88)
Lambert, Elinor, d/o John Lambert, b. Jan 1667 (Q.3)
Lambert, Elizabeth, d/o John Lambert, b. Jan 1667; [Elinor Lambert age 5 in Jan 1672 (E.72)] (P.205)
Lambert, John, s/o John Lambert, b. 5 Feb 1664; [age 8 on 4 Feb 1672 (E.72)] (P.205) (Q.1)
Lambert, Samuel, s/o John Lambert, b. 10 Mar 1671; [age 1 on 10 Mar 1672 (E.72)] (P.205) (Q.4)
Lambert, William, s/o John Lambert, b. 27 Feb 1669; [age 3 in 1672 (E.72)] (P.205) (Q.3)
Lampton, Anne, d/o Marke and Elizabeth Lampton of Portobacco, b. 13 Jan 1689 (Q.15)
Lampton, Elizabeth, d/o Marke Lampton and Elizabeth Lampton of Portobacco, b. 8 Aug 1692 (Q.20)
Lampton, Isable, d/o Marke Lampton and Elizabeth Lampton of Portobacco, b. 15 Dec 1694 (Q.24)
Lampton, John, s/o Marke and Elizabeth Lampton of Portobacco, b. 16 Oct 1687 (Q.13)
Lampton, Marke, s/o Marke and Elizabeth Lampton of the head of Portobacco Creek, b. 6 Oct 1680 (P.206) (Q.7)
Lampton, Mary, d/o Marke and Elizabeth Lampton of the head of Portobacco Creek, b. 24 Jan 1678 (P.206) (Q.6)

Lampton, Victoria, d/o Mark Lampton and Elizabeth Lampton of Portobacco, b. 29 May 1685 (Q.11)

Lampton, William, s/o Marke and Elizabeth Lampton of head of Portobacco Creek, b. 29 Apr 1682 (P.207) (Q.8)

Land, Elizabeth, d/o Richard and Penelope Land of Pickawaxon, b. 4 Apr 1691 (P.212) (Q.17)

Land, John, s/o Richard and Penelope Land of Pickawaxon, b. 12 Jan 1689 (P.212) (Q.15)

Land, Richard, s/o Richard and Penelope Land of Pickawaxon, b. 8 Oct 1687 (P.212) (Q.13)

Land, Susanna, d/o Richard and Penelope Land of Pickawaxon, b. 8 Nov 1694 (Q.25)

Lane, Elizabeth, d/o Wm. Lane, b. last day of May 1668 (P.205)

Langhly, Mary, age 26, swore Thomas Pope father of her child (D.126)

Leete, John, s/o George and Elinor Leete of Portobacco, b. 15 Jan 1687 (Q.12)

Lewis, David, s/o David and Jane Lewis of Pickawaxon, b. 14 Dec 1694 (Q.24)

Lewis, Henry, s/o David and Jane Lewis of Pickawaxon, b. 16 Oct 1687 (P.211) (Q.13)

Lewis, Isable, d/o David and Jane Lewis of Pickawaxon, b. 4 Aug 1690 (P.211) (Q.16)

Lewis, Mary, d/o David and Jane Lewis of Pickawaxon, b. 28 Nov 1692 (P.211) (Q.18)

Lindsey, Edmond, s/o Edmond, dec'd; custody of Wm. Chandler to age 21; Mar 1677/8 (G.129)

Lindsey, James, s/o James Lindsey, b. 10 Feb 1666 [18 Feb; C.253] (P.204) (Q.2)

Ling, Francis, s/o Francis and Mary Ling, b. 9 Oct 1676 (P.207) (Q.5)

Ling, Mary, d/o Francis and Mary Ling, b. 27 Mar 1673 (P.207) (Q.5)

Ling, Michaell, s/o Francis and Mary Ling, b. 22 Jan 1671 (P.207) (Q.4)

Ling, William, s/o Francis and Mary Ling, b. 11 Mar 1669 (P.207) (Q.3)

Ling, William; son-in-law of Richard Hall and natural born son of Mary his wife; 1680 (H.293)
Lomax, Catherine, d/o Cleborne and Blanch Lomax of head of Wicomico River, b. 13 May 1677 (Q.5)
Lomax, Cleborne, s/o Cleborne and Blanch Lomax of the head of Wicomico River, b. 22 Jan 1678 (P.206) (Q.6)
Lomax, John, s/o Cleborne Lomax and Blanch Lomax of the head of Wicomico River, [black]smith, b. 20 Nov 1683 (P.207) (Q.9)
Lomax, Katherine, d/o Cleborne and Blanche; b. 14 or 16 May 1677 (P.206) (G.55)
Lomax, Ralph, s/o Cleborne Lomax and Blanch Lomax at head of Wicomico River, b. last day of July 1673 (P.205) (Q.4)
Lomax, Susanna, d/o Cleborne and Blanch Lomax of head of Wicomico River, b. 3 Apr 1675 (P.206) (Q.5)
Lomax, Thomas, s/o Cleborne Lomax and Blanch Lomax of head of Wicomico, b. 8 Apr 1681 bapt. 4 Jul 1681 (P.206) (Q.8)
Long, Jemima, d/o Robert Long, b. 5 Jan 1667 (P.205) (Q.3)
Love, Elizabeth, d/o William Love, b. last day of May 1668 (Q.3)
Luckett, Ignatius, s/o Samuel and Elizabeth Luckett of Portobacco, b. 30 Jan 1689 (Q.15) (P.210)
Luckett, Samuell, s/o Samuel and Elizabeth Luckett at the head of Portobacco Creeke, b. 10 Oct 1685 (P.207) (Q.11)
Luckett, Thomas, s/o Samuell and Elizabeth Luckett at the head of Portobacco Creeke, b. 12 Aug 1688 (P.208) (Q.14)
Lumbrozo, John, s/o John Lumbrozo, dec'd, b. Jun 1666 (C.266)
Mackmillion, George m. Grace Carr Jan 1669 (P.205) (Q.3)
Mackmillion, Peter, s/o George and Grace Mackmillion, b. Apr 1670 (P.205) (Q.3)
Magitee, James, s/o Patrick Magitee and Rose Magitee of head of Portobacco Creek, b. last week of Mar 1695 (Q.26) (Q.123)
Mankin, Elizabeth, d/o Stephen and Mary Mankin of Portobacco, b. 22 Jun 1682 (P.207) (Q.8)
Mankin, Hope (twin), d/o Stephen Mankin and Mary Mankin of head of Wicomico River, b. 9 Jan 1694 (Q.24)
Mankin, James (twin), s/o Stephen Mankin and Mary Mankin at head of Wicomico River, b. 9 Jan 1694 (Q.24)

Mankin, John, s/o Stephen and Mary Mankin of Portobacco, b. 16 Jan 1686 (P.207) (Q.12)

Mankin, Josiah, s/o Stephen and Mary Mankin of Portobacco, b. 18 Jan 1690 (P.210) (Q.16)

Mankin, Margarett, d/o Stephen and Mary Mankin of Portobacco, b. 20 Mar 1688 (Q.14)

Mankin, Mary, d/o Stephen & Mary of Portobacco, b. 9 Feb 1692 (P.212) (Q.19)

Mankin, Mary, d/o Stephen & Mary, b. 20 Mar 1688 (P.208)

Mankin, Stephen, s/o Stephen and Mary Mankin of Portobacco, b. 4 Jul 1685 (P.207) (Q.11)

Mankin, Tubbman, s/o Stephen and Mary Mankin of Portobacco, b. 9 Apr 1696 (Q.26) (Q.123)

Mannister, Jno., dec'd; father of infant 1 1/2 yrs. old Jun 1681 (I.124)

Maris, Sarah, d/o Thomas Maris, b. 11 Nov 1667 (C266)

Marshall, Barbary, d/o William and Elizabeth Marshall of head of Wicomico River, b. 30 Sep or Oct 1692 (P.210) (Q.18)

Marshall, Elizabeth, d/o William Marshall, b. 15 Apr 1667 (P.204) (Q.3)

Marshall, Thomas, s/o William and Elizabeth Marshall of head of Wicomico River, b. 27 Jan 1694 (Q.24)

Marshall, William, s/o William and Elizabeth Marshall of head of Wicomico River, b. 12 Sep 1690 (P.210) (Q.16)

Martin, Anne, d/o James and Elizabeth Martin of Nanjemy, b. 23 Apr 1686; same date as William (Q.12)

Martin, Catherine, d/o John and Mary Martin of Portobacco, b. 3 Dec 1681 (Q.8)

Martin, Elizabeth, d/o James and Elizabeth Martin of Nanjemy, b. 10 Apr 1683 (Q.9)

Martin, John, s/o Mitchaell and Jillian Martin of Portobacco, b. 15 Mar 1691 (Q.17)

Martin, John, s/o Thomas and Damaris Martin of Wicomico, boatwright, b. 7 Dec 1693 (Q.21)

Martin, Katherine, d/o Joseph & Mary of Portobacco, b. 3 Dec 1681 (P.207)

Martin, Penelope, d/o John Martin, carpenter, & Demaris of
    Wicomico, b. 13 Nov 1690 (P.210) (Q.16)
Martin, William, s/o James and Elizabeth Martin of Nanjemy, b.
    23 Apr 1686; same date as Anne (Q.12)
Mason, Elizabeth, d/o Philip and Mary Mason, b. 6 Oct 1685
    (P.207) (Q.11)
Mason, John, s/o Philip and Mary Mason of Piscataway, b. 19 Jul
    1693 (Q.21)
Mason, Philip, s/o Philip and Mary Mason of Piscataway, b. 2 Jun
    1689 (P.209) (Q.15)
Mason, Samuell, s/o Philip and Mary Mason, b. 18 Apr 1687
    (P.207) (Q.13)
Mason, William, s/o Philip and Mary Mason of Piscataway, b. 23
    Jan 1690 (P.210) (Q.16)
Maston, John, s/o Richard and Mary Maston of Baker's Creek, b.
    last day of Dec 1693 (Q.22)
Mathena, Elizabeth; d/o George Mathena; 1680 (H.293)
Maycocke, Seabright, s/o Seabright Maycocke, d. 5 Sep 1674
    (F.10)
Miller, John, s/o John and Grace Miller of Nanjemy, b. 5 Nov
    1673 (P.209) (Q.4)
Miller, Peter, s/o John and Grace Miller of Nanjemy, b. 7 Jul
    1682 (P.209) (Q.8)
Millsteade, William, s/o Edward and Susanna Millsteade, b. 20
    Jul 1685 (P.208) (Q.11)
Mingoe, Charles, s/o Lewis Joseph and Elizabeth Mingoe of
    Nanjemy, b. 14 Mar 1685 (P.209) (Q.11)
Mingoe, Elizabeth, d/o Lewis Joseph and Elizabeth Mingoe of
    Nanjemy, b. 11 May 1689 (P.209) (Q.15)
Mingoe, Lewis, s/o Lewis Joseph and Elizabeth Mingoe of
    Nanjemy, b. 12 Mar 1681 (P.209) (Q.8)
Mingoe, Thomas, s/o Lewis Joseph and Elizabeth Mingoe of
    Nanjemy, b. 18 Oct 1691 (Q.17)
Moody, Anne, d/o William and Jane Moody of head of
    Wicomico River, b. 2 Mar 1692 (P.212) (Q.19)
Moore, Elizabeth, d/o Henry and Elizabeth Moore, b. 13 Mar
    1664 [30 Mar; E.87] (P.205) (Q.1)

Moore, Henry, s/o Henry and Elizabeth Moore, b. 3 Oct 1665 (P.205) (Q.2)
Moore, John, s/o Henry and Elizabeth Moore, b. 13 Mar 1669 [b. 15 Mar 1674 (D.163)] (P.205) (Q.3)
Moore, Thomas, s/o Henry and Elizabeth Moore, b. 9 Oct 1667 (P.205) (Q.3)
Morrice, child; s/o Richard Morrice, b. 12 Sep, bur. 20 Sep 1667 (C.251)
Morris, Mary, d/o Richard and Penelope Morris of Cedar Point Neck, b. 22 Dec 1680 (P.212) (Q.7)
Morris, Penelope, d/o Richard and Penelope Morris of Cedar Point Neck, b. 13 Nov 1684 (P.212) (Q.10)
Morris, Thomas, s/o Thomas and Anne Morris of Wicomico b. 9 Nov 1693 (Q.21)
Murphey, Dennis, d. at James Lyndsey's 23 Sep 1667 (P.205) (Q.3)
Nevill, [Joan] m.Thomas Hussey by 15 Nov 1665 (D.134)
Newton, Richard, s/o Richard and Jane Newton of Wicomico, b. 1693; bapt. 13 May 1693 (P.212) (Q.21)
OBryan, Elinor, d/o Matthias OBryan, b. 5 Nov 1666 [Obrian; C.222] (P.204) (Q.2)
OBryan, Elizabeth, wife of Matthias OBryan d. 6 May 1670 (P.205) (Q.3)
OBryan, William, s/o Matthias and Magdalen OBryan of Mattawoman, b. 6 Mar 1672 (P.206) (Q.4)
Ord, Anne, d/o Peter and Anne Ord of Wicomico, b. 19 Sep 1694 (Q.23)
Ord, James, s/o Peter and Ann Ord of Wicomico, b. 21 Apr 1690 (P.209) (Q.16)
Ord, Mary, s/o Peter Ord and Anne Ord of Wicomico River, b. 24 Mar 1683 (P.209) (Q.9)
Ord, Thomas, s/o Peter and Anne Ord of Wicomico, b. 19 Nov 1686 (P.209) (Q.12)
Paine, John, m. Marie White 23 Sep 1667 (P.204) (Q.3)
Payne, John; son-in-law of Geo. Godfrey; 1673/4
Peircy, Thomas, d. 5 Nov 1666 (P.204) (Q.2)

Penn, Elizabeth, d/o William and Mary Penn of head of Wicomico River, b. 2 Jun 1695 (Q.26) (Q.123)

Penn, Marke, s/o William & Mary of head of Wicomico, b. 24 Nov 1692 (P.211) (Q.18)

Philpot, Charles s/o Edward Philpot, b. 19 Feb 1667 (P.204) (Q.3)

Philpott, Edward, s/o Edward and Susanna Philpott of head of Wicomico, b. 14 Jan 1687 (P.210) (Q.13)

Philpott, John, s/o Edward and Susanna Philpott of the head of Wicomico River, b. 13 Oct 1692 (P.210) (Q.18)

Philpott, Susanna, d/o Edward and Susanna Phillpott of head of Wicomico River, b. 9 Jun 1690 (P.210) (Q.16)

Pope, John, s/o Francis Pope, dec'd; choses Thomas Harris as guardian (F.230)

Posey, Humphrey, s/o John and Susanna Posey of the head of Wicomico River, b. 1 Feb 1683 (P.211) (Q.9)

Posey, John, s/o John Posey and Susanna Posey of head of the Wicomico River, b. 30 Jul 1685 (P.211) (Q.11)

Posey, Mary, d/o Benjamin and Mary Posey of head of Wicomico River, b. 10 Sep 1693 (Q.22)

Posey, Susanna, d/o Benjamin and Mary Posey of head of Wicomico River, b. 1 Jun 1691 (P.212) (Q.17)

Powell, Robert, s/o Robert and _____ Powell of Pickawaxon, b. 17 Nov 1692 and bapt. 10 Jan 1692 (P.211) (Q.18)

Price, Mary, d/o Robert and Anne Price of Portobacco, b. 12 Nov 1692 (P.211) (Q.18)

Raines, Elizabeth, d/o John and Elizabeth Raines of Mattawoman, b. 26 Jun 1684 (P.209) (Q.10)

Raines, Henry, s/o John and Elizabeth Raines of Mattawoman, b. 3 Sep 1686 (P.209) (Q.12)

Raines, Lucy, d/o John and Elizabeth Raines of Mattawoman, b. 7 Dec 1688 (P.209) (Q.14)

Randall, Richard, d. 7 Sep 1667 (Q.3)

Ratclife, Richard, s/o John and Bathsheba Ratclife of Wicomico, b. 16 Dec 1692 (P.211) (Q.19)

Reason, Elizabeth; had a bastard; court of 12 Jun 1666 (C.30)

Redferne, Mary, d/o James and Faith Redferne of Portobacco, b. 16 Dec 1694 (Q.25)

Regon, Charles, s/o James Regon and Joan Regon of Nanjemy, bricklayer, b. 20 May 1692 (Q.20)

Regon, John, s/o James Regon and Joan Regon of Nanjemy, bricklayer, was b. 24 Mar 1685 (Q.11)

Regon, Margarett, d/o James and Joan Regon of Nanjemy, bricklayer, b. 12 Feb 1684 (Q.23)

Regon, Mary, d/o James and Joan Regon of Nanjemy, bricklayer, b. 28 Aug 1683 (Q.9)

Regon, Matthew, s/o James Regon and Joan Regon of Nanjemy, bricklayer, b. 24 Apr 1687 (Q.13)

Regon, William s/o James Regon and Joan Regon of Nanjemy, bricklayer, b. 31 Jan 1690 (Q.16)

Right, Ellino, d/o George Rights, b. 7 Oct 1683 (P.207)

Robinson, John, m. Elizabeth Browne 21 Mar 1666 (P.204) (Q.2)

Robinson, Mary, d/o Richard and Joyce Robinson of the head of Wicomico River, b. 17 Dec 1679 (P.208) (Q.6)

Robinson, Susanna, d/o Richard and Joyce Robinson at the head of Wicomico River, b. 20 Oct 1677 (P.208) (Q.5)

Rookwood, Edward, s/o Edward and Mary Rookwood of Chingamuxon, b. 25 Dec 1692 (P.211) (Q.19)

Rouse, John, servant to John Cage, d. 25 Jan 1666 (P.204) (Q.2)

Rozer, Mary, d/o Benjamin and Mary Rozer of Portobacco, b. 6 Apr 1675 (P.206) (Q.5)

Rozer, Notley, s/o Benjamin and Mary Rozer, b. 1 Jul 1673 (D.140) (Q.4) (P.205)

Ruelants [or Roolants], Dinah, d/o Robert and Margery Ruelants of Wicomico, b. 2 May 1677 (P.210) (Q.5)

R[andall]?, Richard, d. 7 Sep 1667 [Richard Randall, d. 7 Nov 1667 (C.253)] (P.204)

Sapcoate, Elizabeth, d/o Abram and Rachell Sapcoate of the river side, b. 12 Nov 1677 (P.208) (Q.5)

Saunders, Charles, s/o Edward and Jane Saunders of west side of Portobacco Creek, b. 18 Jul 1690 (Q.15)

Saunders, Edward, s/o Edward and Jane Saunders of the west side of Portobacco Creek, b. 6 Nov 1685 (Q.11)

Saunders, Mary, d/o John and Sarah Saunders of head of Portobacco Creek, b. 19 Apr 1692 (P.212) (Q.18)

Saunders, Thomas, s/o Edward and Jane Saunders of west side of Portobacco Creek, b. 30 Mar 1688 (Q.14)

Scroggin [also Snoggin], Elizabeth, d/o George Scroggin and Susanna Scroggin of Pickawaxon. b. 14 May 1686 (P.211) (Q.12)

Scroggin, George, s/o George Scroggin and Susanna Scroggin of Pickawaxon, b. 13 Nov 1692 (P.211) (Q.18)

Scroggin, John, s/o John and Susanna Scroggin of Pickawaxon b. 27 Dec 1687 (P.211) (Q.13)

Scroggin, Mary, d/o George and Susanna Scroggin of Pickawaxon, b. 16 Mar 1688 (P.211) (Q.14)

Scroggin, Susanna, d/o George and Susanna Scroggin of Pickawaxon, b. 5 Feb 1694 (Q.24)

Shackerley, Edward, s/o John and Francis Shackerley of head of Wicomico River, b. 3 Aug 1694 (Q.23)

Sinnett, Garrett, m. Alice Hunt 21 Nov 1666 (Q.2) (P.204)

Sinnett, Margaret, d/o Garrett Sinnett, b. 24 Oct 1667 (Q.3)

Sinnett, Margarett, d/o Garrett Sinnett, b. 24 Oct 1667 (P.205)

Smallwood, James, s/o James and Esther Smallwood, b. Oct 1668 (P.205) (Q.3)

Smallwood, John, s/o James and Esther Smallwood, b. Jan 1666 (P.205) (Q.2)

Smallwood, Mary, d/o James and Esther Smallwood, b. Jan 1670 (P.205) (Q.4)

Smallwood, Matthew, s/o James and Esther Smallwood, b. Apr 1673 (P.205) (Q.4)

Smith, Alexander; m. _____ Belaine, widow of John Belaine (F.199)

Smith, Arthur, s/o Richard and Anne Smith of Pickawaxon, b. 23 Apr 1692 (Q.20)

Smith, Elizabeth, d/o Richard and Anne Smith of Pickawaxon, b. 12 Sep 1690 (Q.17)

Smith, Henry, s/o Henry and Margery Smith of Portobacco, b. 5 Nov 1694 (Q.24)

Smith, James, s/o Richard and Anne Smith of Pickawaxon, b. 3 Aug 1694 (Q.25)

Smith, Jane, d/o William and Joan Smith of Wicomico, b. 10 Sep 1694 (Q.23)

Smith, John, m. Margarett Barker 14 Feb 1666 (P.204) (Q.2)

Smith, Richard, s/o Richard and Anne Smith of Pickawaxon, b. 11 Jul 1688 (Q.14)

Smith, Richard, s/o Richard Smith, dec'd, choses William Hinsey guardian (F.230)

Smith, Thomas, s/o Henry and Margery Smith of Portobacco, b. 3 Mar 1692 (Q.20)

Smith, William, s/o William and Joan Smith of Wicomico, b. 15 Sep 1691 (Q.17)

Smoote, Edward, s/o Edward and Lydia Smoote of Wicomico, b. 20 Jun 1693 (Q.21)

Smoote, Elizabeth, d/o Richard Smoote, b. 15 Dec 1666 (P.204) (Q.2)

Smoote, Grace, wife of William Smoote d. 14 Jan 1666[1665; C.251] (P.204) (Q.2)

Smoote, John, s/o Edward and Lydia Smoote of Wicomico, b. 22 Nov 1686 (Q.12)

Smoote, Richard; s/o Richard, dec'd; choose Richard Morris as guardian (H.270)

Stigeleer, Jane, d/o James Stigeleer and Mary his wife of Portobacco Parish, b. 4 Jun 1702 (Q.26) (Q.123)

Story, Elizabeth m. Henry Bonner by 15 Nov 1665 (D.134)

Taylor, John, s/o Thomas & Anne of Pickawaxen, b. 8 Jan 1692 (P.211) (Q.19)

Taylor, Thomas, s/o Thomas and Anne Taylor of Pickawaxon, b. 3 Mar 1694 (Q.24)

Theobald, John, s/o John and Mary Theobald of Portobacco, b. __ Sep 1692 (Q.20)

Thompkins, Giles, s/o Giles & Sarah of Pickawaxen, b. 23 Nov 1692 (P.211)

Thompkins, Giles, s/o Giles and Sarah Thompkins of Pickawaxon, b. 6 Dec 1692 (Q.19)

Thompson, Cuthbert, s/o William and Victoria Thompson of head of Wicomico, b. 12 Sep 1692 (Q.20)

Thompson, Jane, d/o William and Victoria Thompson of head of Wicomico River, b. 13 Nov 1690 (Q.15)
Thompson, Mary, d/o John and Mary Thompson of Portobacco, b. 8 Jan 1694 (sic) (Q.25)
Thompson, Mary, d/o William and Victoria Thompson of head of Wicomico River, b. 12 Feb 1694 (sic) (Q.25)
Thompson, Thomas, s/o William and Victoria Thompson at head of Wicomico River, b. 12 Sep 1682 (Q.9)
Thompson, William, s/o William and Mary Thompson of St. Mary's Co., she being d/o William Britton, m. Victoria Matthews, d/o Thomas and Jane Matthews of Charles Co., 11 Apr 1681 (Q.8)
Thompson, William, s/o William and Victoria Thompson at head of Wicomico River, b. 5 Mar 1684 (Q.10)
Turner, Anne bound apprentice to William Marshall to age 16 (C.244)
Turner, Arthur, eldest s/o Arthur Turner, chose Josias Fendall as guardian (C.244)
Turner, Edward bound apprentice to James Bowling to age 21 (C.244)
Turner, female child of Arthur Turner, dec'd, b. ca mid-Oct 1667; to go to Susannah, wife of George Taylor as guardian (C.244)
Turner, James, second s/o Arthur Turner chose Walter Beane as guardian (C.244)
Tymothy, Mabella, d/o William and Mabella Tymothy of Pickawaxon, b. 12 Oct 1693 (Q.22)
Vassall, Thomas, s/o Levy [or Levy] and Elizabeth Vassall, b. 8 Sep 1680 (P.206) (Q.7 & 8)
Wade, child; s/o Zachery Wade, b. 22 Sep 1666 (C.222)
Wade, Edward, s/o Zachary Wade, b. 22 Aug 1672 (P.205) (Q.4)
Wade, Mary, d/o Zachary Wade, b. 21 Apr 1661 (P.204) (Q.1)
Wade, Sarah, d/o Zachary Wade, b. 7 Jul 1662 (P.204)
Wade, William, s/o Zachary Wade, b. 3 Nov 1673; [3 Dec 1673 (E.170)] (P.205) (Q.4)
Ward, Anne, d/o John and Damaris Ward, b. 5 Feb 1663 (Q.1)
Ward, Anne, d/o John and Damaris Ward, b. 10 Apr 1667 (Q.2)
Ward, Anne, d/o John Ward, b. 5 Feb 1663 (P.204)

Ward, Anne, d/o John Ward, b. 10 Apr 1667 (P.204)
Ward, John, s/o John Ward, b. 16 Mar 1671 (P.205) (Q.4)
Ward, John; s/o John Ward; b. 15 Mar 1674 (E.163)
Ward, Mary, d/o John and Damaris Ward, b. 5 Jul 1665 (P.204) (Q.1)
Warner, Christopher; wife Margaret (F.217)
Warren, Benjamin, s/o Humphrey and Margery Warren of Wicomico, b. 23 Jan 1682 (P.210) (Q.8)
Warren, Charles, s/o Humphrey Warren and Margery Warren of Wicomico, b. 10 Nov 1684 (P.210) (Q.10)
Warren, Elinor, d/o Thomas and Mary Warren of Wicomico, b. 7 Mar 1690 (Q.16)
Warren, Humphrey, s/o Humphrey Warren & Margery Warren of Wicomico, b. 15 Nov 1691 (P.210) (Q.17)
Warren, John, s/o Humphrey & Margery Warren of Wicomico, b. 18 Jun 1687 (P.210) (Q.13)
Warren, Notley, s/o Humphrey & Elizabeth Warren of Wicomico, b. 16 Dec 1675 (P.210) (Q.5)
Wharton, Elizabeth; d/o Thomas and Margaret Wharton (H.292)
Wheeler, Ignatius, s/o John and Mary Wheeler, b. May 1665 (P.205) (Q.2)
Wheeler, James, s/o John and Mary Wheeler, b. 9 days before Christmas 1656 (P.205) (Q.1)
Wheeler, John, s/o John and Mary Wheeler; b. 1654 (P.205) (Q.1)
Wheeler, Luke, s/o Ignatius and Francis Wheeler of Portobacco, b. 8 Feb 1693 (Q.22)
Wheeler, Luke, s/o Ignatius and Francis Wheeler of Portobacco, d. 8 Jan 1694 (Q.24)
Wheeler, Mary, d/o John and Mary Wheeler, b. 22 Mar 1658 (P.205) (Q.1)
Wheeler, Thomas, s/o John and Mary Wheeler, b. 18 Mar 1660 (P.205) (Q.1)
Wheeler, Winifrid, d/o John and Mary Wheeler, b. Mar 1663 (P.205) (Q.1)
Whichaley, Jane, wife of Thomas Whichaley of Pickawaxon, d. 7 Nov 1693 (Q.21)

Whichaley, Thomas and Elizabeth Ford, wife of Edward Ford, dec'd, d/o Thomas Allanson of Chingamuxon, dec'd, m. 25 Apr 1694

White, Marie m. John Paine 23 Sep 1667 (C.253)

Whittymore, Anne, d/o Christopher and Anne Whittymore of Portobacco, b. 5 Sep 1690 (Q.16)

Whittymore, Richard, s/o Christopher and Anne Whittymore of Portobacco, b. 2 Sep 1694 (Q.25)

Wilder, Edward, s/o John & Ever Elday Wilder, of Wicomico, b. 27 Nov 1689; bapt. 4 Dec afsd. (P.210) (Q.15)

Wilder, John, s/o John & Ever Elday Wilder, b. 30 Sep 1692; bapt. 2 Oct afsd. (P.210) (Q.16)

Wilkenson, William; servant of Wade, d. in Jun 1666 (C.222)

Wilkinson, Mary, d/o Lancelot and Mary Wilkinson of Mattawoman, b. 15 Oct 1687 (Q.13)

Williams, John, s/o John and Sarah Williams of the river side, b. 2 Aug 1688 (P.208) (Q.14)

Williams, William, s/o John and Sarah Williams of the river side, b. 2 Oct 1685 (P.208) (Q.11)

Witter, Buckley, s/o Thomas and Mary Witter, b. 26 Jul 1675 (P.207) (Q.5)

Witter, George, s/o Thomas and Mary Witter, b. 9 Oct 1683 (P.210) (Q.9)

Witter, Thomas, s/o Thomas and Mary Witter, b. 9 Feb 1672 (P.207) (Q.4)

Witter, William, s/o Thomas and Mary Witter, b. 26 Sep 1678 (P.207) (Q.6)

Wollcock, Christian, d/o Christopher and Mary Woolcock of Portobacco, b. 10 Dec 1694 (Q.24)

Worrell, Robert; wife Margaret (H.55)

Wright, Elinor, d/o George and Anne Wright, b. 7 Oct 1683 (Q.9)

Wynne, Thomas; wife Elizabeth (F.212)

Yates, Charles, s/o Robert and Rebeckah Yates of Pickawaxon, b. 29 Apr 1692 (P.211) (Q.18)

Yates, Robert, s/o Robert and Rebecca Yates of Pickawaxon, b. 10 Apr 1690 (P.211) (Q.16)

Young, John, s/o Lawrence and Sarah Young at head of Baker's
   Creek, b. 4 Dec 1673 (P.206) (Q.6)
Young, Thomas, s/o Lawrence & Sarah, b. 18 May 1678
Young, Thomas, s/o Lawrence and Sarah Young at head of Baker's
   Creek, b. 18 May 1678 (P.206) (Q.6)

Births, Marriages and Deaths
of
CHRIST CHURCH PARISH
Calvert County, Maryland
1688 - 1847

Page 1

Parker, Gabriell, s/o George and Susanna Parker, b. at house of Mr. Gabrill Parrott at the head of South River, Anne Arundel Co., 4 Dec 1697; baptized by Rev. Thomas Cockshett, minister of All Saint's Parish, Calvert Co. (1)

Parker, Elizabeth, d/o George and Susanna Parker, b. at house of her father near head of Fishing Creek in All Saint's Parish on 29 Sep 1700; baptized by Mr. Cockshett

Parker, Susannah, d/o George and Susanna Parker, b. at Clahammon in Christ Church Parish on 13 Jan 1701; bapt. by Mr. Cockshett

Parker, Mary, d/o George and Susanna Parker, b. at Clahammon, 18 Jul 1704; baptized by Mr. Cockshett

Page 2

Parker, William, s/o of George and Susanna Parker, b. at Clahammon on 15 Aug 1707; baptized at the same place by Mr. G__ DeEmilliane 24 Nov 1707; d. at Mr. Sam'l Chew on 24 Jan 1707

Parker, Lansdown, s/o George and Susanna Parker, b. at Clahammon on 5 Sep 1709; d. 11 Sep 1709

Parrott, Elizabeth (mother of Susanna wife of George Parker), d. at house of George Parker 6 Apr 1706; she was wife of Gabriell Parrott

Culpepper, Mary, d/o Mich'll Culpepper and Eliner his wife, b. 10 Nov 1705 **(2)**

Duke, Elizabeth, d/o James and Ma[rtha] Duke his wife, b. 22 Dec 1705

Hernley, Priscilla, d/o Darbey Hernley and Ann his wife, b. 24 Nov 1703

Page 3

Hernley, Edmond, s/o Darbey Hernley and Ann his wife, b. 25 Nov 1703
Reynolds, James, s/o Ros Reynolds and Elizabeth his wife, on 31 Jan 1705/6
Brome, Henry, s/o John Brome and Ann his wife, b. 15 Sep 1705
Hellen, Richard, s/o David Hellen and Susanna his wife, b. 14 Aug 1701
Gabril, Richard, s/o Elizabeth Gabril, b. 6 Dec 1704
Baker, Violetta, d/o Isaack Baker and Ellinor his wife, b. 25 Jun 1704
Dawkins, Joseph, s/o Joseph Dawkins and Sarah his wife, b. 21 Mar 1703/4

Page 4

Turner, Thomas, s/o John Turner and Johana his wife, b. 16 Apr 1706
Johnson, Ann, d/o William Johnson and Sarah his wife, b. 17 Mar 1705/6
Johnson, Joseph, s/o William Johnson and Sarah his wife, b. 6 Apr 1704
Durkhurt, Margret, d/o Alexander Durkhurt and Ann his wife, b. 6 Jul 1705
Swillaven, Daniel, s/o Daniel Swillaven and Prissilla his wife, b. 10 Oct 1705
Avis, Jane, d/o Robert Avis and Ann his wife, b. 18 Apr 1706
Johnson, Elizabeth, d/o John Johnson and Frances his wife, b. 4 Nov 1704 **(3)**
Johnson, John, s/o John Johnson and Frances his wife, b. 2 Mar 1705

Page 5

Hernley, John, s/o Darbey Hernley and Ann his wife, b. 31 May 1706
Easterling, Henry William, s/o John Easterling and Henritta his wife, b. 7 Oct 1704
Veatch, Mary, d/o William Veatch and Jane his wife, b. 21 Aug 1706
Roberts, Benjamin, s/o James Roberts and Elizabeth his wife, b. 8 Apr 1706

John Roberts, s/o James Roberts and Elizabeth his wife, b. 10 Feb 1702

Hazell, Mary, d/o John Hazell and Mary his wife, b. Sunday 9 o'clock at night on 30 Jun 1706

Young, Elizabeth, d/o George Young, Jr. and Mary his wife, b. 26 Aug 1705

Myles, Mary, d/o Tobias Myles and Elizabeth his wife, b. 24 Apr 1672

Page 6

White, Thomas, s/o Richard White and Elizabeth his wife, b. 19 Apr 1705

Allen, William, s/o William Allen and Thomas[in] his wife, b. 1 Aug 1704

Allen, Mary, d/o William Allen and Thomasin his wife, b. 12 Jan 1706/7

Easterling, Martha, d/o Henry Easterling and Elizabeth his wife, b. 26 Aug 1701 **(4)**

Easterling, Elizabeth, d/o Henry Easterling and Elizabeth his wife, b. 3 Jan 1703

Easterling, Mary, d/o Henry Easterling and Elizabeth his wife, b. 30 Aug 1706

Easterling, Henry, s/o Henry Easterling and Elizabeth his wife, b. 24 Mar 1697

Dawkins, James, s/o William Dawkins and Ann his wife, b. 1 Aug 1695

Dawkins, Ann, d/o William Dawkins and Ann his wife, b. 19 Jan 1698

Page 7

Dawkins, Benet, s/o William Dawkins and Ann his wife, b. 2 Oct 1704

Dawkins, Elizabeth, s/o William Dawkins and Rebecca his wife, b. 29 Aug 1728

Dawkins, William, s/o William Dawkins and Ann his wife, b. 13 Sep 1706

Dixon, Benjamin, s/o Robert Dixon and Ruth his wife, b. 28 Feb 1704

Dixon, Mary, d/o Robert Dixon & Ruth his wife, b. 7 Feb 1706/7

Emmatt, John s/o William Emmatt and Alce his wife, b. 24 Dec 1706

Galimore, Ellinor, d/o George Galimore and Jane his wife, b. 21 Dec 1706

Jenifer, Elizabeth, d/o Daniell of St. Thomas Jenifer and Elizabeth his wife, b. 1 Dec 1706

Broome, Mary, d/o John Broome and Ann his wife, b. 21 Sep 1707

Page 8

Simpson, Ann, d/o Jeremiah Simpson and Mary his wife, b. 12 Jul 1707 (5)

Simpson, Jeremiah, d. 2 Jan 1706/7

Barton, Postena, d/o William Barton and Catherine his wife, b. 10 Oct 1707

Demilliane, Elizabeth, d/o Rev. Gabril Demilliane and Ann his wife, b. 8 Jan 1706/7

Collings, Thomas, s/o Robert Collings and Mary his wife, b. 21 Mar 1708

Veach, Jane, d/o William Veach and Jane his wife, b. 21 Jun 1708 at St. Leonard's Creek

Gray, Thomas, s/o William Gray and Martha his wife, b. near head of Battle Creek 29 Jul 1707

Dawkins, James, s/o Joseph Dawkins and Sarah his wife, b. near head of Island Creek on 29 Apr 1708

Page 9

Culpeper, John, s/o Michael Culpeper and Ellinor his wife, b. 7 Jan 1707/8

Holdsworth, Mary, d/o Thomas Holdsworth and Barbara his wife, b. 23 Sep 1713

Holdsworth, Betty, d/o Thomas Holdsworth and Barbara his wife, b. 13 May 1715

Jenifer, Mary, d/o Daniel of St. Thomas Jenifer and Elizabeth his wife, b. 16 Aug 1708 at Battle Creek **(6)**

Croson, John, s/o Charles Crosson and Martha his wife, b. Cecil Co. 18 Aug 1704

Crosen, Mary, d/o Charles Crosen and Martha his wife, b. Christ Church Parish 9 Mar 1706/7

Barrot, Ann, d/o James and Ellinor Barrot, b. 25 Sep 1705

Boyle, Barbara, d/o David and Sarah Boyle, b. 23 May 1704
Page 10
Barton, William, s/o John and Easther Barton, b. 4 Oct 1704
Hazell, John, s/o John and Mary Hazell, b. near head of Island Creek on 11 Aug 1708 about 7 o'clock in the morning one Wednesday
Holdsworth, Rebakah, d/o Thomas Holdsworth and Barbara his wife, b. 30 Jan 1716
Mackall, James John, s/o John Mackall and Susanah his wife, b. 29 Nov 1717; baptized by Rev. Jonath. Cay who with Mr. Thomas How and Madam Cay as sureties
Binnion, Paslo, s/o John and Elizabeth Binnion, b. 13 Mar 1705 **(7)**
Binnion, Thomas, s/o John and Elizabeth Binnion, b. 23 Jul 1703
Broome, John, s/o John and Ann Broome b. 2 Sep 1703
Boyle, Catherine, d/o David and Sarah Boyle, b. 18 Apr 1700
Page 11
Blinkhorne, Mary, d/o Robert and Martha Blinkhorne, b. 18 Oct 1709
Chittam, Charles, s/o John and Mary Chittam, b. 30 May 1701
Demilliane, Gabriel, s/o Rev. Gabril Demilliane and Ann his wife, b. 25 Dec 1705
Dever, Grace, d/o Gilbert and Elizabeth Dever, b. [blank] 1701
Dorman, John, s/o John and Mary Dorman, b. 6 Mar 1701
Emson, Rebeckah, b. James and Rebeckah Emson, b. 12 May 1701
Ellt, Thomas, s/o Henry and Elizabeth Ellt, b. 31 Mar 1704
Forgisson, Mary, s/o John and Elizabeth Forgisson, b. 9 Mar 1704
Freeman, Mary, d/o Richard and Mary Freeman, b. 2 Dec 1701
Page 12
Gardner, Robert, s/o John and Rebeckah Gardner, b. 16 Jul 1701 **(8)**
Garlick, John, s/o John and [blank] Garlick, b. 18 Jul 1701
Howe, Elizabeth, d/o Thomas and Rebeckah Howe, b. 28 Aug 1705
Hernley, Darbey, s/o Darbey and Ann Hernley, b. 18 Jul 1701
Hellen, Peter, s/o David and Susanna Hellen, b. 22 Sep 1697
Hellen, Penellope, d/o David and Susanna Hellen, b. 22 Jan 1695
Hellen, David, s/o David and Susanna Hellen, b. 30 Nov 1692

Hellen, John, s/o David and Susanna Hellen, b. 10 Nov 1690
Hellen, James, s/o David and Susanna Hellen, b. 27 Dec 1688
Page 13
Johnson, Thomas, s/o Thomas and Mary Johnson, bapt. 31 Mar 1703
Johnson, Joseph, s/o William and Sarah Johnson, b. 20 May 1704
Kent, Thomasin, d/o John and Mary Kent, b. 17 Oct 1705
Kelley, John, s/o Patrick and Elizabeth Kelley, b. 30 Mar 1705 **(9)**
Kelley, Sarah, s/o Patrick and Elizabeth Kelly, b. 9 Aug 1702
Leach, Jane, d/o John and Elizabeth Leach, b. 13 Feb 1689
Leach, William, s/o John and Elizabeth Leach, b. 3 Oct 1692
Leach, Effnis, d/o John and Elizabeth Leach, b. 24 Feb 1694
Page 14
Leach, Preserv, d/o John and Elizabeth Leach, b. 31 Jul 1698
Lewis, Mary, d/o Griffin and Ann Lewis, b. 18 Dec 1704
Mackabe, Thomas, s/o James and Elizabeth Mackabe, b. 8 May 1703
Mackabe, James, s/o James and Elizabeth Mackabe, b. 10 Mar 1700
Mauldin, Sarah, d/o Francis and Elizabeth Mauldin, b. 3 Jul 1698
Mackabe, Ann, d/o James and Elizabeth Mackabe, b. 19 June 1697
Mackabe, Rachel, d/o James and Elizabeth Mackabe, b. 7 Sep 1694
Mauldin, William, s/o Francis and Elizabeth Mauldin, b. 16 May 1689
Mauldin, Margrett, d/o Francis and Elizabeth Mauldin, b. 3 Feb 1692
Page 15
Mauldin, James, s/o Francis and Elizabeth Mauldin, b. 16 Jul 1695 **(10)**
Parker, William Henry, s/o William and Mary Parker, b. 17 Jan 1797
Parker, Elizabeth, d/o William and Mary Parker, b. 5 Jul 1700
Parker, Fealder, s/o William and Mary Parker, b. 1 Sep 1702
Rigden, Elizabeth, d/o John and Ann Rigden, b. 27 Aug 1699
Ridgen, John, s/o John and Ann Rigden, b. 6 Apr 1701
Rouland, Thomas, s/o Thomas and Ann Rouland, b. 4 Apr 1705

Spencer, James, s/o Francis and Mary Spencer, b. 29 Oct 1704
Stinnet, Elizabeth, d/o William and Elizabeth Stinnet, b. 29 Jan 1704
Page 16
Simpson, John, s/o Jeremiah and Mary Simpson, b. 1 Apr 1704
Stirmey, William, s/o William and Katherine Stirmey, b. 2 May, 1701
Stirmey, Mary, d/o William and Catherine Stirmey, b. 27 Jan 1692
Stirmey, Priscilla, d/o William and Catherine Stirmey, b. 16 Mar 1685
Smith, Sarah, d/o Humpry and Ann Smith, b. 24 Apr 1701
Turner, John, s/o John and Johanna Turner, b. 5 Jun 1704 **(11)**
Turner, John, s/o John and Elizabeth Turner, b. 19 Apr 1706
Veach, Eunis, d/o William and Jane Veach, b. 20 Jan 1704
Willis, Mary, d/o John and Mary Willis, b. 4 May 1701
Page 17
Williams, Francis, s/o Francis and Ann Williams, b. 13 May 1701
Wilkinson, Mary, d/o William and Rebecca Wilkinson, b. 17 Jul 1701
Williams, William, s/o William and Sarah Williams, b. 20 May 1704
Willis, Samuel, s/o Richard and Martha Willis, b. 21 Aug 1704
Chilton, John, s/o Cuthbird and Mary Chilton, b. 17 Nov 1708
Allen, Elizabeth, d/o William and Thomazin Allen, b. 25 Jan 1708; d. same day
Young, Mary, d/o George Young, Jr. and Mary his wife, b. 1 Feb 1707
Swan, George, d/o Edward and Elizabeth Swan, b. 6 Jan 1702
Page 18
Jones, William, s/o William Jones and Jennit Oswell, b. 15 Jul 1708 **(12)**
Miller, Ellinor, d/o William and Grace Miller, b. 5 Aug 1708
Bagnall, Sarah, d/o Ralph and Rebecka Bagnall, b. 4 Oct 1704
Bagnall, Samuel, s/o Ralph Bagnall and Rebecka his wife, b. 26 Apr 1707

Roberts, James, s/o James and Elizabeth Roberts, b. 22 May 1707
Roberts, Jacob, s/o James and Elizabeth Roberts, 8 Jan 1708/9
Avis, Dorcas, d/o Robert and Ann Avis, b. Isle Land Creek 21 Nov 1708
Urquahart (Aurkhutt), James, s/o Alexander and Ann Aurkhutt, b. 19 Jul 1708

Page 19

Parran, Mary, d/o Alexander and Mary Parran, b. near St. Leonard's Creek on 27 Oct 1699
Parran, John, s/o Alexander Parran and Mary his wife, b. near St. Leonard's Creek on 26 Sep 1702
Parran, Alexander, s/o Alexander Parran and Mary his wife, b. near St. Leonard's Creek on 20 Jan 1704; d. 12 Feb 1704
Parran, Jane, d/o Alexander Parran and Mary his wife, b. near St. Leonard's Creek 29 Apr 1706 **(13)**
Parran, Alexander, Jr., s/o Alexander Parran and Mary his wife, b. near St. Leonard's Creek on 8 Dec 1707
Williams, John, s/o William Williams and Sarah his wife, b. 20 Dec 1706
Spellman, William, s/o Richard and Elizabeth Spellman, b. 12 Feb 1789 [should this be 1708/9?]

Page 20

Spellman, Richard, s/o Richard Spellman and Elizabeth, b. 6 Dec 1704
Cobb, James, s/o Paul Cobb and Sarah his wife, b. 13 Nov 1708; bapt. 24 Apr 1709
Barton, John and Sarah Barton, twin son and dau. of John Barton and Easther his wife, b. on the Clifts on 4 Feb 1707/8
Boyle, David, s/o David Boyle and Sarah his wife, b. St. Leonard's Creek on 19 Jan 1706
Howerton, Martha, d/o John and Elizabeth Howerton, b. on the Clifts on 8 Jun 1695
Howerton, Elizabeth, d/o John and Elizabeth Howerton, b. on the Clifts on 2 Mar 1701

Page 21

Forgisson, Christian, d/o John and Elizabeth Forgisson, b. on the Clifts 28 Jun 1706 **(14)**

Forgisson, Ellinor, d/o John and Elizabeth Forgisson, b. on the Clifts on 23 Jun 1709
Cammell, William, s/o James and Bridgitt Cammell, b. 9 Aug 1705
Smith, Mary, d/o John and Mary Smith, b. 28 Apr 1709
Maynard, Diana, d/o Thomas and Ann Maynard, b. [blank] 1696
Ellt, Elizabeth, d/o Henry and Elizabeth Ellt, b. 18 Oct 1703
Ellt, Ellinor, d/o Henry and Elizabeth Ellt, b. 24 Oct 1709
Davis, Thomas, s/o John and Martha Davis, b. 8 Mar 1703

Page 22

Davis, William, s/o John and Martha Davis, b. 23 Sep 1707
Freeman, Isaac, s/o George and Rachel Freeman, b. 13 Dec 1705
Freeman, Cassander, d/o George and Rachel Freeman, b. 11 Dec 1707
Money, Ann, d/o Isaac and Elizabeth Money, b. 4 Apr 1700
Money, William, s/o Isaac and Elizabeth Money, b. 21 May 1702
Money, Abraham, s/o Isaac and Elizabeth Money, b. 28 Aug 1706
(15)
Money, Elizabeth, d/o Isaac and Elizabeth Money, b. 20 May 1709
Mackabe, Lacey, s/o James and Elizabeth Mackabe, b. 4 Oct 1705
Mackabe, Abraham, s/o James and Elizabeth Mackabe, b. 10 Nov 1708

Page 23

Wade, Rachel, d/o George and Catherine Wade, b. 6 Mar 1694
Wade, George, s/o George and Catherine Wade, b. 31 May 1696
Wade, John, s/o George and Catherine Wade, b. 21 Apr 1699
Wade, Elizabeth and Catherine Wade, twin daus. of George and Catherine, b. 25 Sep 1703
Wade, Ann, d/o George and Catherine Wade, b. 20 Apr 1706
Johnson, Thomas, s/o John and Francis Johnson in St. Leonard's Town on 4 Nov 1709
Appleton, John, s/o John and Elizabeth Appleton, b. on the Clifts on 23 Oct 1709
Veatch, Virlinnea, d/o William and Jane Veatch, b. at St. Leonard's Creek on 28 Jan 1709

Page 24

Croson, Martha, d/o Charles and Martha Croson, b. at mouth of Patuxon River on 16 Mar 1709/10

Johnson, Elizabeth, d/o William and Sarah Johnson, b. 28 Jan 1709/10 **(16)**

Kelley, Rebecka, d/o Patrick and Elizabeth Kelley, b. 29 Dec 1706

Kelley, Randall, s/o Patrick and Elizabeth Kelley, b. 14 Jan 1709/10

Henley, James, s/o Edward and Ezabell Henley, b. 17 Mar 1709/10

Dixon, Obed, s/o Robert and Ruth Dixon, b. 20 May 1709

Douglas, Ann, d/o James and Sarah Douglas, b. St. Leonard's Creek on 17 Mar 1710/11

Page 25

Hernley, Ann, d/o Darbey and Ann Hernley, b. 31 Oct 1697

Hernley, Mary, d/o Darbey and Ann Hernley, b. 17 Jul 1711

Miller, William, s/o William and Grace Miller, b. 14 Mar 1710

Franklin, Elizabeth, d/o Thomas and Grace Franklin, b. 6 Dec 1711

Bourn, Elizabeth, d/o Thomas and Elizabeth Bourn, b. at mouth of Patuxon on 27 Dec 1711

Shekon, Elizabeth, d/o John and Jane Shekon, b. 31 Jan 1711 **(17)**

Greves, Elizabeth, d/o Robert and Margaret Greves, b. 9 Mar 1711

Page 26

James, John, s/o John and Hannah James, b. St. Leonard's on 13 Jan 1711/12

How, Thomas, s/o Thomas and Rebeckah How, b. 2 Jan 1689

How, Sarah, d/o Thomas and Rebecka How, b. 7 Sep 1693

How, Mauldin, d/o Thomas and Rebecka How, b. 24 Jan 1697

How, Rebecka, s/o Thomas and Rebecka How, b. [no date] 1699

How, Elizabeth, d/o Thomas and Rebecka How, b. 8 Aug 1705

How, Mary, d/o Thomas and Rebecka, b. 20 Feb 1709

Page 27

Freeman, George, s/o George and Rachel Freeman, b. 10 Mar 1709/10 **(18)**

Freeman, Abraham, d/o George and Rachel Freeman, b. 10 Jun 1712
Crafford, Susanna, d/o Addam and Mary Crafford, b. 8 Jun 1711
Fowler, Dorothy, d/o Peter and Agnis Fowler, b. 7 Jan 1710/11
Mills, Elizabeth, d/o John and Elizabeth Mills, d. 5 Nov 1707
Mills, John, s/o John and Elizabeth Mills, b. 26 Nov 1711
Swillaven, Priscilla, d/o Daniel and Priscilla Swillaven, b. 26 Feb 1707/8

Page 28

Brome, Thomas, s/o John and Ann Brome, b. 2 Jan 1709
Brome, Ann, d/o John and Ann Brome, b. 2 Apr 1712
Avis, Jarvis, s/o Robert and Ann Avis, b. 18 Feb 1711/12
Gooldsberrey, Thomas Maynard, s/o Robert and Dianna Gooldsberrey, b. 12 Jul 1713 **(19)** [O'Brien says this is twins]
Spellman, Ann, d/o Richard and Elizabeth Spellman, b. 28 Aug 1711
Spellman, Mary, d/o Richard and Elizabeth Spellman, b. 2 Mar 1712/13
Dungerman, Rennis Rennar, d/o Christopher and Elizabeth Dungerman, b. 13 Oct 17[12]

Page 29

Ailing, Margaret, d/o Jane [James] and Elizabeth Ailing, his second wife, 5 Jul 1706
Young, Elizabeth, d/o William and Rebekah Young, b. 9 Feb 1712
Young, William, s/o William and Rebekah Young, b. 9 Aug 1711
Young, George, s/o Wm. and Rebecca Young, b. 9 Jan 1709
Young, Samuel, s/o Wm. and Rebecca Young, b. 11 Mar 1706
Young, Grace, d/o Henry and Mary Grace Young, b. 16 Oct 1709
Young, Phillemon, s/o Henry and Anne Young, b. 1 Aug 1712
Rhodin, John, s/o John and Elizabeth Rhodin, b. 4 Mar 1707
Rhodin, William, s/o John and Elizabeth Rhodin, b. 11 Oct 1710
Rhodin, Sarah, s/o John and Elizabeth Rhodin, b. 16 Nov 1713
  (20)

Page 30

Tucker, Priscilla, d/o Tho's and Rebekah Tucker, b. 8 Mar 1711
Garner, James, s/o Matthew and Elizabeth Garner, b. 2 Apr 1709

Garner, Dorcas, s/o Mattw and Elizabeth Garner, b. 27 Nov 1710
Garner, Rachel, d/o Matthew and Elizabeth Garner, b. 17 Dec 1712
Winnul, William, s/o John and Elizabeth Winnul, b. 7 Jul 1706
Winnul, Sarah, d/o Jno. and Elizabeth Winnul, b. 7 Jul 1706
Garner, Mary, d/o Jacob and Anne Grner, b. 26 Nov 1704
Garner, Sarah, d/o Jacob and Anne Garner, b. 29 Sep 1707
Mauldin, Frances, s/o Thomas and Ludah Mauldin, b. 2 Apr 1705
Pierreviell, Jas. Gideon, and Ann Elizabeth Pierreviell, son and dau. of John and [blank] Pierreviell, twins, b. 14 Jan 1714
Tucker, Grace, d/o Thomas Tucker and Rebekah his wife, b. 15 Feb 1714

Page 31

Dungerman, Lothea Renard, d/o Stephen Dungerman and Elizabeth his wife, b. 4 Jun 1716
Beckett, Rebekah, d/o John and Susannah Beckett, b. 4 Feb 1714
Young, Sarah, d/o Geo. Young, Jr. and Mary his wife, b. 14 Aug 1712
Young, Parker, s/o Geo. Young, Jr. and Mary his wife, b. 19 Feb 1714/15
Taylor, Mary, d/o John and Ann Taylor, b. 16 Aug 1714 (sic) (21)
Taylor, Elizabeth, d/c John and Ann Taylor, b. 26 Jan 1714 (sic)
Webster, Ann, d/o John and Mary Webster, b. 24 Jun 1715
Ellt, William, s/o William and Eleanor Ellt, b. 9 Feb 1715
Ellt, Mary, d/o William and Eleanor Ellt, b. 10 Oct 1715
Macknew, Cathrine, d/o David Macknew and Elliner his wife, b. 5 May 1716 (?)

Page 32

Macknew, David, s/o David Macknew and Elliner his wife, b. 22 Sep 1716 (?)
Heseltine, Ann, d/o Charles Haseltine and Elener his wife, b. 14 Aug about 11 o'clock in the forenoon 1721 and on the 18th following was baptized by Rev. Jona. Cay rector of Christ Church according to the tenets of the Church of England
Mackeath, Sarah, d/o Benj. Mackeath and Barbara his wife, b. 12 May 1720
Parker, George, s/o Gab. and Eliza. his wife, b. 25 Jun 1714

Parker, Susannah, d/o Gab. Parker and Ann, b. 21 Nov 1716
Parker, Sarah, d/o Gab. Parker and Ann, b. 12 Sep 1719
Kidd, Gidian, s/o William and Ann Kidd, b. 23 Oct 1721
Collenbr, Elizabeth, d/o Tho's and Alce Collenbr, b. 16 Dec 1714
Page 33
Collenbr, Rebaca, d/o Tho's and Alce Collenbr, b. 25 Dec 1717
Collenbr, Thomas, s/o Thomas and Alce Collenbr, b. 6 Apr 1719
Collenbr, John, s/o Thomas and Alce Collenbr, b. 9 Jan 1723
Mackall, Benja., s/o Benja. Mackall and Barbara his wife, b. 16 Feb 1723 **(22)**
Hesletine, Catherine, d/o Charles and Eleanor Hesletine, b. 13 7ber 1724, between 6 & 7 o'clock in the afternoon; bapt. 22 Nov 1724 by Rev. Jona. Cay
Young, Eleanor, d/o John Young and Mary his wife, b. 10 Aug 1723
Somervell, Rebeca, d/o James Somervell and Sarah his wife, b. 20 Nov 1724; bapt. following Dec
Crichard, Tommison, d/o John Crichard and Tommison his wife, b. 19 April 1717
Page 34
Allsup, Rachell, d/o Richard Allsup and Mary his wife, b. 15 Jan 1717
Allsup, Rich'd, s/o Rich'd Allsup and Mary his wife, b. 28 Feb 1721
Allsup, Prisela, d/o Rich'd Allsup and Mary his wife, b. 15 Sep 1721
Allsup, Sarah, d/o Rich'd Allsup and Mary his wife, b. 6 Jul 1724
Young, Rich'd, s/o John Young and Mary his wife, b. 22 Jun 1725
Hesletine, Charles, s/o Charles and Eleanor Hesletine, b. 22 Jul 1727; bapt. 14 Sep 1727 by Rev. James Williamson, rector of All Saint's Parish, Calvert Co.
Kirshaw, Francis, s/o James and Margaret Kirshaw, b. 24 Jun 1727; bapt. 13 Sep 1727 by Rev. James Williamson of All Saint's
Page 35
Kentt, Thomazen, d/o John Kentt and Jannett Kentt his wife, b. 30 Dec 1722
Kentt, Jane, d/o John Kent and Jannett Kentt his wife, b. 30 Jul 1724

Parran, Alexd'r intermarried with Mary Ashcomb **(23)**
Parran, John, s/o Alexd'r Parran and Mary his wife, b. 26 Sep 1702
Parran, Jane, d/o Alexd'r and Mary his wife, b. 29 Apr 1706
Parran, Alexd'r, s/o Alexd'r and Mary and his wife, b. 8 Sep 1707
Parran, Alexd'r intermarried with Mary Young and Young Parran, s/o Alexd'r and Mary his wife, b. 5 Oct 1711
Parran, Moses, s/o Alexd'r and Mary his wife, b. 28 Sep 1713
Parran, Ann, d/o Alexd'r and Mary his wife, b. 26 Dec 1715
Page 36
Parran, Sarah, d/o Alexd'r Parran and Mary his wife, b. 23 Nov 1729
Parran, Samuell, s/o Alexd'r and Mary his wife, b. 28 Sep 1717
Parran, Benjamin, s/o Alexd'r Parran and Mary his wife, b. 4 Jan 1719
Parran, Mary, d/o Alexd'r Parran and Mary his wife, b. 20 May 1722
Parran, Phillip, s/o Alexd'r Parran and Mary his wife, b. 5 Nov 1724
Parran, Elizabeth, d/o Alexd'r Parran and Mary his wife, b. 6 Feb 1726
Hellen, Peter intermarred to Jane Parran 24 Nov 1726
Young, Richard, s/o John Young and Mary his wife, b. 21 Jun 1725
Hellen, Alexd'r, s/o Peter and Jane Parran, b. 20 Nov 1728
Page 37
Young, Richard, Gent., and ?Jr. and Mary Broome, spinster, obtained license to marry dated 25 Mar 1725; /s/ Jonathan Cay; married same date by Rev. Cay; /s/ Char. Allen, clerk **(24)**
Parker, Ann, d/o Gabrill Parker and Ann his wife, b. 1 Oct 1722
Parker, Gabrill, s/o Gabrill Parker and Ann his wife, b. 1 Jun 1724
Page 38
Parker, Hutchinson, s/o Gabrill Parker and Ann his wife, b. 27 Jul 1726
Parker, Mary, d/o Gabrill Parker and Ann his wife, b. 14 Jun 1728

Royston, Abel m. Elizabeth Robinson 2 Mar 1727 according to the rites of the Church of England
Royston, Alce, d/o Abel and Eliza., b. 23 Mar 1728
Richardson, Thomas, s/o John , b. 20 Jul 1711
Slater, Ellis and Sarah Delamere, m. 12 Jul 1729 by Rev. Cay
(25)
Slater, Jonathan, s/o Ellis Slater and Sarah his wife, b. Thursday 21 Jul 1730; bapt. Sunday 20 Sep 1730 by Rev. Cay
Hellen, Susan, d/o Peeter Hellen and Jane his wife, b. 25 Mar 1731
Ellt, Benja., s/o Will'm Ellt and Ellener his wife, b. 16 Mar 1715;
Page 39
 baptized at Midlam Chappell, Church of England by Rev. Cay 9 Mar 1731
Barton, Will'm, s/o John Barton and Eve his wife, b. 5 Oct 1729; bapt. __ Jun 1730
Bates, Sarah, d/o Rich'd Bates and Sarah his wife, b. 13 Feb 1725
Bates, Mary, d/o Rich'd and Sarah Bates, b. 8 Jan 1726/7
Bates, James, s/o Rich'd and Sarah Bates, b. 28 Jan 1728
Bates, Grace, d/o Rich'd and Sarah Bates, b. 1 Feb 1730
Manning, Sarah, d/o Thomas and Jochan Manning, b. 8 Oct 1714
Manning, Grace, d/o Thomas and Jochan Manning, b. 27 Dec 1716
Manning, Anne, d/o Thomas and Jochan Manning, b. 27 Nov 1720
Page 40
Manning, Mary, d/o Thomas and Joshan Manning, b. 23 Jun 1724
Manning, Thomas, s/o Thomas and Joshan Manning, b. 6 Sep 1728
(26)
Manning, John, s/o Thomas and Joshan Manning, b. 7 Dec 1731
Manning, Sarah, b. Virginia and registered at Fairfield Church
Manning, Grace, b. Virginia and registered in WecoCommoco Northings
Mackall, Mary, d/o James Mackall and Mary his wife, b. 25 Nov 1731; bapt. 19 Apr following in Church of England
Ellt, Rebekah, d/o Henry Ellt and Eliza. his wife, b. 10 Apr 1712
Turner, Sarah, d/o Rich'd and Eliza. his wife, b. 25 Jan 1722
Turner, Sophia, d/o Rich'd Turner and Eliza. his wife, b. 11 Sep 1727

Ellt, Mary, b. 2 Oct 1728

Page 41

Pecock, Joseph, s/o Sam'll and Eliza. his wife, b. 13 Apr 1732

Appelton, James, s/o John Appleton and Eliza. his wife, b. 8 Dec 1718

Appelton, Mary, d/o John Appelton and Eliza. his wife b. 18 Aug 1722

Bellsom, Sarah, d/o Jona'n Beellsom and Eliza. his wife, b. 6 May 1732

Slater, David, s/o Ellis Slater and Sarah his wife, b. at Prince Frederick Town 30 Nov 1732; bapt. by Rev. Cay at the Court House Sunday 23 Feb 1732

Kent, Thomazin, d/o John Kentt and Jannett his wife, b. 18 Dec 1726

Kentt, Isaac and Rebackh Kentt, son and dau. of John Kentt and Jannett his wife, b. 22 Dec 1731

Holdsworth, Ann, d/o Tho's and Barbara, b. 1 Nov 1719 **(27)**

Hellen, Mary, d/o Peeter Hellen and Jane his wife, b. 11 Oct 1733

Page 42

Dorrumple, Grace, d/o John Dorrumple and Grace his wife, b. 7 Aug 1719; d. 16 day same month

Dorrumple, John, s/o John Dorrumple and Grace his wife, b. 2 Mar 1720

Dorrumple, William, s/o John Dorrumple and Grace his wife, b. 12 Feb 1723

Dorrumple, Betty, d/o John Dorrumple and Grace his wife, b. 1 Dec 1727

Dorrumple, Rebecca, d/o John Dorrumple and Grace his wife, b. 22 Jan 1730

Mackall, James, second s/o James Mackall and Mary his wife, b. 30 Jan 1734; bapt. Rev. Cay on 6 Apr 1735

Mackall, John, s/o James Mackall and Mary his wife, b. 22 Oct 1738

Dawkins, Anne, d/o William Dawkins and Mary his wife, b. 2 Aug 1721

Page 43

Dawkins, Sarah, d/o William Dawkins and Mary his wife, b. 18 Sep 1722; d. 10 Apr 1730

Dawkins, Elizabeth, d/o William Dawkins and Mary his wife, b. 19 Apr 1725

Dawkins, James, s/o William Dawkins and Mary his wife, b. 15 Jan 1726

Dawkins, Joseph, s/o William Dawkins and Mary his wife, b. 22 Jan 1728

Dawkins, Mary, d/o William Dawkins and Mary his wife, b. 10 Nov 1730

Dawkins, Dorcas, d/o William Dawkins and Mary, b. 20 Mar 1731

Dawkins, William, d/o William Dawkins and Mary his wife, b. 3 Aug 1734

Tucker, John, s/o James Tucker and Sarah his wife, b. 18 Jul 1735

Page 44

Dawkins, Joseph, s/o James Dawkins, Jr., and Mary his wife, b. 15 Nov 1737

Fowler, George, s/o Joseph Fowler and Catherine his wife, b. 29 Mar 1724 **(29)**

Fowler, Joseph, d/o Joseph Fowler and Catherine his wife, b. 6 Mar 1725

Fowler, Parker, s/o Joseph Fowler and Catherine his wife, b. 23 Jun 1728

Hellen, David, s/o Peter Hellen and Jane his wife, b. 18 Apr 1736

Dawkins, Charles, s/o William Dawkins and Mary his wife, b. 22 Aug 1736

Dawkins, Rebecca, d/o William Dawkins and Mary his wife, b. 3 May 1738

Howard, John, d/o George Howard and Margaret his wife, b. 18 Nov 1734

Dawkins, Benjamin, s/o William Dawkins of Calvert Co. and Mary his wife, b. 4 Jun 1740

Page 45

Crane, Jane, d/o John Crane of Calvert Co., cordwinder, and Elizabeth his wife, b. 23 Dec 1732

Crane, Mary, d/o John Crane and Elizabeth his wife, b. 15 Oct 1738 **(30)**

Robinson, Margaret, d/o Samuel Robinson and Mary his wife, b. 11 Jan 1731

Dawkins, Jesse, s/o William Davkins and Mary his wife, b. 31 Jul 1742

Mackall, Benjamin, d/o James Mackall and Mary his wife, b. 4 Jan 1741

Ellt, Ellinor, d/o Benjamin Ellt and Anne his wife, b. 10 Jun 1742

Crompton, Mary, d/o Thomas Crompton and Mary his wife, b. 10 Jan 1740

Crompton, Catherine, d/o Thomas Crompton and Mary his wife, b. 7 May 1742

Page 46

Dorsey, James, s/o Phillip Dorsey and Anne his wife, b. 18 Sep 1735

Dorsey, Elizabeth, d/o Phillip Dorsey and Anne his wife, b. 26 Jul 1738

Dorsey, Anne, d/o Phillip Dorsey and Anne his wife, b. 9 Apr 1741

Dorsey, Rebecca, d/o Phillip Dorsey and Ann his wife, b. 5 Mar 1742 **(31)**

Bourn, Eleanor, d/o Jesse Bourn and Elizabeth his wife, b. 9 Nov 1740

Bourn, Jesse, s/o Jesse Bourn and Eliz'th his wife, b. 1 Dec 1742

Gray, Margrett, d/o John Gray and Jane his wife, b, b. 1741 John Gray and Jane his wife, b. 15 Sep 1735

Page 47

Gray, Samuel, s/o John Gray and Jane his wife, b. 31 Dec 1737

Gray, Jane, d/o John Gray and Jane his wife, b. 7 May 1740

Gray, Elizabeth, d/o John Gray and Jane his wife, b. 21 Oct 1742; d. 9 Dec following about 8 o'clock at night **(32)**

Gray, Rebeca, d/o John Gray and Jane his wife, b. 18 Oct 1743

Hungerford, Edmund, s/o James Hungerford and Eliza. his wife, b. 25 Apr 1741

Hungerford, Jane, d/o James Hungerford and Eliza. his wife, b. 9 Feb 1743/4

Hungerford, James, s/o Benjamin Hungerford and Jane his wife, b. 26 Apr 1742

Sedwick, Mary, d/o Benjamin Sedwick and Mary his wife, b. 23 Jul 1739

Page 48

Sedwick, Benja., s/o Benja. Sedwick and Mary his wife, b. 3 Jan 1740

Somervell, James, s/o James Somervell and Sarah his wife, b. 4 Jul 1731 **(33)**

Somervell, Alexander, s/o James Somervell and Sarah his wife, b. 9 Aug 1734

Somervell, John, s/o James Somervell and Sarah his wife, b. 25 Nov 1726

Seavern, John Dewick, s/o James Seavern and Sarah his wife, b. Thursday 17 Mar about 7 o'clock at night 1742

Seavern, James, s/o James Seavern and Sarah his wife, b. Friday 16 Nov at 12 o'clock in the day 1744

Gray, James, s/o John Gray and Jane his wife, b. 26 Apr 1746

Bourn, Sarah, d/o Jesse Bourn and Rebeccah his wife, b. 13 Feb 1745/6

Page 49

Day, Benjamin, d/o Dan'l Day and Eleanor his wife, b. 24 Sep 1735

Ivey, Mary, d/o John Ivey and Eleanor his wife, b. 16 Jun 1738 **(34)**

Ivey, Abigail, d/o John Ivey and Eleanor his wife, b. 15 May 1740

Ivey, John, s/o John Ivey and Eleanor his wife, b. 24 Aug 1743

Ivey, Elizabeth, d/o John Ivey and Eleanor his wife, b. 12 Aug 1745

Gray, Rebeccah, d/o John Gray and Jane his wife, d. Saturday 16 Sep 1749 about 12 o'clock in the night in her 6th year

Gray, Elizabeth, d/o John Gray and Jane his wife, b. 17 Aug 1748

Mackall, Ann, d/o James Mackall and Mary his life, b. 9 Dec 1748

Page 50

Newton, Ward, s/o Thomas Newton and Grace his wife, b. 1 Mar 1746/7 **(35)**

Clagett, Richard Dorsey, s/o Sam'l and Elizabeth Clagett, b. 24 Apr 1749

Taylor, Brian, s/o Everard Taylor and Sarah his wife, b. 11 May 1741; (note on the side of this page: this entry in error; see Liber A of Parish Record Books for correct entry of 1742)

Taylor, Mary, d/o Everard and Sarah his wife, b. 1 Jan 1744

Taylor, Sarah, d/o Everard and Sarah, b. 22 Mar 1746/7

Hooper, Abraham, s/o Jacob Hooper and Betty his wife, b. 5 Oct about 10 o'clock in the night 1742

Young Francis, s/o Parker Young and Sarah his wife, b. 25 Jan 1749

Young, Jane, d/o Parker Young and Sarah his wife, b. 27 Mar 1753

Page 51

Hellen, Mary, d/o Richard Hellen and Eliza. his wife, b. 19 Dec 1746 **(36)**

Dixon, Mary, d/o Obed Dixon and Sarah his wife, b. 2 Aug 1741

Dixon, Robert, s/o Obed and Sarah his wife, b. 17 Sep 1743

Dixon, Sarah, d/o above, b. 1 Feb 1745

Dixon, Ruth, d/o Obed and Sarah, b. 7 Jan 1748/9

Dixon, Benja., s/o Obed and Sarah, b. 6 Feb 1750

Hungerford, Jno., s/o Benja. and Jean his wife, b. 18 Feb 1750

Ivey, James, s/o Jno. and Eleanor his wife, b. 30 Sep 1747

Bourne, Sarah, d/o Jesse Bourne and Rebecca his wife, b. 13 Feb 1745 **(37)**

Somervell, Sarah, d/o Thomas How and relict of James Somervell, d. 22 Mar 1755

Page 52

Somervell, James and Susanna Dare, m. 5 Aug 1755

Smith, Walter, s/o Walter Smith of Parker's Creek and Sarah his wife, b. 12 Aug 1747

Smith, Alethea, d/o Walter and Sarah his wife, b. 23 Oct 1748

Mackall, Susanah, d/o James John Mackall and Mary his wife, b. 14 Jan 1737

Mackall, John, s/o James John Mackall and Mary his wife, b. 10 May 1740

Mackall, Mary, s/o James John Mackall and Mary his wife, b. 20 May 1742

Mackall, Elizabeth, d/o James John Mackall and Mary his wife, b. 14 Jan 1743 **(38)**

Mackall, Benjamin, s/o James John Mackall and Mary his wife, b. 14 Aug 1745

Page 53

Mackall, James, s/o James John Mackall and Mary his wife, b. 31 Oct 1747

Mackall, Richard, s/o James John Mackall and Mary his wife, b. 4 Apr 1749

Mackall, Thomas, s/o James John Mackall and Mary his wife, b. 31 Aug 1751

Mackall, Sarah, d/o James John Mackall and Mary his wife, b. 4 Jul 1752

Mackall, Ann, d/o James John Mackall and Mary his wife, b. 12 Mar 1753

Mackall, Margaret and Barbary, daus. and twins of James John Mackall and Mary his wife, b. 14 May 1755 "whom God preserve"

Page 54

Freeman, John, s/o John Freeman and Elizabeth his wife, b. 24 Jul 1755 **(39)**

Young, George Parker, s/o Parker Young and Sarah his wife, b. 26 Mar 1755 **(40)**

Young, Mary, d/o Parker Young and Sarah his wife, b. 4 Sep 1757

Young, William Miles, s/o Parker Young and Sarah his wife, b. 4 Dec 1760

Somervill, John, s/o James Somervell and Susanna his wife, b. 15 May 1756

Somervill, James, s/o James Somervell and Susanna his wife, b. 19 Apr 1758

Somervell, Sarah, d/o James Somervell and Susanna his wife, b. 22 Sept 1760

Somervell, Howe, s/o James Somervell and Susanna his wife, b. 10 Dec 1762

Beveridge, John, s/o John Beveridge and Margaret his wife, b. 17 Feb 1758; bapt. 4 Apr following by Rev. George Cook; Godfathers John Johnson and Alexander Somervell; God-mother Miss Jane Johnson

Page 55

Clare, John, s/o Isaac Clare and Elizabeth his wife, b. 13 Feb 1747

Clare, Rebecca, d/o Isaac Clare and Elizabeth his wife, b. 9 Jan 1749

Clare, William, s/o Isaac Clare and Elizabeth his wife, b. 6 Dec 1750

Clare, Elizabeth, d/o Isaac Clare and Elizabeth his wife, b. 11 Jun 1753 **(41)**

Clare, Ann, d/o Isaac Clare and Elizabeth his wife, b. 10 Feb 1757

Mackall, Prissilla, d/o James John Mackall and Mary his wife, b. 19 May 1758

Page 56

Kirshaw, Francis and Rebecca Brady, m. 12 Sep 1756

Kirshaw, Margaret, d/o Francis Kirshaw and Rebecca his wife, b. 18 Nov 1757

Kirshaw, Dinah, d/o Francis Kirshaw and Rebecca his wife, b. 24 Feb 1759

Kirshaw, Francis, s/o Francis Kirshaw and Rebecca his wife, b. 18 Nov 1760

Kirshaw, Joshua, s/o Francis Kirshaw and Rebecca his wife, b. 17 Jan 1762

Dawkins, Rebecca, d/o William Dawkins and Dorcas his wife, b. 20 Jul 1741

Somervell, Alexander and Rebecca Dawkins, m. 2 Dec 1759

Somervell, Thomas, s/o Alexander Somervell and Rebecca his wife, b. 24 Sep 1760 **(42)**

Page 57

Somervell, William, s/o Alexander Somervell and Rebecca his wife, b. 30 Jan 1763

Dossey, Philip, s/o Philip Dossey and Martha his wife, b. 11 Aug 1759 [should this be Dorsey?]

Vanswaringgen, Joseph, and Eleanor Byrn, m. 26 Jul 1757

Vanswaringgen, Martha, d/o Joseph Vanswaringgen and Eleanor his wife, b. 30 Mar 1760

Mackall, John, and Margaret Gough, m. 11 Mar 1758

Mackall, Mary, d/o John Mackall and Margaret his wife, b. 16 May 1759

Mackall, Thomas Howe, s/o John Mackall and Margaret his wife, b. 23 Mar 1761

Page 58

Mackall, Rebecca, d/o John Mackall and Margaret his wife, b. 11 Feb 1763 **(43)**

Somervell, Rebecca, d/o Alexander Somervell and Rebecca his wife, b. 28 Mar 1765

Mackall, John, s/o John Mackall and Margaret his wife, b. 20 Aug 1764

Mackall, Ann, d/o John Mackall and Margaret his wife, b. 7 Mar 1766

Day, Elizabeth, d/o William Day and Jane his wife, b. 28 Jan 1762

Day, William, s/o William Day and Jane his wife, b. 23 Mar 1763

Day, Rebecca, d/o William Day and Jane his wife, b. 9 Nov 1764

Day, Jane, d/o William Day and Jane his wife, b. 16 Jul 1766

Fraizer, Margarett, d/o James Fraizer and Catherine his wife, b. 28 Apr 1747

Page 59

Fraizer, Anne, d/o James Fraizer and Catherine his wife, b. 7 Mar 1752 **(44)**

Fraizer, Chaney, d/o James Fraizer and Catherine his wife, b. 23 Feb 1755

Fraizer, Mary, d/o James Fraizer and Catharine his wife, b. 1 Sep 1757

Fraizer, Charles, s/o James Fraizer and Catharine his wife, b. 26 Oct 1760

Fraizer, Elizabeth, d/o James Fraizer and Catherine his wife, b. 24 Jan 1763

Fraizer, James Hasletine, s/o James Fraizer and Catharine his wife, b. 6 Feb 1767

Egan, Henrietta Reeder, d/o Barnaby Egan and Henrietta his wife, b. 13 Mar 1764

Egan, Thomas Henry, s/o Barnaby Egan and Henrietta his wife, b. 11 Feb 1767

Page 60

Fryar, John Edward Henry, s/o William Fryar and Mary his wife, b. 29 Jul 1761 **(45)**

Fryar, Zachariah, s/o William Fryar and Mary his wife, b. 8 Apr 1764

Mackall, James, s/o John Mackall and Margaret his wife, b. 2 Nov 1767

Mackall, Benjamin, s/o John Mackall and Margaret his wife, b. 2 Nov 1767

Mackall, Benjamin, s/o James Mackall and Mary his wife, d. 17 Jul 1767

Allen, Elizabeth, d/o William Allen and Mary his wife, b. 12 Mar 1758

Allen, Mary, d/o William Allen and Eleanor his wife, b. 13 Jul 1764

Allen, William, s/o William Allen and Eleanor his wife, b. 17 Oct 1766

Page 61

Hellen, Peter, s/o James Hellen and Ann his wife, b. 14 Aug 1724 **(46)**

Pattison, Penelope, s/o James Pattison, b. 24 Nov 1724

Hellen, Peter and Penelope Pattison, m. 14 Mar 1746/7

Hellen, James, s/o Peter Hellen and Penelope his wife, b. 24 Dec 1747

Hellen, Ann, d/o Peter Hellen and Penelope his wife, b. 14 Jan 1749/50

Hellen, Peter, s/o Peter Hellen and Penelope his wife, b. 28 Mar 1752

Hellen, William, s/o Peter Hellen and Penelope his wife, 20 Nov 1754

Hellen, Mary, d/o Peter Hellen and Penelope his wife, b. 21 Jan 1757

Hellen, Benjamin, s/o Peter Hellen and Penelope his wife, b. 20 Jun 1759

Page 62

Hellen, Barbara, d/o Peter Hellen and Penelope his wife, b. 29 Mar 1762

Monett, Isaac, s/o Isaac, b. 18 Dec 1746 **(47)**

Monett, Isaac and Ann Hellen, m. 9 Feb 1768

Monett, Penelope, d/o Isaac Monett and Ann his wife, b. 23 Apr 1769

Hellen, Richard, s/o James Hellen and Ann his wife, b. 28 Sep 1722

Mackall, Benjamin, s/o John Mackall of St. Leonards and Margaret his wife, b. 6 Apr 1769

Vanswearinggen, Kezia, d/o Joseph Vanswearinggen and Eleanor his wife, b. 4 Jun 1763

Egan, Susanna, d/o Barnaby Egan and Henrietta his wife, b. 26 Aug 1770

Page 63

Hoopper, Abraham and Mary Hellen, m. 8 Jan 1764 **(48)**

Hoopper, Jacob, s/o Abraham Hoopper and Mary his wife, b. 17 Sep 1764

Hoopper, Abraham, s/o Abraham Hoopper and Mary his wife, b. 6 Nov 1766

Hoopper, Isaac, s/o Abraham Hoopper and Mary his wife, b. 19 Jun 1769

Pardoe, John, s/o Peter and Ann his wife, b. 14 Jan 1741/2

Pardoe, John, s/o Peter and Ann his wife, and Margaret Fraizer, m. 23 Nov 1769

Pardoe, Catherine Hesletine, d/o John Pardoe and Margaret his wife, b. 5 Dec 1770

Mackall, Margaret, d/o John Mackall of St. Leonards and Margaret his wife, b. 28 Jan 1771

Page 64

Kent, John and Elizabeth Dare, m. 6 Jul 1758

Kent, Isaac, s/o John Kent and Eliza. his wife, b. 19 May 1759

Kent, Kessah, d/o John Kent and Elizabeth his wife, b. 18 Dec 1760 **(49)**

Kent, John, s/o John Kent and Elizabeth his wife, b. 6 Sep 1762
Kent, Richard, s/o John Kent and Elizabeth his wife, b. 15 Oct 1764
Kent, Joseph, s/o John Kent and Elizabeth his wife, b. 30 Oct 1766
Kent, Jennet, d/o John Kent and Elizabeth his wife, b. 27 Nov 1768
Kent, Gideon Dare, s/o John Kent and Elizabeth his wife, b. 16 Sep 1770
Page 65
Taylor, Brian and Barbara Dawkins, m. 7 May 1772
Coe, William, s/o Samuel and Elizabeth his wife, b. 9 Nov 1757
Coe, Ann, d/o Samuel Coe and Elizabeth his wife, b. 25 Mar 1760
Hungerford, James, s/o Edmund Hungerford and Mary his wife, b. 2 Jan 1764 **(50)**
Hungerford, Ann, d/o Edmund Hungerford and Mary his wife, b. 20 May 1766
Hungerford, Benjamin, s/o Edmund Hungerford and Mary his wife, b. 14 Feb 1769
Mackall, Sarah, d/o John Mackall of St. Leonards and Margaret his wife, b. 24 Jun 1772
Page 66
Taylor, Sarah, d/o Brian Taylor and Barbara his wife, b. 24 Feb 1773
Taylor, William Dawkins, s/o Brian Taylor and Barbara his wife, b. 22 Apr 1774
Pardoe, James, s/o John Pardoe and Margaret his wife, b. 25 Jan 1774
Mackall, Dorcas, d/o John Mackall of St. Leonards and Margarett his wife, b. 12 Jul 1774
Hoopper, Elizabeth Downs, d/o Abraham Hoopper and Mary his wife, b. 9 Aug 1773 **(51)**
Young, Thomas, s/o Parker Young and Sarah his wife, b. 14 Mar 1765
Young, Miles, s/o Parker Young and Sarah his wife, b. 22 May 1771
Page 67
Monett, Abraham, s/o Isaac Monett and Ann his wife, b. 26 Mar 1774
Sedwick, John and Elizabeth Lander Cook, m. 1 Mar 1764

Sedwick, Ann, d/o John Sedwick and Elizabeth Lander his wife, b. 10 Dec 1764

Sedwick, Elizabeth, d/o John Sedwick and Eliza. Lander his wife, b. 20 May 1767

Sedwick, Joshua, s/o John Sedwick and Elizabeth Lander his wife, b. 2 Jul 1770

Sedwick, Isabella, d/o John Sedwick and Elizabeth Lander his wife, b. 18 Feb 1773 **(52)**

Gray, William, s/o Thomas Gray and Elizabeth his wife, and Rebecca Gardner, m. 20 Oct 1761

Page 68

Gray, Thomas, s/o William Gray and Rebecca his wife, b. 23 Dec 1762

Gray, Elizabeth, d/o William Gray and Rebecca his wife, b. 11 Jan 1764

Gray, Sarah, d/o William Gray and Rebecca his wife, b. 10 Jan 1766

Gray, Mary, d/o William Gray and Rebecca his wife, b. 16 Jun 1768

Gray, John, s/o William Gray and Rebecca his wife, b. 2 Mar 1771

Hellen, Benjamin, b. reg. p. (46), d. Monday 24 Jul 1775 about 4 o'clock in the morning, age 16 years, one month and 4 days

Taylor, Everard, s/o Brian Taylor and Barbara his wife, b. 10 Nov 1775

Page 69

Taylor, Brian and Barbara Dawkins, both of same parish, m. 7 May 1772, by Rev. Francis Lander, Rector of Christ Church; witnessed by Thomas Johnson, Jr., James Mackall Sollers **(53)**

Broome, John and Betty Heighe Gantt, m. 24 Nov 1774

Broome, John, s/o John Broome and Betty Heighe his wife, b. 21 Oct 1775

Broome, James Mackall, s/o John Broome and Betty Heighe his wife, b. 2 June 1778

Taylor, James Mackall, s/o Brian Taylor and Barbara his wife, b. 26 Aug 1778

Sedwick, John, s/o John Sedwick and Elizabeth Lander his wife, b. 13 Sep 1775

Page 70

Sedwick, Mary, d/o John Sedwick and Elizabeth Lander his wife, b. 19 Jan 1778

Pardoe, John, s/o John Pardoe and Margaret his wife, b. 5 May 1772 **(54)**

Pardoe, Anne, d/o John Pardoe and Margaret his wife, b. 5 Feb 1776

Pardoe, Peter, s/o John Pardoe and Margaret his wife, b. 5 Jun 1778

Boney, Mary Dale Davidson, d/o Thomas Boney and Jane his wife, b. 2 Dec 1777 at Prince Frederick Town in Christ Church Parish

Ogg, Alexander and Jane Hellen of Calvert County; license granted 29 Mar 1781 by Patrick Sim Smith according to the law of the state of Maryland; lawfully married in the Church of England; dated 1 Jun 1782; /s/ Walter Magowan, Rector of St. James Parish

Page 71

Sedwick, Mary, d/o John Sedwick and Elizabeth Lander his wife, b. 19 Feb 1778

Sedwick, Benjamin, s/o John Sedwick and Elizabeth Lander his wife, b. 2 Jul 1781; d. 20 Jul 1781 **(55)**

Sedwick, James Cook, s/o John Sedwick and Elizabeth Lander his wife, b. 26 Jan 1786

Hellen, Mary, d/o James Hellen and Ann his wife, b. 1 Jan 1730/1

Blackburn, Sarah, d/o Benjamin Blackburn and Barbara his wife, b. 9 Nov 1786

Dawkins, Ann, d/o Charles Dawkins and Rebecca his wife, b. 13 May 1775

Dawkins, Rebecca, d/o Charles Dawkins and Rebecca his wife, b. 23 Mar 1777

Dawkins, Dorcas, d/o Charles Dawkins and Rebecca his wife, b. 1 Feb 1779

Page 72

Dawkins, William, s/o Charles Dawkins and Rebecca his wife, b. 31 Dec 1781

Kershaw, John, s/o Francis Kershaw and Rebecca his wife, b. 10 Apr Thursday forenoon 1767

Buckingham, Mary, d/o John Buckingham and Sarah his wife, b. 2 Oct 1776 **(56)**

Buckingham, Anne, d/o Jno. Buckingham and Sarah his wife, b. 8 Dec 1778; d. 8 Nov 1781

Buckingham, Rebeccah, d/o Jno. Buckingham and Sarah his wife, b. 16 Feb 1781

Buckingham, Martha, d/o Jno. Buckingham and Sarah his wife, b. 8 Jan 1783

Buckingham, Katharine, d/o Jno. Buckingham and Sarah his wife, b. 11 Sep 1784

Buckingham, Thomas, s/o Jno. Buckingham and Sarah his wife, b. 28 Sep 1786

Page 73

Buckingham, Sarah, d/o Jno. Buckingham and Sarah his wife, b. 28 Sep 1788

Sedwick, John, Jr. and Elizabeth Rawlings, m. 1 Dec 1796 **(57)**

Sedwick, Caroline Elisabeth, d/o John Sedwick, Jr. and Elisabeth his wife, b. 28 Sep 1797

Sedwick, Eloisa Mary, d/o John and Elisabeth his wife, b. 31 Jan 1800

Sedwick, Daniel Rawlings, s/o John and Elisabeth his wife, b. 20 Jun 1802

Sedwick, Rebecker Prisciller, d/o John and Elizabeth his wife, b. 17 Jun 1805

Wilson, John, s/o William and Mary Wilson, b. 19 Jun 1805

Hooper, Isaac and Elisabeth Hollyday, m. 10 Nov 1770 **(58)**

Page 74

Hooper, Priscilla, of Isaac Hooper and Elisabeth his wife, b. 23 Aug 1774

Hooper, John, of Isaac Hooper and Elisabeth his wife, b. 23 Jan 1777

Hooper, James, of Isaac Hooper and Elisabeth his wife, b. 25 Nov 1780

Hooper, Anne, of Isaac Hooper and Elisabeth his wife, b. 2 May 1782

Hooper, Isaac, of Isaac Hooper and Elisabeth his wife, b. 23 Aug 1784

Hooper, William, of Isaac Hooper and Elisabeth his wife, b. 21 Jun 1787

Hooper, Benjamin, of Isaac Hooper and Elisabeth his wife, b. 23 Mar 1790

Hooper, Abraham, of Isaac Hooper and Elisabeth his wife, b. 12 Dec 1791

Hooper, Rachael, of Isaac Hooper and Elisabeth his wife, b. 18 Mar 1794

Page 75

Askew, James, of Henry Askew and Dinah his wife, b. 14 Jan 1790 **(59)**

Bowen, Benjamin and Elenor, twins of John Bowen of Basil and Martha his wife, b. 22 Dec 1781

Bowen, Barbara, of John Bowen of Basil and Dinah his wife, b. 22 Oct 1796

Bowen, Rebeccah, of John Bowen of Basil and Dinah his wife, b. 28 May 1798

Bowen, Basil, of John of Basil and Dinah his wife, b. 3 Feb 1801

Bowen, John, of John of Basil and Dinah his wife, b. 19 Jun 1802

Kirshaw, Benjamin Wright, s/o Margaret Kirshaw, b. 21 Jan 1782

Mackenney, John, of Alexander Mackenney and Margaret his wife, b. 23 Dec 1787

Mackenny Priscilla, of Alexander and Margaret, b. 28 Mar 1791

Makenny, Dorcas, of Alexander and Margaret his wife, b. 15 Feb 1794

Page 76

Wood, Rebeccah Miles, d/o Sabret Wood and Sarah his wife, b. 5 Jan 1799; christened 21 Apr following; sponsors Charles Bowen and Mary Bowen of Parker **(60)**

Hance, John, s/o Francis Hance and Ann his wife, b. 16 Jan 1793; bapt. 1 Sep 1799

Hance, Harriet, d/o Francis Hance and Ann his wife, b. 2 May 1795; bapt. 1 Sep 1799

Hance, Mary Ann, d/o Francis Hance and Ann his wife, b. 5 May 1798; bapt. 1 Sep 1799

Kirshaw, John, s/o James Kirshaw and Kesya his wife, b. 11 Dec 1789 **(61)**
Kirshaw, Cavey R., d/o James Kirshaw and Kesya his wife, b. 18 Nov 1791
Kirshaw, Joseph S., s/o James Kirshaw and Kesya his wife, b. 20 Feb 1794; d. 17 Aug 1798
Kirshaw, Rebecca, d/o James Kirshaw and Kesya his wife, b. 17 May 1796
Kirshaw, Patsey, d/o James Kirshaw and Kesya his wife, b. 29 May 1799; bapt. 1 Sep 1799
Kershaw, James L., s/o John Kershaw and Rebecca Kirshaw, b. 7 Nov 1815
Page 77
Kirshaw, John and Pricale Kirshaw, m. 11 Nov 1819
Askew, Michael, of Joseph and Susannah Askew, b. 8 Apr 1761 **(62)**
Askew, Mary, of Michael and Anne Askew his wife, b. 13 Aug 1786
Kirshaw, Francis and Ann P. Duke, m. 22 Jul 1784; [he] d. 15 Mar 1820
Kirshaw, Benjamin D., s/o Francis and Ann Kirshaw, b. 22 Sep 1780; d. 24 Jun 1792
Kirshaw, Sarah A., of Fras. and Ann Kirshaw, b. 23 Jan 1787
Kirshaw, Cortiana, d/o Frans. and Ann Kirshaw, b. 21 Mar 1789; d. 16 Jan 1793
Kirshaw, Priscilla, d/o Frans. and Ann Kirshaw, b. 11 Jun 1791; d. 20 Apr 1820
Kirshaw, Joshua, s/o Frans. and Ann Kirshaw, b. 22 Jul 1793; d. 3 Jul 1794
Kershaw, Francis, s/o Frans. and Ann Kershaw, b. 26 Apr 1795
Page 78
Kershaw, Cortinia Ann, d/o Frans. and Ann Kershaw, b. 5 Apr 1798; d. age ca 6 mos
Kirshaw, Osburn, s/o Frans. and Ann Kershaw, b. 14 Oct 1799; twin; d. 18 Oct 1802; age 3 years and 4 days
Kirshaw, Armeneco, s/o Frans. and Ann Kershaw, b. 14 Oct 1799; twin; d. 19 Oct 1802; age 3 years and 5 days

Kirshaw, John, of Frans. and Ann Kirshaw, b. Apr 1802; d. 3-4 hrs.
Kirshaw, William, s/o Frans. Kirshaw and Ann Kirshaw, b. 28 Sep 1803
Kirshaw, James D., s/o Francis and Ann Kirshaw, b. 12 Oct 1806
Williams, John, of John Williams and Sarah his wife, b. 2 Nov 1777 **(63)**
Hellen, Joseph Johnson, s/o Thos. Hellen and Rebeker his wife, b. 3 Dec 1796
Hellen, Thos. John, s/o Thos. and Rebeker Hellen, b. 23 Nov 1798
Hellen, Walter, s/o above, b. 26 Sep 1800
Hellen, Maria, s/o Thos. and Rebeker, b. 7 Jul 1804

Page 79

Yoe, Benjamin, and Sarah A. Kirshaw, m. 5 Feb 1807 by Rev. N. W. Lane, Rector Christ Church Parish
Slye, John, of Samuel and Ann, b. May 1778; m. Martha Buckingham of John and Sarah 24 Dec 1801 **(64)**
Missing page number **(65)**
Yoe, John, s/o Robert Yoe and Mary his wife, b. 29 Jul 1750 **(66)**
Yoe, John and Catharine Skinner, m. 19 Mar 1781
Yoe, Benjamin Skinner, of John and Catharine, b. 4 Sep 1782
Yoe, Catharine, d. 15 Sep 1782 in the 25th year of her age
Yoe, John and Susannah Miller, m. 9 Jan 1785
Miller, Susannah, of Rousby, b. 12 Sep 1759
Yoe, John, of John and Susannah his wife, b. 5 Oct 1785
Yoe, Robert, of John and Susannah his wife, b. 12 Jul 1787
Yoe, Mary, of John and Susannah his wife, b. 24 Jun 1789
Yoe, Ann, of John and Susannah his wife, b. 27 Aug 1791
Yoe, William, of John and Susannah his wife, b. 28 Jan 1793
Yoe, James, of John and Susannah his wife, b. 28 Aug 1795
Yoe, Hariet, of John and Susannah his wife, b. 28 Jan 1799
Yoe, Walter, of John and Susannah his wife, b. 16 Nov 1800
Bourne, James E., s/o Jesse Jacob and Ann Bourne, b. 12 Aug 1781 **(67)**
Duke, Basil, s/o Jas. and Rebecca Duke, b. 39 Jan 1790
Gibson, Peter, s/o Peter Gibson, b. 6 Jan 1797

Page 80

Gibson, James Richard, s/o Peter Gibson and Elizabeth his wife, b. 3 Sep 1825
Duke, Nathaniel, s/o Jas and Rebecca Duke, b. 2 Apr 1799
King, Thomas B., s/o Benj'n and Susanna King, b. 1 Feb 1794
Duke, Sarah Broome, s/o Nathaniel and Mary Duke, b. 22 Jan 1826
Duke, James, s/o N. Duke and Mary Duke, b. 5 Sep 1828
Duke, Sarah, b. 16 Mar 1787; m. John L. Bond 28 Feb 1806 **(68)**
Bond, Thos. H., s/o John L. Bond and Sarah H. Bond his wife, b. 15 Dec 1807
Bond, Jas. A., b. 7 Feb 1812
Bond, Juliet Ann, b. 28 Nov 1809; d. 15 May 1814
Bond, John, b. 15 Nov 1814
Bond, Basil Duke, b. 15 Apr 1817
Bond, Mary Rebecca, b. 15 Sep 1819; d. 11 Sep 1822
Bond, Sarah Howe, b. 28 Sep 1821
Bond, Elizabeth Masiah, b. 20 Aug 1821; d. 6 Mar 1822
Bond, Benson, b. 28 Dec 1827
Laveille, Uriah, b. 8 Jan 1800
Laveille, John L., b. 12 Sep 1821

Page 81

Bond, Thos. Holdsworth, Dr., killed by lightning on night of 11 Aug 1838 at home of his uncle, Dr. James Duke, in the 31st year of his age. He was a worthy man and greatly beloved by all who knew him. May he rest in peace. What I do thou knowest not now but thos shalt know hereafter.
Rawlings, Thomas, b. 22 Feb 1789 **(69)**
Bacome, James T., b. 14 Jul 1791
Missing page number **(70)**
Bond, James Alexander and Sarah Elizabeth Chesley Hance, m. by Rev. Olcott Bulkley, Rector of Christ Church Parish, 20 Nov 1838 **(71)**
Bond, John Thos., s/o Jas. and Sarah Bond, b. 16 Apr 1840
Bond, Jas. Alex. Chesley, s/o Jas. and Sarah Bond, b. 3 Sep 1845
Bond, Benjamin Young Hance Bond, s/o Jas. and Sarah, b. Jul 1847

Page 82

Confirmed on Sunday, 4 May 1794 by the Right Rev'd Doct'r Clagget, Bishop of Maryland (98)

Skinner, Elisabeth
Belt, Mary Skinner
Pitcher, Rebecca
Fraizer, Betty H.
Bourne, George
Harris, Elisabeth
Roberts, Mary Howe
Kirshaw, Kesya
Griffin, Mary
Hellen, Anne
Sedwick, Anne
Winnull, Jno.
Harris, Joseph
Moore, Thomas
Dotron, Elenor
Sedwick, Jno
Edmons, Easorn
Jenkins, Thomas
Jenkins, Mary
Baden, Jeremiah
Baden, Elisabeth
Pasture, Rebecca
Bowen Isaac Godsgrace
Bowen, Isaac
Bowen, Elisabeth Godsgrace
Bowen, Sarah
Dixon, Lydia
Day, Eleanor
Helen, Mary
Williams, Jno.
Page 83
Moody, Sarah
Gantt, Mary
Skinner, Orphap
Skinner, Lethe
Everist, Mary
Wood, Elisabeth
Grover, Priscilla
Monett, Abraham
Askew, Dinah
Bowen, Rebeca
Roberts, Anne
Wilson, Elisabeth
Duke, Mary
Harris, William
Harris, Betty
Sedwick, Elisabeth
Brook, Anne
Bowen, David
Edmonds, Dolly
Wilson, Mary
Mills, Chaney
Tucker, Susannah
Bowen, Martha
Barze, Mary
Freeman, Israel
Young, Susanna
Day, Sarah
Tanner, Mary
Askew, Anne
Cullember, Casse
Bowen, Elisabeth
Sedwick, Isabel
Hollyday, Eleanor
Skinner, Christiana

Kersahw, James
Hutchings, Elisabeth
Denton, Jno
Denton, Priscilla
Spencer, Martha
Bond, Sarah
Spencer, Francis
Kirshaw, Rebecca
Wilkinson, Sarah
Davis, Sarah
Bowen, Benj'm G.
Bowen, James G.
Watson, Anne
Bowen, Susannah
Wilson, Sarah
Bowen, Elisabeth
Shrive, Martha

Page 84

The Records of Marriages of Christ Church Parish, Calvert County
Bussey, Edward and Martha Evans, m. 10 Aug 1701
Holshot, Jno. and Dorothy Ireland, m. 10 Aug 1701
Kelley, Patrick and Elizabeth Simmons, m. 15 Nov 1701
Delimere, David and Elizabeth Mauldin, m. 29 Feb 1701
Chilton, Cuthbert and Mary Baker, m. 29 Jul 1703
Barton, John and Hester Holmes, m. 1 Jun 1703
Wheeler, Roger and Elizabeth Gibson, m. 16 Apr 1704
Lee, Robert and Elizabeth Munday, m. 16 Apr 1704
Hobs, John and Mary Wilde, m. 20 Aug 1704
Roberts, Jno. and Deborah Roberson, m. 17 Sep 1704
Gardner, Jno. and Ann Birmingham, m. 27 Jan 1704
Hazell, John and Mary Nevitt, m. 7 Nov 1704
White, Tho. and Mary Lane, m. 6 Feb 1704
Demilliane, Gabriel (Minister) and Ann Young, m. 31 Jan 1704
Fowler, Peter and Agnes Gray, m. 10 Oct 1704
Dixon, Robert and Ruth Manning, m. 20 Apr 1703
Swillaven, Daniel and Priscilla Stirney, m. 24 Apr 1705
Turner, Jno. and Elizabeth Hodges, m. 6 Oct 1705

Martin, Wm. and Elizabeth Chapple, m. 21 Oct 1705
Culpeper, Michael and Elliner Fidgarrill, m. 14 Jan 1705
Barton, Wm. and Catherine Place, m. 9 Apr 1705
Aurkhutt, Alexander and Ann Barton, m. 9 Apr 1705
Hebedine, Thomas and Elizbeth Raymie, m. 11 Aug 1706
Jones, Thomas and Dorothy Chittham, m. 18 Apr 1706
Harbutt, Jno. and Rebecka Williams, m. 21 Jul 1706
Brabant, Wm. and Mary Gyatt, m. 24 Apr 1706
Gray, Wm. and Martha Duke, m. 16 Oct 1706
Bumnalley, Andrew and Elizabeth Blackett, m. 6 May 1707
Roberts, Jno. and Grace Mannin, m. 3 Sep 1707
Richards, Tho. and Margrett Delaine, m. 25 Dec 1707
Williams, Joseph and Easther Creed, m. 6 Oct 1707

Page 85

Greeves, James and Catherine Barton, m. 8 Apr 1707
Glover, Richard and Mary Jones, m. 23 Nov 1707
Miller, William and Grace Young, m. 21 Oct 1707
Ashcom, Nathaniel and Margret Bigger, m. 26 Dec 1706
Greves, Robert and Margrett Howe, m. 7 Nov 1707
Parran, Alexander and Mary Ashcom, m. 16 Feb 1693
Makgill, David and Grace Boon, m. 6 Mar 1708/9
Williamson, John and Mary Rurk, m. 21 Aug 1709
Crafford, Richard and Mary Covene, m. 17 Sep 1709
Smith, John and Mary Simpson, m. 4 Dec 1708
Maynard, Thomas and Ann Smith, m. 25 Aug 1693
Ellt, Henry and Elizabeth Topin, m. 21 Jun 1703
Morgan, Thomas and Margrit Ellt, m. 14 Dec 1708
Collings, Robert and Mary Watson, m. 1 Jan 1704/5
Baker, John and Hannah Williams, m. 18 May 1710
Mackenney, Alexander and Catherine Plunkitt, m. 4 Sep 1710
Holdsworth, Thos. (Mr.) and Barbara Smith, m. 1 Jan 1712
Andrew, Patrick (Mr.) and Mrs. Ann Bigger, m. 30 Jun 1715
Jenifer, Michael m. Mary Parker, d/o George Parker and Susanna his wife on 9 Jan 1718
Derrumple, John and Grace Constable, m. by Rev. Thomas Cockshutt 10 Jul 1718

Derrumple, John and Ellinor Allen, m. by Rev. Jonathan Cay on __ Feb 1733/4

Gray, John and Jane Abbott, m. by Rev. Jonathan Cay on 1 Dec 1731

Buckingham, John m. Sarah Cullember, d/o Thomas and Mary Cullember on 31 Jan 1776

Mackenny, Alexander m. Margaret Kirshaw, d/o Francis and Rebecca Kirshaw, 18 Feb 1787

Page 86

Kirshaw, James and Kesya Vansweringen, m. 25 Dec 1788

Jerrcons, Edward and Elizabeth Piscood, m. 13 May 1711

Smith, William and Elizabth Gardner, m. 13 May 1711

Franklin, Thomas and Grace Currant, m. 27 May 1711

Austin, John and Jane Sparks, m. 6 Jan 1712

Holdsworth, Thomas and Barbara Smith, m. 1 Jan 1712

Taylor, John and Rachel Holmes, m. 9 Nov 1713

Godgrace, John and Mary Grover, m. 27 Dec 1713 by Rev. Gabril DeEmmilliane

Kemp, William and Hannah Warren, m. 27 May 1715

Heseltine, Charles and Eleanor Webb, m. 7 7ber 1720 by Rev. Rob't Scot, Record of All Faith's Parish, St. Mary's Co.

Davkins, William and Mary Mackall, m. 9 Aug 1720

Somervall, James and Sarah Howe, m. 1 Jan 1722

Kirshaw, James and Margett Malden, m. 21 Aug 1725 by Rev. Cay

Peecock, Sam'l and Eliza. Ellt, m. 6 Jan 1731

Ambler, Thos. and Mary Burton Shair, m. __ Jan 1733

Page 87

Burialls

Allen, Charles, d. at his house on the Clifts in Calvert Co. 12 Oct 1734

Somervell, James, Dr., d. Friday 15 Feb 1750/1 between 2 & 3 o'clock in the morning in his 58th year; being maried 28 years to his second spouse, Sarah Howe

Clare, John, s/o Isaac and Elizabeth Clare, d. 12 Apr 1804, age 57 years, 2 months, 1 day

Calvert County Marriages
by
Rev. Francis Louder

Mills, Leonard m. China Fraser	4 Dec 1777
Young, George m. Mary Hellen	16 Dec 1777
Sedgwick, Thomas m. Anne Rigby	21 Dec 1777
MacKinnie, John m. Mary Kershaw	28 Dec 1777
Hutchings, Thomas m. Elizabeth Hellen	1 Jan 1778
Hellen, James m. Lydia Blackburn	5 Jan 1778
Gardiner, Isaac m. Rebecca Baker	13 Jan 1778
Gardiner, Kinsey m. Martha Games	15 Jan 1778
Parran, Benjamin m. Dorcas Hellen	15 Jan 1778
Wood, Jesse m. Hannah Ward	20 Jan 1778
Dare, Nathaniel m. Jean Gray	22 Jan 1778
Jones, Benjamin m. Sarah Gibson	1 Feb 1778
Parran, Alexander m. Mary King	10 Feb 1778
Powell, William m. Alice Evans	12 Feb 1778
Wilkinson, Richard m. Mary Askey	19 Feb 1778
Platford, David m. Sarah Cotton	23 Apr 1778
Brown, William m. Dorcas Woodward	26 Apr 1778
Gough, Salathael m. Elizabeth Sheredine Gray	26 Apr 1778
Baker, Nathaniel m. Anne Grover	30 Apr 1778
Hudson, Richard m. Jane James	25 Jun 1778
Smith, William m. Alice Stallings	4 Aug 1778
Wood, Edward m. Rebecca Gray	15 Sep 1778
Denton, Edward m. Mary Games	20 Oct 1778
Gray, Thomas m. Anne Bowen	3 Nov 1778
Bowen, John m. Sarah Tucker	5 Nov 1778
Cullember, Nathaniel m. Cassandra Bowen	8 Nov 1788
Hungerford, John m. Mary Cowen	24 Nov 1778
Allein, William m. Elizabeth Cowen	1 Dec 1778
Wilson, Nathaniel m. Anne Brome	3 Dec 1778
Hance, Samuel, Jr. m. Sarah Allnutt	6 Dec 1778
Tanner, Henry m. Mary Games	10 Dec 1778
King, Richard m. Sarah Rawlings	17 Dec 1778
Gough, Thomas m. Margaret Gray	22 Dec 1778

Bannister, Benjamin m. Grace Holland	24 Dec 1778
Chesly, John m. Mary Aschum Parran	5 Jan 1779
Hutchins, Joseph m. Mary Hardesty	5 Jan 1779
Jefferson, John m. Mary Gray	5 Jan 1779
Ramsey, William, m. Rebecca Jefferson	7 Jan 1779
Boguet, James m. Elizabeth Saxe	17 Jan 1779
Breedin, Joseph m. Susanna Stallions	21 Jan 1779
Hellen, William m. Dorcas Johnson	4 Feb 1779
Truman, Thomas m. Sarah Mitchell	6 Apr 1779
Ireland, George m. Mary Dare	11 Apr 1779
McDowell, John m. Mary Willin	13 Apr 1779
Younger, Joseph m. Jean Charlton	15 Apr 1779
Sollers, James Marshall m. Rebecca Elt	25 Apr 1779
Bowen, Charles m. Martha Gray	16 Apr 1779
Tabbs, Barton m. Elizabeth Bond	20 Jun 1779
Barrs, Leonard m. Mary Griffin	14 Nov 1779
Wilson, James m. Rebecca Skinner	25 Nov 1779
Harris, Richard m. Margaret Hance	19 Dec 1779
Willin, Thomas m. Elizabeth Wood	9 Jan 1780
Allein, Richard m. Phebe Dixon	23 Jan 1780
Ramsey, John m. Susanna Wood	1 Feb 1780
Rolle, Robert m. Martha Freeland	30 Mar 1780
Hance, Benjamin m. Sarah Dare	2 Apr 1780
Talbot, Thomas m. Susanna Rhodes	15 Apr 1780
Scarf, James m. Mary Hollandshead	20 Apr 1780
Gardiner, William m. Keziah Willin	29 Jun 1780
Beveridge, John m. Ann Cobbart	16 Jul 1780
Tucker, John m. Rebecca Williams	27 Jul 1780
Allsep, Richard m. Keziah Howse	28 Sep 1780
Davies, Joseph m. Sarah Miller	31 Oct 1780
Ramsay, William m. Rebecca Bond	31 Oct 1780
Boney, Thomas m. Sarah Fleet	31 Oct 1780
Thompson, Thomas m. Elizabeth Jones	2 Nov 1780
Button, Roger m. Ally Sebree (of Eastern Shore)	4 Nov 1780
Ivy, John m. Elizabeth Powell	12 Nov 1780
Avis, John m. Sarah Aisquith	23 Nov 1780

Marriages
by
Rev. Thomas John Clagget, Calvert County

Lee, Charles m. Mary Leach	28 Jul 1777
Smith, James m. Barbara White	12 Aug 1777
Owens, Charles m. Betty Barton	__ Oct 1777
Beckett, Humphrey m. Lydia Sunderland	31 Oct 1777
Page, Daniel m. Leonora Piles	16 Nov 1777
Dusheel, Benjamin m. Ann Yoe	25 Dec 1777

License granted Baltimore Co.; recorded Calvert Co.:
Dilworth, William m. Kisia Greenfield 16 Sep 1777

Births, Marriages, and Deaths
of
ST. ANDREW'S PARISH
St. Mary's County, Maryland

Page 1

Hellen, George Aisquith, s/o David Hellen and Susannah his wife, b. 18 Sep 1759 (7)
Hellen, Ann Parran, d/o above, b. 19 Jan 1762
Hellen, Jane, d/o above, b. 10 Nov 1763
Hellen, Thomas, s/o above, b. 10 Oct 1765
Hellen, Susanna Aisquith, d/o above, b. 25 May 1766
Wise, Cuthbert, s/o John Wise and Margaret his wife, b. 9 Apr 1765
Thomas, Samuel, s/o Mark Thomas and Elizabeth his wife, b. 10 Apr 1769
Joy, Henrietta, d/o John Joy, Jr. and Eleanor his wife, b. 3 Aug 1769
Taylor, Henrietta, s/o Ignatius Taylor and Elizabeth his wife, b. 5 May 1768
Hall, Dorothy, d/o Joseph Hall and Mary his wife, b. 18 Apr 1767
Hall, Thomas, s/o above, b. 5 Sep 1769
Abell, Sarah, d/o Peter Abell and Lucy his wife, b. 25 Oct 1769
Long, Margaret, d/o John Long and Barbara his wife, b. 25 Oct 1769
Bowes, Joseph, s/o Timothy Bowes and Mary his wife, b. 23 Feb 1769
Anderson, Ann, d/o Thomas Anderson and Henrietta his wife, b. 15 Apr 1764
Anderson, Mary, d/o above, b. 2 Jan 1766
Anderson, John, s/o Thomas Anderson and Chloe, b. 18 Sep 1768
Armsworthy, John, s/o Abraham Armsworthy and Eleanor his wife, b. 4 Nov 1769

Page 2

Latham, Margaret Ann, d/o Matthew and Susanna Latham, b. 25 Dec 1761
Latham, William, s/o above, b. 25 Jun 1765

St. Andrew's Parish

Latham, Mary, d/o above, b. 8 Mar 1767
Smart, Susanna, d/o William and Frances his wife, b. 9 Nov 1769
Bradburn, Mary, d/o Benjamin Bradburn and Ann his wife, b. 4 Jun 1765
Bradburn, Matthew, s/o above, b. 10 Feb 1767
Bradburn, Anastatia, d/o above, b. 16 Oct 1768
Stone, Ignatius, s/o Ignatius and Monica his wife, b. 6 Feb 1762
Stone, Matthew, s/o above, b. 8 Sep 1764
Wilkinson, Mary Thomas, s/o William Wilkinson and Nancy, b. 12 Jul 1765
Wilkinson, Winifred, d/o above, b. 24 Oct 1762
Wilkinson, James, s/o above, b. 18 Feb 1769
Thompson, Johnson, s/o James Thompson and Elizabeth his wife, b. 9 Dec 1761
Thompson, Elizabeth, d/o above, b. 14 May 1764
Thompson, James, s/o above, b. 6 May 1766
Thompson, Janet, d/o above, b. 5 Nov 1768
Downes, Ignatius, s/o Joseph Downes and Ann his wife, b. 18 Nov 1759
Downes, John, s/o above, b. 25 May 1762
Downes, Mary, d/o above, b. 26 May 1764
Downes, Elizabeth, d/o above, b. 23 Jun 1766
Downes, Ann, d/o above, b. 24 Oct 1768
Wootton, John, s/o Joseph Wootton and Mary his wife, b. 5 Nov 1759 **(8)**
Wootton, Thomas, s/o above, b. 5 Feb 1762

Page 3

Wootton, Elizabeth, d/o above, b. 19 Mar 1764
Wootton, Joseph, s/o above, b. 30 Sep 1766
Clarke, John, s/o Robert Clarke and Ann his wife, b. 15 Oct 1751
Clarke, Mary, d/o above, b. 29 Oct 1755
Clarke, Robert, s/o above, b. 17 Nov 1757
Clarke, Ann, d/o above, b. 17 Aug 1760
Clarke, Eleanor, d/o above, b. 22 May 1764
Wise, Caleb, s/o Richard Wise and Mary his wife, b. 6 Nov 1752
Wise, Jane, d/o above, b. 6 Feb 1755
Wise, Dorothy, d/o above, b. 18 Sep 1760

Wise, Margaret, d/o above, b. 25 Nov 1763
Armsworthy, Ann, d/o James Armsworthy and Susanna his wife, b. 5 Aug 1765
Armsworthy, Barton, s/o above, b. 2 Sep 1767
Wise, James, s/o Adam Wise and Frances his wife, b. 17 Mar 1767
Silence, Enoch, s/o John Silence, Sr. and Mary his wife, b. 6 Mar 1760
Silence, Jeremiah, s/o above, b. 19 Oct 1762
Silence, Austin, s/o above, b. 11 Apr 1765
Silence, John, s/o John Jr., and Elizabeth his wife, b. 24 Mar 1761
Silence, Ann, d/o above, b. 27 Dec 1766
Thomas, Elizabeth, d/o Abell Thomas and Sarah his wife, b. 2 Mar 1769
Thompson, Joseph and Zachariah, sons of Thomas Thompson and Ann his wife, b. 7 Feb 1769

Page 4

Winsatt, Priscilla, d/o John Winsatt and Henrietta his wife, b. 5 Apr 1769
Tennison, John, s/o Absolom Tennison and Susanna his wife, b. 10 Mar 1754
Tennison, Jesse, s/o above, b. 13 Oct 1765
Tennison, Susanna, d/o above, b. 10 Oct 1758
Tennison, Eleanor, d/o above, b. 10 Oct 1763
Tennison, Ann, d/o above, b. 26 May 1766
Tennison, Margaret, d/o above, b. 14 Sep 1768
Goldsbury, Charles, s/o Jonathan Goldsbury and Christian his wife, b. 4 Mar 1765
Wise, Clarke, s/o John Wise and Margaret his wife, b. 7 Jan 1753
Wise, Eleanor, d/o above, b. 27 Dec 1754
Wise, Rhode, s/o above, b. 15 Mar 1756
Wise, John, d/o above, b. 10 Feb 1758
Wise, James Manning, s/o above, b. 17 Apr 1762
Cole, Winifred, d/o Francis Cole and Ann his wife, b. 3 Sep 1766
Cooke, Susannah, d/o Thomas Cooke and Jane his wife, b. 19 Sep 1755
Cooke, Thomas, s/o above, b. 13 Jan 1757

Cooke, Benjamin, s/o above, b. 6 Oct 1759
Cooke, Jane, d/o above, b. 27 Sep 1763
Cooke, Joanna, d/o above, b. 2 Nov 1765 **(9)**
Cooke, Catharine, d/o above, b. 18 Mar 1768
Joy, Joseph, s/o John Joy and Mary his wife, b. 20 Sep 1755
Page 5
Joy, Mary, s/o above, b. 20 Sep 1755
Joy, Winifred, s/o John Joy and Sarah his wife, b. 20 Feb 1762
Joy, Thomas Tarlton, s/o above, b. 23 May 1765
Joy, Elizabeth, d/o above, b. 17 May 1768
Thomas, Luke, s/o Abell Thomas and Sarah his wife, b. 24 Nov 1763
Lake, Susanna, d/o John Lake and Elizabeth his wife, b. 28 Jul 1766
Lake, John, s/o above, b. 28 Mar 1768
Bohanan, Jonathan, s/o George Bohanan and Eliz'th his wife, b. 20 Jul 1767
Fish, Thomas, s/o James Fish and Elizabeth his wife, b. 14 Aug 1763
Fish, Bennet, s/o above, b. 15 Dec 1765
Hutchens, Jane [?James], s/o Robert Hutchens and Ann his wife, b. 30 May 1763
Hall, Bennet, s/o Benjamin Hall and Ann his wife, b. 25 Nov 1765
Hall, Joseph, s/o above, b. 12 Aug 1769
Hall, Priscilla, d/o above, b. 20 Aug 1761
Hall, Mary, d/o above, b. 1 Dec 1763
Hall, Elizabeth, d/o above, b. 12 Dec 1768
Kirby, Richard, s/o Peter Kirby and Henrietta his wife, b. 22 Feb 1754
Kirby, Rebecca, d/o above, b. 4 Jan 1762
Hopewell, Richard, s/o Joseph Hopewell and Dorcas his wife, b. 26 Feb 1753
Hopewell, George, s/o above, b. 28 Jan 1757
Hopewell, John, s/o above, b. 3 Jun 1763
Page 6
Tarlton, Jeremiah, s/o William Tarlton and Jane his wife, b. 12 May 1761

Kirby, Hopewell, d/o William Kirby and Elizabeth his wife, b. 22 Apr 1756
Jones, Uel, s/o Johnson Jones and Elizabeth his wife, b. 19 Aug 1764
Breeden, Aaron, s/o James Breeden and Sarah his wife, b. 12 Oct 1766
Hammet, Johnson, s/o Robert Hammet and Rebecca his wife, b. 1 Dec 1766
Dogan, Jeremiah, s/o Thomas Dogan and Monica his wife, b. 2 Feb 1763
Wise, Dorcas, s/o Jemima Wise, b. 3 Jun 1763
Wise, Edward Swann, s/o above, b. 10 Apr 1768
Saunders, Elizabeth, d/o Sinnot Saunders and Ann his wife, b. 24 Jan 1768
Armsworthy, Thomas, s/o George Armsworthy and Rebecca his wife, b. 17 Aug 1756
Armsworthy, Mack, s/o above, b. 3 Apr 1758
Armsworthy, Bennet, s/o above, b. 5 Apr 1760
Armsworthy, Sarah, d/o above, b. 15 Feb 1762
Armsworthy, Daniel, s/o above, b. 17 Jun 1764
Sticklin, Jeremiah, s/o Josias Sticklin and Joanna his wife, b. 11 May 1767
Warren, William, s/o Edward Warren and Elizabeth his wife, b. 25 May 1755 **(10)**
Warren, Mary, d/o above, b. 20 Nov 1759
Warren, Britanina, d/o above, b. 9 Mar 1762
Thomas, Stanhope Rule, s/o Mary Thomas, b. 24 Dec 1755
Thomas, Sarah, d/o above, b. 15 Jan 1765
Page 7
Files, Ann, d/o Thomas Files and Sarah his wife, b. 18 Dec 1756
Files, William, s/o above, b. 13 Feb 1760
Files, Thomas, s/o above, b. 1 Feb 1758
Files, Sarah, d/o above, b. 7 Feb 1763
Files, John, s/o above, b. 24 Dec 1765
Bates, John, s/o Lowry Bates and Susanna his wife, b. 10 Nov 1758
Bates, Ann, d/o above, b. 3 Dec 1764
Joy, William, s/o John Joy and Eleanor his wife, b. 18 Jul 1760

Joy, Benedict, s/o above, b. 10 Apr 1763
Martin, Thomas, s/o William Martin and Mary Ann his wife, b. 13 Jun 1757
Martin, William, s/o above, b. 13 Feb 1759
Martin, George, s/o above, b. 10 May 1761
Martin, Ann, d/o Thomas Martin and Jane his wife, b. 27 Mar 1759
Martin, John Curry, s/o above, b. 17 Feb 1761
Martin, Jane Dorothy, d/o above, b. 17 Feb 1764
Thomas, Ann, d/o John Thomas and Dorothy his wife, b. 16 Dec 1764
Thomas, John, s/o above, b. 1 Nov 1766
Armsworthy, Henrietta, d/o Jonathan Armsworthy and Ann his wife, b. 15 Jun 1758
Chrisman, John, s/o Luke Chrisman and Elisabeth his wife, b. 13 Apr 1766
Adams, Enoch, s/o Abraham Adams and Ann his wife, b. 18 Sep 1757
Adams, Austin, s/o above, 3 Apr 1759

Page 8

Adams, Elizabeth, d/o above, b. 13 Jan 1762
Adams, Abraham, s/o above, b. 13 Oct 1764
Dogan, Eleanor, d/o John Dogan and Ann his wife, b. 13 Apr 1761
Dogan, William, s/o above, b. 10 May 1763
Dogan, James, s/o above, 5 Nov 1765
Dogan, John, s/o above, 15 Apr 1768
Abell, Caleb, s/o Cuthbert Abell, b. 10 Apr 1742
McClain, John Vowles, s/o William McClain and Mary his wife, b. 25 Dec 1767
Abell, Elizabeth, d/o Caleb Abell and Mary his wife, b. 12 Nov 1767
Medcalf, John Kenelin, s/o Ignatius Medcalf and Sarah his wife, b. 25 Oct 1760
Thompson, George Matthews, s/o William Thompson and Susanna his wife, b. 11 Dec 1767
Latham, James, s/o Matthew Latham and Susanna his wife, b. 27 Oct 1770

Nuthall, Ann Roach, d/o Margaret Nuthall, b. 28 Feb 1761
Thompson, Eleanor, d/o Robert Thompson and Elizabeth his wife, b. 7 Aug 1757 (11)
Thompson, Charles James, s/o above, b. 14 Jul 1760
Thompson, Bennet, s/o above, b. 3 Jun 1763
Thompson, Mary, d/o above, b. 22 Nov 1765
Thompson, James, s/o above, 13 Dec 1767
Cissell, John, s/o John Cissell and Henrietta his wife, b. 15 Oct 1757

Page 9

Cissell, Delbert, s/o above, b. 30 Jul 1763
Boarman, John, s/o Francis Boarman and Batris his wife, b. 8 Oct 1758
Boarman, Francis Ignatius, s/o above, b. 14 Mar 1762
Boarman, Sarah, d/o above, b. 1 Mar 1764
Spink, Joseph, s/o Edward Spink and Monica his wife, b. 22 Apr 1759
Spink, Mary, d/o above, b. 29 Jul 1762
Peake, Augustine, s/o John Peake and Susanna his wife, b. 23 Jan 1757
Peake, Robert, s/o above, b. 23 Nov 1755
Meken, Susanna, d/o Augustine Meken and Margaret his wife, b. 4 May 1761
Meken, Margaret, d/o above, b. 26 Aug 1764
Thompson, Ignatius, s/o Mark Thompson and Margaret his wife, b. 29 Oct 1761
Thompson, Mary, d/o above, b. 12 Aug 1767
Payne, Ann, d/o Charles Payne and Monica his wife, b. 15 Sep 1767
Thompson, Thomas Alexius, s/o Thomas Thompson and Ann his wife, b. 3 Nov 1761
Thompson, Eleanor, d/o above, b. 26 Mar 1763

Page 10

Thompson, Joseph Edward, s/o above, b. 16 May 1766
Payne, Francis Exlinerus, s/o Richard Payne and Priscilla his wife, b. 12 Sep 1756
Payne, James, s/o above, b. 28 Feb 1759

Thompson, James, s/o Robert Thompson and Ann his wife, b. 14 Nov 1757

Thompson, Mary Ann, d/o above, b. 20 Feb 1760

Benden, Elizabeth, d/o John Benden and Monica his wife, b. 8 Jan 1762

Medley, Augustine, s/o George Medley and Ann his wife, b. 26 Sep 1763

Cissell, Ann, d/o Baptist Cissell and Rebecca his wife, b. 2 Feb 1766

Cissell, William, s/o above, b. 10 Aug 1767

Cissell, James Rodolph, s/o Ignatius Cissell and Elizabeth his wife, b. 8 Apr 1762

Cissell, Ignatius, s/o above, b. 12 Mar 1764

Cissell, Joseph, s/o above, b. 28 Jun 1766

Cissell, Peter, s/o James Cissell and Elizabeth his wife, b. 29 Jun 1764

Payne, Henry Berryman, s/o Leonard Payne and Monica his wife, b. 12 May 1756

Payne, Elizabeth, d/o above, b. 18 Aug 1758

Payne, Monica, d/o above, b. 13 Mar 1763

Page 11

Mareman, Richard, s/o Joseph Mareman and Elizabeth his wife, b. 3 Feb 1768 (12)

Woolingham, John Baptist, s/o John Woolingham and Appolonia his wife, b. 1 Nov 1758

Woolingham, Ann, d/o above, b. 1 Mar 1763

Wimsat, Ralph, s/o John Wimsat and Henrietta his wife, b. 1 Oct 1754

Wimsat, Williams, s/o above, b. 16 May 1757

Wimsat, Elizabeth, d/o above, b. 14 Nov 1759

Wimsat, Robert Henry, s/o above, b. 9 May 1762

Wimsat, Ann, d/o above, b. 27 Dec 1764

Howard, Mary Ann, d/o Henry Howard and Mary his wife, b. 24 Jul 1758

Howard, Charles, s/o above, b. 24 Nov 1762

Howard, Joseph, s/o above, b. 3 May 1764

Taylor, Mary, d/o Ignatius Taylor and Elizabeth Spink his wife, b. 1 Oct 1764
French, Bennet, s/o John French and Monica his wife, b. 27 Jun 1757
French, Ann, d/o above, b. 16 Sep 1759
French, Bernadine, s/o above, b. 20 Dec 1761
French, Elizabeth, d/o above, b. 3 May 1764
Nottingham, Raphael Ignatius, s/o Matthias Nottingham and Mary his wife, b. 9 Jun 1754
Nottingham, Mary Ann, d/o above, b. 2 Aug 1757
Nottingham, Elizabeth, d/o above, b. 5 Jan 1761
Nottingham, Ignatius, s/o above, b. 12 Apr 1765
Cissell, Shedrick, s/o John Cissell and Margaret his wife, b.18 Nov 1754

Page 12

Cissell, Dorothy, d/o above, b. 17 Apr 1756
Booth, Ignatius, s/o Thomas Booth and Mary his wife, b. 4 Nov 1754
Booth, Rebecca, d/o above, b. 4 Jun 1756
Booth, Leonard, s/o above, b. 5 Mar 1758
Booth, Mary, d/o above, b. 7 Sep 1760
Booth, Eleanor, d/o above, b. 17 Jun 1761
Booth, Sarah, d/o above, b. 20 Jun 1763
Booth, George, s/o above, b. 11 Jul 1765
Finnacy, Mary Ann, d/o Stephen Finnacy and Ann his wife, b. 13 Oct 1760
Finnacy, John Archibald, s/o above, b. 1 May 1765
Finnacy, Joseph Normand Mack, s/o above, b. 1 Feb 1768
Wheatley, Rebecca, d/o James Wheatley and Henrietta his wife, b. 18 Sep 1755
Wheatley, James, s/o above, b. 23 Sep 1758
Wheatley, Joseph, s/o above, b. 27 May 1761
Wheatley, Edward, s/o above, b. 23 Dec 1765
Russell, Catharine, d/o John Russell and Susanna his wife, b. 27 Jun 1771
Bowes, Mary, d/o Timothy Bowes and Mary his wife, b. 3 Mar 1763

Bowes, Eleanor, d/o above, b. 9 Jun 1766
Norris, Mary Ann, d/o Thomas Norris and Ann his wife, b. 1 Nov 1756 **(13)**
Norris, Philip, s/o above, b. 1 May 1758
Norris, Mary, d/o above, b. 22 Oct 1759
Page 13
Norris, William, s/o above, b. 7 Jun 1761
Norris, Joseph, s/o above, b. 29 Jul 1764
Peake, Henry Barton, s/o Edward Peake and Ann his wife, b. 7 Nov 1754
Peake, Henrietta, d/o above, b. 3 Feb 1757
Peake, Kenelm, s/o above, b. 11 Mar 1760
Peake, Mary, d/o above, b. 4 Apr 1762
Peake, Francis, d/o above, b. 4 Feb 1764
Peake, Charles, s/o above, b. 8 Oct 1767
Daft, Mary, d/o William Daft and Elizabeth his wife, b. 6 Apr 1762
Inge, Vincent, s/o Vincent Inge and Susanna his wife, b. 13 Oct 1758
Inge, John, s/o above, b. 29 Oct 1761
Inge, Ambrose, s/o above, b. 23 Oct 1765
Inge, Ann Maria, d/o above, b. 2 Apr 1768
Browne, Dorothy, d/o Anthony Browne and Mary his wife, b. 27 Mar 1755
Browne, Benedict, s/o above, b. 7 Jun 1758
Browne, Susanna, d/o above, b. 12 Sep 1761
Browne, Frances, d/o above, b. 6 Mar 1764
Browne, Anthony, s/o above, b. 7 Apr 1768
Clarke, Richard Langhorn, s/o John Clarke and Eleanor his wife, b. 19 Jan 1753
Greenwell, Joshua Leonard, s/o John Basil Greenwell and Eleanor his wife, b. 5 Nov 1756
Greenwell, James, s/o above, b. 15 Jan 1761
Wheatley, William, s/o James Wheatley and Eleanor his wife, b. 8 Jan 1763
Page 14
Wheatley, Benedict, s/o above, b. 3 Nov 1766

Payne, Bernard, s/o Henry Payne and Jane his wife, b. 27 Nov 1762
Payne, Allelusia, d/o above, b. 17 Apr 1765
Hackett, Joshua, s/o Rhodolph Hackett and Mary his wife, b. 13 Nov 1763
Hackett, Mary Magdalene, d/o above, b. 10 Dec 1766
Sanson, William, s/o John Sanson and Mary his wife, b. 3 Oct 1767
Thomas, Robert, s/o James Thomas and Elizabeth his wife, b. 25 Jul 1756
Thomas, Jemima, d/o above, b. 4 Mar 1761
Edwards, Elizabeth, d/o John Edwards and Henrietta his wife, b. 25 Feb 1762
Edwards, Ann Chloe, d/o above, b. 4 May 1763
Forrest, Richard, s/o Zachariah Forrest and Ann his wife, b. 15 Nov 1767
Beverly, Anastatia, d/o George Beverly and Mary his wife, b. 2 Feb 1756
Beverly, Jemima, d/o above, b. 2 Sep 1763
Breeden, Elizabeth, d/o Enoch Breeden and Elizabeth his wife, b. 9 May 1768
Gough, Jane, d/o James Gough and Susanna his wife, b. 9 Oct 1755 (14)
Gough, Elizabeth, d/o above, b. 18 May 1757
Gough, Anastatia, d/o above, b. 9 Apr 1760
Gough, John Baptist, s/o above, b. 18 Feb 1764
Gough, Matthew, s/o above, b. 30 Jun 1766
Browne, Jereboam, s/o Peter Browne and Frances his wife, b. 16 Nov 1764

Page 15

Browne, Ann, d/o above, b. 9 Apr 1768
Payne, Winifred, d/o Baptist Payne and Ann his wife, b. 14 Apr 1763
Payne, Mary, d/o above, b. 22 Sep 1765
Payne, Elizabeth, d/o above, b. 17 Apr 1768
Howard, Sarah, d/o George Howard and Ann his wife, b. 19 Jan 1761

Howard, Ignatius, d/o (sic) above, b. 2 Mar 1765
Howard, Francis, d/o above, b. 6 Mar 1767
Bradburn, John Baptist, s/o Mark Bradburn and Susanna his wife, b. 27 Sep 1757
Bradburn, Elizabeth, d/o above, b. 27 Oct 1759
Booth, Elizabeth, d/o John Booth and Mary his wife, b. 14 Mar 1762
Booth, Jane, d/o above, b. 14 Aug 1763
Booth, Rodolph, s/o above, b. 30 Nov 1765
Booth, John Baptist, s/o above, b. 10 Mar 1768
French, Rodolph, s/o William French and Rinah his wife, b. 1 Aug 1755
French, Jeremiah, s/o above, b. 13 Oct 1761
French, Susanna, d/o above, b. 14 Oct 1766
Norris, Philip, s/o John Norris and Mary his wife, b. 25 Dec 1754
Norris, Henry Elijah, s/o above, b. 14 Mar 1758
Norris, Arnold, s/o above, b. 26 Jun 1761
Norris, Barbara, d/o above, b. 17 Mar 1766
Greenwell, Emma Ransean Anna, d/o Henry Greenwell and Frances his wife, b. 10 Jan 1754

Page 16
Greenwell, Richard, s/o above, b. 9 Jan 1760
Greenwell, Joseph, s/o above, b. 17 Apr 1764
Jarboe, Frances, d/o Clement Jarboe and Ann his wife, b. 15 Jun 1762
Jarboe, Eleanor, d/o above, b. 30 Jul 1764
Jarboe, Monica, d/o above, b. 26 May 1767
Norris, Enoch, s/o Joseph Norris and Elizabeth his wife, b. 27 Feb 1765
Norris, Luke, s/o above, b. 3 Jan 1767
Norris, Susanna, d/o above, b. 27 Sep 1769
Sewell, Clement, s/o Henry Sewall and Mary his wife, b. 10 Jun 1757
Sewall, Mary Smith, d/o above, b. 7 Jul 1762
Sewell, Henry, s/o above, b. 3 Jun 1764
Sewell, Charles, s/o above, b. 20 Jul 1767
Abell, Elizabeth, d/o John Abell and Jane his wife, b. 3 Dec 1759

Abell, Jane, d/o Edward Abell and Susanna his wife, b. 6 Nov 1760 **(15)**
Abell, Benjamin, s/o above, b. 7 Apr 1764
Abell, Catharine, d/o above, b. 22 Apr 1766
Abell, Samuel, s/o above, b. 23 Jan 1768
Vanreshwick, Thomas, s/o John Vanreshwick and Appolonia his wife, b. 15 Oct 1752
Vanreshwick, Mary, d/o above, b. 23 Mar 1755
Vanreshwick, Joseph, s/o above, b. 15 Aug 1757
Vanreshwick, Francis, s/o above, b. 4 Nov 1763
Vanreshwick, George, s/o above, b. 10 May 1756
Vanreshwick, John Basil, s/o above, b. 12 Oct 1762

Page 17

Abell, George, s/o George Abell and Elizabeth his wife, b. 27 Jul 1768
Harris, Zachariah, s/o Samuel Harris and Elizabeth his wife, b. 5 Nov 1763
Harris, Austin, s/o above, b. 13 Oct 1766
Long, John Read, s/o John Long and Barbara his wife, b. 23 Jul 1754
Long, Reuben, s/o above, b. 22 Dec 1756
Long, Nicholas, s/o above, b. 15 Dec 1759
Long, Hannah, d/o above, b. 10 Jan 1762
Long, Gabriel, s/o above, b. 1 Oct 1765
Long, William, s/o above, b. 28 Feb 1768
Wathen, Francis Hudson, s/o Henry Hudson Wathen and Ann his wife, b. 3 Nov 1764
Wathen, Henry Hudson, s/o above, b. 11 May 1766
Hammett, Richard, s/o McKelvie Hammett and Henrietta his wife, b. 12 Jan 1754
Hammett, Henry, s/o above, b. 10 Feb 1757
Hammett, Dolly, s/o above, b. 12 Aug 1759
Hammett, Mary, d/o above, b. 5 Feb 1762
Hammett, Frances, d/o above, b. 25 Nov 1764
Hammett, Sarah, d/o above, b. 1 Mar 1767
Young, James, s/o John Abell Young and Ann his wife, b. 26 Jun 1766

Young, John Standfill, s/o above, b. 16 Jan 1768
King, Adam, s/o Edward King and Eleanor his wife, b. 17 Oct 1757
Greenwell, John, s/o Charles Greenwell and Eleanor his wife, b. 2 Oct 1760
Page 18
Greenwell, Jane, d/o above, b. 20 Mar 1763
Greenwell, Richard, s/o above, b. 7 Oct 1765
Greenwell, Edward, s/o above, 30 Jan 1768
Heard, Mary, d/o John Heard and Ann his wife, b. 9 Jul 1764
Heard, Ann, d/o above, b. 5 Apr 1766
Heard, Hellen, d/o above, b. 29 Sep 1767
Greenwell, Bennet, s/o James Greenwell and Hannah his wife, b. 28 Aug 1755
Greenwell, William, b. 12 Jul 1757
Greenwell, Joseph, s/o above, b. 3 Aug 1759 **(16)**
Greenwell, Elizabeth, d/o above, b. 23 Jul 1763
Gough, Charles, s/o Benjamin Gough and Susanna his wife, b. 25 May 1755
Gough, Mary, d/o above, b. 24 Jun 1762
Gough, Rebecca, d/o above, b. 5 Jun 1766
Wootton, Susanna, d/o Thomas Wootton and Susanna his wife, b. 7 Mar 1759
Wootton, Isaac, s/o above, b. 9 Jun 1761
Wootton, Bennet, s/o above, b. 10 Jul 1762
Wootton, Frances, d/o above, b. 9 May 1765
Pyke, Mary Ann, d/o James Pyke and Ann his wife, b. 14 May 1753
Pyke, Henry, s/o above, b. 5 Feb 1756
Pyke, James, s/o above, b. 18 Apr 1759
Hackett, Henrietta, d/o Rhode Hackett and Mary his wife, b. 14 Aug 1757
Page 19
Hackett, Ann, d/o above, b. 7 Nov 1758
Medley, Eleanor, d/o Clement Medley and Mary his wife, b. 27 Feb 1761
Medley, Joseph, s/o above, b. 3 Nov 1764

Medley, Matthew, s/o above, b. 16 Feb 1766
Medley, Ann Elizabeth, d/o above, b. 1 Feb 1768
Nottingham, Mary Ann, d/o Athana Notthingham and Mary his wife, b. 18 Nov 1762
Nottingham, Ann, d/o above, b. 3 Sep 1763
Nottingham, Enoch, s/o above, b. 25 Dec 1766
Greenwell, William, s/o Ignatius Greenwell and Jane his wife, b. 26 Nov 1752
Greenwell, Ignatius, s/o above, b. 23 Dec 1754
Manning, Monica, d/o Cornelius Manning and Jane his wife, b. 26 Oct 1759
Manning, Frances, d/o above, b. 10 Jan 1762
Smith, Ann, d/o John Smith and Elizabeth his wife, b. 3 May 1756
Greenwell, Thomas, s/o Philip Greenwell and Mary his wife, b. 4 Sep 1754
Greenwell, Mary, d/o Philip Greenwell and Winifred, b. 17 Oct 1762
Greenwell, Ann, d/o above, b. 6 Jun 1767
Armsworthy, Aaron, s/o William Armsworthy and Mary his wife, b. 3 Sep 1765
Armsworthy, Eleanor, d/o above, b. 2 Sep 1767
Fish, William, s/o William Fish and Jennet his wife, b. 30 May 1765

Page 20

Fish, Ann, d/o above, b. 11 May 1768
Mills, Justinian, s/o Nicholas Mills, b. 2 Apr 1728
Mills, Mary, wife of Justinian Mills, b. 1 Sep 1736
Mills, John, s/o Justinian Mills and Mary his wife, b. 5 Feb 1753
Mills, Elizabeth, d/o above, b. 9 May 1755
Mills, Winifred, d/o above, b. 30 Oct 1757
Mills, Margaret, d/o above, b. 30 Jan 1760
Mills, Joseph, s/o above, b. 26 Feb 1762 **(17)**
Mills, Justinian and Mary, son and dau. of above, b. 7 Oct 1764
Mills, Ann, d/o above, b. 5 Dec 1767
Mills, Charles, s/o above, b. 24 Aug 1770
Bean, Bennet, s/o Robert Bean and Margaret his wife, b. 5 Aug 1771

Silence, Edmund, s/o John Silence and Elizabeth his wife, b. 9 Mar 1771

Reeves, Susanna, d/o George Reeves and Mary his wife, b. 7 Aug 1771

Hammet, Margaret, d/o Cartwright Hammet and Elizabeth his wife, b. 17 Oct 1771

Browne, Monica, d/o Anthony Browne and Mary his wife, b. 22 May 1771

Norris, Susanna, d/o John Norris and Mary his wife, b. 14 Mar 1771

Fish, Robert, s/o William Fish and Jennet his wife, b. 11 Oct 1771

Page 21

Armsworthy, Bennet, s/o Abraham Armsworthy and Eleanor his wife, b. 26 Dec 1771

Taylor, Ann, d/o Ignatius Taylor and Elizabeth his wife, b. 15 Sep 1770

King, Jane, d/o Thomas King and Eleanor his wife, b. 29 Jan 1772

Hammet, Ann, d/o William Hammet and Ann his wife, b. 19 Nov 1771

Peake, John, s/o Edward Peake and Ann his wife, b. 8 Oct 1771

Hammet, Frances, d/o John Hammet and Margery his wife, b. 26 Feb 1771

West, George William, s/o Rev. William West and Mrs. Susanna his spouse, b. 22 Jan 1770

Payne, Joseph, s/o Vincent Payne and Mary his wife, b. 8 Dec 1771

Bradburn, Mary Ann, d/o James Bradburn and Margaret, b. 15 May 1772

Bradburn, Sarah, d/o Benjamin Bradburn and Ann his wife, b. 25 May 1772

Bradburn, Catherine, d/o Notley Bradburn and Eleanor his wife, b. 14 Mar 1772

Payne, Frances, d/o Leonard Payne and Teresia his wife, b. 12 Sep 1772

Vowles, Susanna, d/o James Vowles and Priscilla his wife, b. 7 Jun 1772

Cissell, Thomas, s/o John Baptist Cissell and Rebekah his wife, b. 14 Apr 1762
Page 22
Cissell, James, s/o Ignatius Cissell and Elizabeth his wife, b. 22 May 1768
Cissell, Mary, d/o above, b. 10 Mar 1770
Cissell, Wilford, s/o above, b. 10 Jul 1772
Tomkins, Mary Attaway, d/o John Tomkins and Mary his wife, b. 17 Sep 1771
Tierce, Eleanor, d/o Andrew Tierce and Catharine his wife, b. 7 Mar 1772
Thompson, Mary, d/o Mark Thompson and Margaret his wife, b. 12 Aug 1767
Hopewell, Richard, s/o Bennet Hopewell and Teresia his wife, b. 23 May 1759
Hopewell, Jane, d/o Bennet Hopewell and Mary Ann his wife, b. 22 Dec 1763
Hopewell, Joshua, s/o above, b. 23 May 1765
Hopewell, Bennet, s/o above, b. 4 Oct 1766
Hopewell, Francis, s/o above, b. 20 Feb 1770
Hopewell, Mary Ann, d/o above, b. 1 May 1772
Howard, Elizabeth, d/o George Howard and Anastatia Spink, b. 14 Jun 1772
Taylor, Ann, d/o Ignatius Taylor and Elizabeth his wife, b. 15 Dec 1770
Payne, Eleanor, d/o John Baptist Payne and Ann his wife, b. 30 May 1771
Abell, Rachel, d/o Caleb Abell and Mary his wife, b. 29 Sep 1772
Hammet, John, s/o McKelvie Hammet and Ann his wife, b. 16 May 1775
Page 23
Peake, Joseph, s/o John Peake and Susanna his wife, b. 11 Dec 1772 **(20)**
Vowles, Mary, d/o Cyrus Vowles and Victoria his wife, b. 20 Nov 1772

Tarlton, John, s/o James Tarlton and Mary Ann his wife, b. 23 Sep 1772

Hammet, Frances, d/o McKelvie Hammet and Ann his wife, b. 24 Jan 1773

Russell, Eleanor, d/o Ignatius Russell and Mildred his wife, b. 22 May 1773

Hammet, Bennet, s/o John Hammet, Jr. and Margery his wife, b. 6 Mar 1772

Gowndril, Katherine, d/o Rev. George Gowndril and Hannah his wife, b. 16 Nov 1770; bapt. "by himself" 17 Nov 1770

Gowndril, George, s/o above, b. 2 Jul 1772, bapt. 19 Jul 1772

Gowndril, George: He came to Maryland in May 1770; was Vicar of Kilnsea and Curate of Essington; s/o Rev. George Gowndril, Rector of Sproatley in Yorkshire near Hull; was married to Hannah Simpson d/o William Simpson of Datrington in the same Parish

Buchanan, Rebecca, d/o George Buchanan and Elizabeth his wife, b. 15 Jun 1772

Mareman, Lydda, d/o William Mareman and Mary his wife, b. 23 Jun 1773

Page 24

Clarke, Eleanor, d/o Joshua Clarke and Mary his wife, b. 12 Aug 1773

Cissell, Jeremiah, s/o John Baptist Cissell and Rebecca his wife, b. 26 Sep 1773

Kelshew, Mary Ann, d/o James and Elizabeth Kelshew, b. 25 Sep 1773

Mareman, James, s/o Joshua and Susanna Mareman, b. 18 May 1767

Mareman, Mary, d/o above, b. 29 Oct 1769

Mareman, John Baptist, s/o above, 27 Mar 1771

Mareman, Mary Attaway, d/o above, b. 6 Apr 1773

Jarboe, Abner, s/o Joshua and Jean Jarboe, b. 9 Dec 1763

Jarboe, Bennet, s/o above, b. 2 Jan 1767

Jarboe, Eleanor, d/o above, b. 2 Nov 1768

Jarboe, Charles, s/o above, b. 21 Jun 1773

Norris, Rebecca, d/o Thomas Norris and Mary his wife, b. 18 Sep 1771

Norris, Dorothy, d/o above, b. 24 Aug 1773

Thompson, Mary Ann, d/o Thomas Thompson and Ann his wife, b. 1 Apr 1773

Thompson, John Barton, s/o Raphael Thompson and Anastatia his wife, b. 24 Apr 1773

Stone, John, s/o Joseph Stone and Dorothy his wife, b. 13 Nov 1773

Payne, Rosa Ann, d/o John Baptist Payne and Ann his wife, b. 12 Sep 1773

Hamilton, Philemon, s/o Jonathan and Margaret Abell, b. 8 Mar 1774

Page 25

Medley, Mary, d/o Clement Medley and Mary his wife, b. 9 Mar 1770

Thompson, Joseph, s/o Raphael Thompson and Susanna his wife, b. 9 Dec 1764

Thompson, Mary, d/o above, b. 9 Mar 1767

Thompson, James Aloisus, s/o above, b. 27 Jan 1769 (21)

Thompson, Charles, s/o above, b. 1 Oct 1770

Thompson, William, s/o above, b. 24 Sep 1774

Baxter, Francis, s/o Francis Baxter and Margaret his wife, b. 20 Jan 1773 at 2 o'clock in the morning

King, Bennet, s/o Margaret King, b. 14 Jul 1764

Thompson, Sarah, d/o John Baptist Thompson and Susanna his wife, b. 18 Feb 1774

Henry, James, s/o Martin Henry and Mary his wife, b. 17 Jun 1774

Browne, Eleanor, d/o Peter Browne and Frances his wife, b. 4 Jul 1774

Mugg, Peter, s/o Walter Mugg and Priscilla his wife, b. 6 May 1773

Payne, Elizabeth, d/o Raphael Payne and Tabitha his wife, b. 9 Apr 1772

Payne, Sarah, d/o above, b. 26 Jan 1775

Peacock, John Barton, s/o Ignatius Peacock and Ann his wife, b. 12 Dec 1774

St. Andrew's Parish

Vowles, Richard, s/o James Vowles and Priscilla his wife b. 6 Mar 1774
Page 26
Cissell, Matthew, s/o John Baptist Cissell and Ann his wife, b. 20 Feb 1775
Cissell, Joseph, s/o John Cissell and Mary his wife, b. 27 Dec 1772
Newton, Elizabeth, d/o Bernard Newton and Mary Ann his wife, b. 24 Jul 1771
Wimsatt, Joseph Zachariah, s/o Stephen Wimsatt and Mary his wife, b. 24 May 1773
Wimsatt, Frances, d/o above, b. 5 Mar 1774
Rishwick, Joseph, s/o Thomas Rishwick and Mary his wife, b. 19 Sep 1774
Anderson, Margaret, d/o William Anderson and Elizabeth his wife, b. 27 Apr 1775
Hammet, John, s/o McKelvie and Ann Hammet, b. 16 May 1775
Adams, Hatton George, s/o James Adams and Mary his wife, b. 11 Apr 1775
Merrell, Mary Ann, d/o Joshua Merrell and Mary his wife, b. 21 Dec 1769
Merrell, Philip, s/o above, b. 22 Oct 1762
French, Mary, d/o Ignatius French and Elizabeth his wife, b. 28 Oct 1769
French, Joseph, s/o above, b. 27 Sep 1771
French, Ignatius, s/o above, b. 14 Oct 1773
Watts, Ann, d/o Willoughby Watts and Jemima his wife, b. 5 Jun 1773
Watts, William, s/o above, b. 26 Jun 1775
Mareman, Ann, d/o Joseph Mareman and Elizabeth his wife, b. 18 May 1775
Tomkins, Aletha, d/o John Tomkins and Mary his wife, b. 31 May 1775
Ford, Clare, d/o Philip Ford and Eleanor his wife, b. 5 Jul 1771
Page 27
Ford, Charles, s/o Philip Ford and Eleanor his wife, b. 2 Jan 1773

Cissell, Matthew, s/o John Baptist Cissell and Ann his wife, b. 20 Feb 1775

Clarke, Susanna, d/o Joshua Clarke and Mary his wife, b. 19 Sep 1775

Mareman, Elizabeth, d/o William Mareman and Mary his wife, b. 3 Jul 1776

Mareman, William, s/o Zachariah Mareman and Ann his wife, b. 26 Nov 1775

French, Philip, s/o John French and Jane his wife, b. 27 Nov 1774

French, Peter, s/o above, b. 12 May 1776

French, Elizabeth, d/o Ignatius French and Elizabeth his wife, b. 27 Nov 1775

Mareman, Joseph, s/o Joshua Mareman and Susanna his wife, b. 12 Aug 1775 **(22)**

Clarke, Mary, d/o Thomas Clarke and Elizabeth his wife, b. 21 Jan 1771

Clarke, Ann, d/o above, b. 2 Mar 1773

Clarke, Thomas, s/o above, b. 3 Mar 1775

Austin, Elizabeth, d/o George Austin and Eleanor his wife, b. 24 Feb 1774

Austin, Priscilla, d/o above, b. 11 Sep 1775

Bould, Elizabeth, d/o William Bould and Mary his wife, b. 9 Mar 17767

Wheeler, William, s/o Francis Wheeler and Ann his wife, b. 18 Sep 1776

Brown, Martin, s/o Peter Brown and Susanna his wife, b. 16 Nov 1775

Page 28

Russell, John Baptist, s/o William Russell and Dryden his wife, b. 14 Feb 1776

Abell, Francis, s/o George Abell and Elizabeth his wife, b. 20 Jun 1774

Merrell, Mills Eleanor, d/o Joshua Merrell and Mary Ann his wife, b. 4 Nov 1775

Brown, Dryden, d/o Leonard Brown and Ann his wife, b. 25 May 1760

Brown, Chloe, d/o above, b. 20 Feb 1762

Brown, Leander, d/o above, b. 27 May 1765
Brown, Allusia, d/o above, b. 13 Aug 1769
Brown, Lucy, d/o above, b. 11 Apr 1775
Brown, Raphael, s/o John Baptist Brown and Heneretta his wife, b. 4 Oct 1761
Brown, Rebecca, d/o above, b. 4 Apr 1767
Brown, Winifred, d/o above, b. 16 Sep 1772
Brown, John Barton, s/o Nicholas Brown and Eleanor his wife, b. 6 Mar 1775
Finnacy, Rosanna, d/o Stephen Finnacy and Ann his wife, b. 12 Dec 1771
Russell, Philip, s/o Ignatius Russell and Mildred his wife, b. 15 Sep 1775
Walker, Margaret, d/o Roger Walker and Elizabeth his wife, b. 7 Dec 1776
Hammet, James, s/o John Hammet and Marjery his wife, b. 11 Apr 1775

Page 29

Hammet, John, s/o above, b. 7 Feb 1777
Hutchens, John, s/o John Hutchens and Rachel his wife, b. 27 Jan 1777
Armsworthy, Mary, d/o Wm. Armsworthy and Mary his wife, b. 12 Feb 1777
Henning, Sarah, d/o Jeremiah Henning and Ann his wife, b. 24 Dec 1776
Thompson, Mary, d/o James Thompson and Elizabeth his wife, b. 11 Jun 1771
Thompson, Elijah, s/o above, b. 12 Feb 1774
Vowles, Elizabeth, d/o Cyrus Vowles and Victoria his wife, b. 9 Jun 1777
Abell, Pollard, s/o George Abell and Elizabeth his wife, b. 20 Sep 1777
Payne, Anastatia, d/o Raphael Payne and Tabitha his wife, b. 23 Dec 1777
Mattingly, Catharine, d/o Robert Mattingly and Mary Ann his wife, b. 28 Mar 1778

Russell, Allusia, d/o Ignatius Russell and Mildred his wife, b. 24 Dec 1777

Bould, Mary Ann, d/o William and Mary Bould, b. 1 Jun 1778 **(23)**

Brown, Peter, s/o Peter Brown and Frances his wife, b. 25 Sep 1779

Henry, Philip, s/o Martin Henry and Mary his wife, b. Feb 1776

McWherter, Elizabeth, d/o Andrew and Mary McWherter, bapt. 2 Apr 1780

Page 30

Beane, Barton, s/o George and Anne Beane, bapt. 7 May 1780

Forrest, Uriah, s/o Zachariah and Nancy Forrest, bapt. 14 May 1780

King, James, s/o William King, bapt. 21 May 1780

White, Jesse, s/o William and Veache White, bapt 18 Jun 1780

Wise, George, s/o Adam and Frances Wise, bapt. 16 Jul 1780

Fowler, Margaret, d/o Sarah Fowler, bapt. 16 Jul 1780

Buchanan, William Thompson, s/o Moses and Eleanor Buchanan, bapt. 24 Dec 1780

Hamett, Catharine, d/o John Hammett, Jr., bapt. 18 Mar 1781

Hall, Catharine, d/o Arthur and Rebecca Hall, bapt. 22 Jul 1781

Stone, Francis, s/o Joseph and Winifred Stone, bapt. 6 Aug 1781

Abell, Jean, d/o John and Elizabeth Abell, bapt. 23 Sep 1781

Hilton, Elizabeth, d/o Thomas and Anne Hilton, bapt. 30 Sep 1781

Rigill, Mary, d/o Thomas and Statia Rigill, bapt. 21 Oct 1781

Messenger, Mary, d/o Rev. Joseph Messenger and Mary his wife, b. 14 Jan 1776; bapt. 7 Apr 1776

Messenger, William and John Feron, twin brothers and sons of above, b. 25 Nov 1777; bapt. 26 Nov 1777

Abell, Jonathan, s/o John and Elizabeth Abell, bapt. 4 May 1783

Abell, Janet, d/o Edmund and Elizabeth Abell, bapt. 4 May 1783

McCartney, Fanny, d/o Edward MacCartney and Mary his wife, b. 9 Jun 1779

McCartney, Sarah, d/o above, b. 9 Apr 1781

McCartney, Ann, d/o above, b. 10 Mar 1784

Abell, John, s/o Edward Abell and Susannah his wife, b. 23 Dec 1769
Page 31
Abell, Mary, d/o above, b. 3 Nov 1771
Abell, Barbara, d/o Edward Abell and Stasia his wife, b. 10 Jul 1777
Abell, Pharmel, d/o above, b. 8 Jun 1780
Abell, Eleanor, d/o above, b. 10 Mar 1782
Thomas, Edward, s/o Thomas Thomas and Jane his wife, b. 13 Mar 1782
Thomas, Mary, d/o above, b. 31 Mar 1784
Thomas, James, s/o above, b. 16 Oct 1786
Vowles, Henry, s/o Matthew Vowles and Ann his wife, b. 6 Jun 1787
McCartney, Susanna, d/o Edward McCartney and Mary his wife, b. 26 Aug 1787
Wise, William Cornelius Francis, s/o James Wise and Allethea his wife, b. 25 May 1799; bapt. 11 Oct 1799 (24)
Evans, Ann, d/o Richard Evans and Jane his wife, b. 30 Oct 1798; bapt. 9 Sep 1799
Corum, John Rollins, s/o Isaac Corum and Barbara his wife, b. 20 Nov 1799; bapt. 3 Aug 1800
Crane, James, s/o James A. Crane and Mary his wife, b. 9 Jun 1800; bapt. 3 Aug 1800
Abell, Elizabeth, d/o Samuel Abell and Sarah his wife, b. 29 Nov 1799; bapt. 3 Aug 1800
Thornton, Harriet, d/o Vincent Thornton and Priscilla his wife, b. 29 Mar 1800; bapt. 3 Aug 1800
Cissell, Mary, d/o William Cissell and Catharine his wife, b. 8 Mar 1800; bapt. 3 Aug 1800
Matheny, Thomas, s/o Thomas Matheny and Elizabeth his wife, b. 1 Aug 1803; bapt. 1 Aug 1803
Page 32
Evans, Daniel, s/o Richard Evans and Jane his wife, b. 15 Oct 1805; bapt. 28 Nov 1805
Biscoe, James Lewis, s/o Richard Biscoe and Eleanor his wife, b. 7 Oct 1811; bapt. 1 Nov 1811 by Rev. Jos. Jackson

Wise, Joseph Adam, s/o Adam Wise and Mary his wife, b. 6 Sep 1810; bapt. 30 May 1812

Wise, Charles, s/o above, b. 19 Apr 1812; bapt. 30 May 1812

Harris, Martha, d/o Joseph Harris and Susanna his wife, b. 4 Oct 1811; bapt. 16 Feb 1812

Causens, Jane Pope Row, d/o Gerard N. Causens and Eleanor his wife, b. 20 Mar 1812

Watts, George Nelson, s/o Joshua Watts and Eleanor his wife, b. 15 Aug 1812; bapt. 25 Oct 1812

Adams, John, s/o George, Adams and Sarah his wife, b. 28 Jul 1812; bapt. 25 Oct 1812

Adams, Ann, d/o Abraham Adams and Elizabeth his wife, b. 19 Oct 1812; bapt. 5 Nov 1812

Hammett, George Alexander, s/o Robert Hammett and Catharine his wife, b. 30 Mar 1813; bapt. 23 May 1813

Heath, Ann Elizabeth, d/o Thomas Heath and Kitty his wife, b. 15 Feb 1813; bapt. 23 May 1813

Harris, Jane, d/o Joseph Harris and Susanna his wife, b. 21 Jan 1813; bapt. 3 Jun 1813

Hopewell, James Robert, s/o James Hopewell and Angelica his wife, b. 27 Oct 1813; bapt. 19 Dec 1813 **(25)**

Page 33

Abell, James Crane, s/o Matthew Abell and Elizabeth his wife, b. 27 Nov 1813; bapt. 24 Dec 1813

Biscoe, Ann Clarke, d/o Richard Biscoe and Eleanor his wife, b. 8 Dec 1813; bapt. 15 May 1814

Adams, Dorothy, d/o George Adams and Sarah his wife, b. 10 Jan 1814; bapt. 15 May 1814

Wise, Eleanah, s/o Adam Wise and Mary his wife, b. 28 Feb 1814; bapt. 15 May 1814

Wise, William Robert, s/o George Wise and Sophia his wife, b. 25 Mar 1814; bapt. 15 May 1814

Thompson, Benjamin, s/o Elijah Thompson and Elizabeth his wife, b. 5 Oct 1813; bapt. 18 Sep 1814

Crane, William Samuel, s/o James A. Crane and Mary his wife, b. 15 Sep 1814; bapt. 6 Nov 1814

Plater, Edward, s/o John R. Plater and Elizabeth his wife, b. 28 Jul 1814; bapt. 18 Mar 1815

Watts, Eleanor Delilah, d/o Joshua Watts and Eleanor his wife, b. 7 Mar 1815; bapt. 26 Mar 1815

Hammett, Sarah, d/o Robert Hammett and Catharine his wife, b. 18 Mar 1815; bapt. 26 Mar 1815

Evans, Jane Abell, d/o Richard Evans and Jane Elizabeth his wife, b. 18 Jan 1815; bapt. 7 May 1815

Evans, Sarah, d/o John B. Evans and Patty his wife, b. 14 Mar 1815; bapt. 7 May 1815

Page 34

Wise, James Clinton, s/o George Wise and Sophia his wife, b. 18 Mar 1815; bapt. 7 May 1815

Bennett, William Clayton and James Lewis, twin sons of William B. Bennett and Pheebe his wife, b. Sep 1815; bapt. 3 Sep 1815

Wise, John Clinton, s/o John Wise and Mary his wife, b. 2 Sep 1815; bapt. 1 Oct 1815

Adams, Susan, d/o George Adams and Sarah his wife, b. 15 Sep 1815; bapt. 12 Nov 1815

Abell, Mary Elizabeth, d/o Francis Abell and Ann his wife, b. 10 Dec 1815; bapt. 1 Jan 1816

Redman, Rosanna, d/o Zachariah Redman and Fanny his wife, b. 1 Jan 1816; bapt. 17 Mar 1816 **(26)**

Armsworthy, _____, d/o Thomas Armsworthy and Elizabeth his wife, b. 30 Nov 1815; bapt. 19 May 1816

Martin, Laura Sophia, d/o Stephen Martin and Elizabeth his wife, b. 21 Jan 1816; bapt. 19 May 1816

Goldsbury, Athanatius, s/o Athantius Goldsbury and Mary his wife, b. 27 Dec 1815; bapt. 19 May 1816

Hammett, Luther, s/o Robert Hammett and Catharine his wife, b. 15 Aug 1817; bapt. Sep 1817

Hammett, Catharine Hebb, d/o above, b. 12 Aug 1819; bapt. 19 Sep 1819

Dent, James Thomas, s/o Hezekiah Dent and Martha Matilda his wife, b. 24 Oct 1822; bapt. 10 Nov 1822

Dent, Sarah Matilda, d/o Thomas E. Dent and Susanna his wife, b. 27 Dec 1828; bapt. 7 Jun 1829

Page 35
Dent, James Hammett, s/o above, b. 6 May 1833; bapt. 7 Jul 1833
Dent, Joseph Chappelear, s/o above, b. 13 Mar 1835; bapt. 7 Jun 1835
Dent, Martha Ann, d/o above, b. 20 Sep 1837; bapt. 7 Jan 1838
Dent, Thomas, s/o above, b. 21 Oct 1839; bapt. 20 Nov 1839
Dent, Benjamin, s/o above, b. 12 Jun 1842; bapt. 31 Jul 1842
Fitzhugh, William, s/o William Fitzhugh and Mary E. Chesley, b. 26 Jul 1881; bapt. privately 21 Sep 1881
Somerville, Margaret Alverta (col.), d/o Francis Somerville and Louisa his wife, b. 9 Jan 1886; bapt. 30 Jun 1886 by Rev. W. H. Vaughan

---

Lucas, Joshua, s/o William Lucas and Rachel his wife, b. 9 Feb 1755
Jenkins, John, s/o Joseph Jenkins and Mary his wife, b. 5 May 1744
Jenkins, Agusutine, s/o above, b. 12 Jan 1746/7
Jenkins, Thomas, s/o above, b. 28 Jun 1749
Jenkins, Edmund Courtney, s/o above, b. 1 Oct 1752
Russell, William, s/o William Russell and Ann his wife, b. 29 Apr 1747
Page 36
Russell, Ignatius, s/o above, b. 10 Mar 1748/9
Russell, James, s/o above, b. 6 Dec 1755
Hasler, Henrietta, d/o William and Elizabeth Hasler, b. 9 Feb 1752
Hasler, William, s/o above, b. 19 May 1755
Hasler, Richard, s/o above, b. 5 Feb 1757
Vowles, Walter, s/o Thomas and Susanna Vowles, b. 25 Mar 1749
Vowles, Henry, s/o above, b. 25 Sep 1752
Vowles, Ann, d/o above, b. 10 Oct 1754
[?Daley], Susanna, d/o Daniel and _____, b. 29 Jul 1752
[?Daley], Charles, s/o above, b. 25 Sep 1746
[?Daley], Eleanor, d/o above, b. 16 Oct 1748
Parsons, James, orphan at John Dorans, b. 1 Apr 1744
Cooper, Mary, d/o Henry Cooper and Susanna, b. 30 Oct 1749

Cooper, William, s/o above, b. 5 Nov 1751
Cooper, Henrietta, d/o above, b. 10 Jan 1754
Cissell, Anastatia, d/o John Cissell and Henrietta his wife, b. 11 Feb 1745
Cissell, Mary, d/o above, b. 4 Jan 1750
Cissell, James, s/o above, b. 24 Jan 1753
Vowles, Jane, d/o Cyrus and Victoria Vowles, b. 25 Dec 1754
Thompson, Susanna, d/o Robert Thompson and Elizabeth his wife, b. 7 Jul 1747
Thompson, Athanasius, s/o above, b. 6 Sep 1749
Thompson, Elisabeth, d/o above, b. 9 Apr 1752
Thompson, Mary, d/o above, b. 10 Feb 1755
Mareman, Zachariah, d/o John and Ann Mareman, b. 16 Dec 1751

Page 37

Mareman, Joseph, s/o above, b. 6 Jul 1748
Mareman, Joshua, s/o above, b. 15 Jun 1746
Payne, John Barton, s/o Richard Payne and Priscilla his wife, b. 3 Aug 1754
Payne, Priscilla, d/o Leonard Payne and Monica his wife, b. 19 May 1753
Birchmore, Rebekah, d/o William and Margaret Birchmore, b. 8 Dec 1746
Mattingly, Thomas, s/o Clement Mattingly and _____ his wife, b. 28 Mar 1738
Mattingly, John Baptist, s/o above, b. 28 Jan 1745
Mattingly, Elisabeth, d/o above, b. 7 Jun 1736
Mattingly, Mary Ann, d/o above, b. 6 Oct 1741
Mattingly, Ann, d/o above, b. 6 May 1747
Mattingly, Ruth, d/o above, b. 23 Jun 1749
Russell, Mary Ann, d/o William Russell and Ann, b. 20 Mar 1757
Carpenter, William, s/o George and Elizabeth Carpenter, b. 21 Mar 1757
Watson, Elizabeth, s/o John and Elinor Watson, b. 27 Mar 1757
Cole, Susanna, d/o Francis and Ann Cole, b. 27 Feb 1757
James, George, s/o Thomas and Mary James, b. 14 Jul 1753
James, Chloe, d/o above, b. 2 May 1755

Beverley, William, s/o George and Mary Beverley, b. 14 Feb 1757
Wellman, Joshua, s/o Michel and Elizabeth Wellman, b. 9 Oct 1753
Wellman, Jared, s/o above, b. 13 Sep 1755

Page 38

Abell, Samuel, s/o Samuel and Elinor Abell, b. 13 Jan 1755
Abell, Robert, s/o above, b. 8 May 1757
Inge, Mary, d/o Vincent and Ann Inge, b. 29 Jun 1756
French, Ignatius, s/o Ignatius and Susanna French, b. 26 Mar 1757
French, Mary, d/o above, b. 14 Jan 1755
Thompson, John Gerard, s/o Mark and Margarett Thompson, b. 16 Apr 1753
Thompson, Mary Ann, d/o above, b. 17 Feb 1757
Howard, Austin, s/o Joshua and Mary Howard, b. 8 Oct 1755
Howard, Henrietta, d/o above, b. 8 Oct 1753
Reshwick, Wilford, s/o Thomas and Ann Reshwick, b. 12 Jan 1756
Spink, Mary, d/o Edward and Monica Spink, b. 21 Dec 1765
Thompson, Mary, d/o Thomas and Ann Thompson, b. 27 Sep 1754
Thompson, John Barton, s/o above, b. 12 Jun 1757
French, Anastatia, d/o John French, Jr., and Monica his wife, b. 29 Jul 1750
Watson, William, s/o Benjamin Watson and Susanna his wife, b. 29 Aug 1756
Reshwick, Monica, d/o Thomas and Ann Reshwick, b. 19 Aug 1753
Armsworthy, Katey, d/o John and Frances Armsworthy, b. 10 Nov 1757
James, Champion, s/o Thomas and Mary James, b. 13 Jun 1757
Greaves, Jeremiah Adkey, s/o Thomas and Ann Greaves, b. 15 Jan 1758
Craigg, Elizabeth, d/o Jesse and Sarah Craigg, b. 7 Jul 1747
Craigg, Peter, s/o above, b. 6 Sep 1749
Craigg, Eleanor, d/o above, b. 17 Jan 1752
Craigg, Rachel, d/o above, b. 17 Feb 1754

Page 39

Craigg, Reuben, s/o above, b. 25 Apr 1756

Wattson, Catherine and Sarah, daus. of Benjamin Wattson and Susanna his wife, b. 18 Jul 1759

Abell, Abner, s/o Samuel and Elinor Abell, b. 29 Jul 1759

Russell, Charles, s/o William and Ann Russell, b. 12 Oct 1759

Adkinson, Mary Brent, d/o Joshua and Susanna Adkinson, b. 25 Aug 1759; granddau. to Brent Nutthall who was s/o Mary Brent, sister to William Brent, Esq. who died in Great Britain

Spong, James, s/o Francis and Elizabeth his wife, b. 8 Sep 1760

Daft, John Baptist, s/o William and Elizabeth his wife, b. 15 Mar 1760

Payne, Jeremiah, s/o Leonard and Monica his wife, b. 29 Sep 1760

Cissell, Bernard, s/o James and Elizabeth his wife, b. 12 Feb 1759

Cissell, Susanna, d/o above, b. 28 Jan 1760

Cissell, Edmund Barton, s/o Ignatius and Elizabeth his wife, b. 25 Jun 1760

Anderson, James, s/o John Baptist and Tabitha his wife, b. 6 Jan 1758

Anderson, John, s/o above, b. 16 Jun 1761

Clow, John, s/o James Clow and Mary his wife, b. 6 Sep 1761

Clow, James, s/o above, b. 17 Oct 1763

Page 40

Turnbull, John, s/o James Turnbull and Margaret his wife, b. 2 Mar 1764

Buchannan, Aaron, s/o George Buchannan and Margaret his wife, b. 6 Apr 1764

Wise, Jeremiah, s/o Thomas Wise and Mary his wife, b. 15 Apr 1764

Kirby, Elizabeth, d/o Thomas Kirby and Mary his wife, b. 2 Jan 1764

Abell, Allethea, d/o Richard Abell and Ann his wife, b. 22 Apr 1764

Knott, Ignatius, s/o Bennett Knott and Eleanor his wife, b. 18 Oct 1754

Knott, James, s/o above, b. 6 Oct 1757

King, Bennett, s/o Margaret King, b. 19 Jul 1764

Lewis, James, s/o Charles Lewis and Jane his wife, b. 13 Oct 1764

Wellman, Rhoda (m), s/o Michael Wellman and Elizabeth his wife, b. 28 Nov 1758

Wellman, Jemima, d/o above, b. 3 Mar 1762

Wellman, Elijah, s/o above,b. 28 Oct 1764

Walker, Nathaniel, s/o Bowen Walker and Elizabeth his wife, b. 31 Jan 1763

Tarlton, Ignatius, s/o James Tarlton and Mary Anne his wife, b. 16 Jul 1762

Tarlton, Elijah, s/o above, b. 20 Jan 1765

Page 41

Wilkinson, Mary, d/o William and Nancy Wilkinson, b. 23 Jun 1771

Wise, Nancy, d/o Joseph Wise and Sarah his wife, b. 7 Nov 1755

Wise, Henrietta, d/o above, 31 Aug 1762

Breeden, Robert Hammett, s/o Enoch and Elizabeth Breeden, b. 12 Nov 1762

Breeden, Sarah, d/o Enoch Breeden and Elizabeth his wife, b. 4 Mar 1765

Fish, Robert, s/o Robert and Priscilla Fish, b. 9 Mar 1765

McClane, Richard, s/o William McClane and Mary his wife, b. 14 Apr 1765

McClane, Enoch, s/o above, b. 26 Feb 1758

McClane, William, s/o above, b. 23 Apr 1760

McClane, Arthur, s/o above, b. 22 Dec 1763

Redman, George, s/o William Redman and Ann his wife, b. 7 Oct 1763

Redman, John, s/o above, b. 11 Apr 1765

Walker, Mary, d/o John Walker and Mary his wife, b. 16 May 1765

Vowles, John, s/o Cyrus and Victoria Vowles, b. 1 Feb 1758

Vowles, Matthew, s/o above, b. 27 May 1762

Vowles, Ann, s/o above, b. 11 Feb 1765

Hall, Frances, d/o Henry Hall and Catharine his wife, b. 11 Jul 1765

Wilkinson, Mark Thomas, s/o William and Ann Wilkinson, b. 12 Jul 1765

Page 42

St. Andrew's Parish 119

McGill, Jannett, d/o Abell McGill and Marianne his wife, b. 4 Dec 1765

Abell, Elizabeth, d/o George Abell and Elizabeth his wife, b. 24 Jan 1766

Hutchens, Frances, d/o Francis Hutchens and Susanna his wife, b. 10 Oct 1763

Hutchens, Alathea, d/o above, b. 16 Dec 1765

Wise, Ransean, d/o Thomas Wise and Mary his wife, b. 29 Jan 1766

Kirby, Henrietta, d/o Thomas Kirby and Mary his wife, b. 17 Apr 1766

Abell, Jeremiah Williams, s/o Caleb Abell and Mary his wife, b. 2 Apr 1766

Wellman, James, s/o Michael Wellman and Elizabeth his wife, b. 19 Jul 1767

Vowles, Thomas, s/o Cyrus Vowles and Victoria his wife, b. 26 Jan 1767

McClane, John Vowles, s/o William and Mary McClane his wife, b. 25 Dec 1767

Medcalf, John Kenelin, s/o Ignatius Medcalf and Sarah his wife, b. 25 Oct 1760

Thompson, George Matthews, s/o William Thompson and Susanna his wife, b. 11 Dec 1767

Latham, James, s/o Matthew Latham and Susanna his wife, b. 27 Oct 1770

Page 43

Thompson, Eleanor, d/o Robert Thompson and Elizabeth his wife, b. 7 Aug 1757

Thompson, Charles James, s/o above, b. 14 Jul 1760

Thompson, Bennett, s/o above, b. 3 Jun 1763

Thompson, Mary, d/o above, b. 22 Nov 1765

Thompson, James, s/o above, b. 13 Dec 1767

Cissell, John, s/o John Cissell and Ann his wife, b. 18 Oct 1757

Cissell, Delbert, s/o above, b. 30 Jul 1763

Boarman, John, s/o Francis Boarman and Batris his wife, b. 8 Oct 1758

Boarman, Francis Ignatius, s/o above, b. 14 Mar 1762

Boarman, Sarah, d/o above, b. 1 Mar 1764
Spink, Joseph, s/o Edward Spink and Monica his wife, b. 22 Apr 1759
Spink, Mary, d/o above, b. 29 Jul 1752
Peake, Augustine, s/o John Peake and Susanna his wife, b. 23 Nov 1755
Peake, Robert, s/o above, b. 23 Nov 1755
Mekin, Susanna, d/o Augustine Mekin and Margaret his wife, b. 4 May 1761
Mekin, Margaret, d/o above, b. 26 Aug 1764
Thompson, Ignatius, s/o Mark Thompson and Margaret his wife, b. 29 Oct 1761
Thompson, Mary, d/o above, b. 12 Aug 1767
Payne, Ann, d/o Charles Payne and Monica his wife, b. 15 Sep 1767
Thompson, Thomas Alexius, s/o Thomas Thompson and Ann his wife, b. 3 Nov 1761
Thompson, Eleanor, d/o above, b. 26 Mar 1763
Thompson, Joseph Edmund, s/o above, b. 16 May 1766
Payne, Francis Exhuerus, s/o Richard Payne and Priscilla his wife, b. 21 Sep 1756
Payne, James, s/o above, b. 28 Feb 1759
Thompson, James, s/o Robert Thompson and Ann his wife, b. 14 Nov 1757
Thompson, Mary Ann, d/o above, b. 28 Feb 1760
Benden, Elizabeth, d/o John Benden and Monica his wife, b. 8 Jan 1762
Medley, Augustine, s/o George Medley and Ann his wife, b. 26 Sep 1763
Cissell, Ann, d/o Baptist Cissell and Rebecca his wife, b. 2 Feb 1766
Cissell, William, s/o above, b. 10 Aug 1767
Cissell, James Rodolph, s/o Ignatius Cissell and Elizabeth his wife, b. 8 Apr 1762

Page 45

Cissell, Ignatius, s/o above, b. 12 Mar 1764
Cissell, Joseph, s/o above, b. 28 Jun 1766

Cissell, Peter, s/o James Cissell and Elizabeth his wife, b. 29 Jun 1764
Payne, Henry Berryman, s/o Leonard Payne and Monica his wife, b. 21 Mar 1756
Payne, Elizabeth, d/o above, b. 18 Aug 1758
Payne, Monica, d/o above, b. 13 Mar 1763
Mareman, Richard, s/o Joseph Mareman and Elizabeth his wife, b. 3 Feb 1768
Nuthall, Ann Roach, d/o Margaret Nuthall, b. 28 Feb 1761
Woolingham, John Baptist, s/o John Woolingham and Appolonia his wife, b. 1 Nov 1758
Woolingham, Ann, d/o above, b. 1 Mar 1763
Wimsatt, Ralph, s/o John Wimsatt and Henrietta his wife, b. 1 Oct 1754
Wimsatt, William, s/o above, b. 16 May 1757
Wimsatt, Elizabeth, d/o above, b. 14 Nov 1759
Wimsatt, Robert Henry, s/o above, b. 9 May 1762
Wimsatt, Ann, d/o above, b. 27 Dec 1764
Howard, Mary Ann, d/o Henry Howard and Mary his wife, b. 24 Jul 1758
Howard, Charles, s/o above, b. 24 Nov 1762
Howard, Joseph, s/o above, b. 3 May 1764
Taylor, Mary, d/o Ignatius Taylor and Elizabeth Spink his wife, b. 1 Oct 1764
French, Bennett, s/o John French and Monica his wife, b. 27 Jun 1757

Page 46
French, Ann, d/o above, b. 16 Sep 1759
French, Bernadine (m), s/o above, b. 20 Dec 1761
French, Elizabeth, d/o above, b. 3 May 1764
Nottingham, Raphael Ignatius, s/o Mathias Nottingham and Mary his wife, b. 9 Jun 1754
Nottingham, Mary Ann, d/o above, b. 2 Aug 1757
Nottingham, Elizabeth, d/o above, b. 5 Jan 1751
Nottingham, Ignatius, s/o above, b. 21 Apr 1763
Cissell, Shedrick, s/o John Cissell and Margaret his wife, b. 18 Nov 1754

Cissell, Dorothy, d/o above, b. 17 Apr 1756
Booth, Ignatius, s/o Thomas Booth and Mary his wife, b. 4 Nov 1754
Booth, Rebecca, d/o above, b. 4 Jun 1756
Booth, Leonard, s/o above, b. 5 Mar 1758
Booth, Mary, d/o above, b. 7 Sep 1760
Booth, Eleanor, d/o above, b. 17 Jun 1761
Booth, Sarah, d/o above, b. 20 Jun 1763
Booth, George, s/o above, b. 11 Jul 1765
Booth, Justinian, s/o above, b. 12 Nov 1767
Finnacy, Mary Ann, d/o Stephen and Ann his wife, b. 31 Oct 1760
Finnacy, John Archibald, s/o above, b. 1 May 1765
Finnacy, Joseph Normand Mack, s/o above, b. 1 Feb 1768
Wheatly, Rebecca, d/o James Wheatly and Henrietta his wife, b. 18 Sep 1755

Page 47

Wheatly, James, s/o above, b. 23 Sep 1758
Wheatly, Joseph, s/o above, b. 27 May 1761
Wheatly, Edmund, s/o above, b. 23 Dec 1765
Russell, Catharine, d/o John Russell and Susanna his wife, b. 27 Jun 1771
Bowes, Mary, d/o Timothy Bowes and Mary his wife, b. 3 Mar 1763
Bowes, Eleanor, d/o above, b. 9 Jun 1766
Norris, Mary Ann, d/o Thomas Norris and Ann his wife, b. 1 Nov 1756
Norris, Philip, s/o above, b. 1 May 1758
Norris, Mary, d/o above, b. 22 Oct 1759
Norris, William, d/o above, b. 7 Jun 1761
Norris, Joseph, s/o above, b. 29 Jul 1764
Peake, Henry Barton, s/o Edward Peake and Ann his wife, b. 7 Nov 1754
Peake, Henrietta, d/o above, b. 3 Feb 1757
Peake, Kenelm, s/o above, b. 11 Mar 1760
Peake, Mary, d/o above, b. 4 Apr 1762
Peake, Francis, s/o above, b. 4 Feb 1764
Peake, Charles, s/o above, b. 8 Oct 1767

Daft, Mary, d/o William Daft and Elizabeth his wife, b. 6 Apr 1762

Inge, Vincent, s/o Vincent Inge and Susanna his wife, b. 31 Oct 1758

Page 48

Inge, John, s/o above, b. 29 Oct 1761

Inge, Ambrose, s/o above, b. 23 Oct 1765

Inge, Ann Maria, d/o above, b. 2 Apr 1768

Browne, Dorothy, d/o Anthony Browne and Mary his wife, b. 27 Mar 1753

Browne, Benedict, s/o above, b. 7 Jun 1758

Browne, Susanna, d/o above, b. 21 Sep 1761

Browne, Frances, d/o above, b. 6 Mar 1764

Browne, Anthony, s/o above, b. 7 Apr 1768

Clarke, Richard Langham, s/o John Clarke and Eleanor his wife, b. 19 Jan 1753

Greenwell, Joshua Leonard, s/o John Basil and Eleanor his wife, b. 5 Nov 1756

Greenwell, James, s/o above, b. 15 Jan 1761

Wheatley, William, s/o James Wheatley and Eleanor his wife, b. 8 Jan 1763

Wheatley, Benedict, s/o above, b. 2 Nov 1766

Payne, Bernard, s/o Henry and Jane his wife, b. 27 Nov 1762

Payne, Alllelusia, d/o above, b. 17 Apr 1765

Hackett, Joshua, s/o Rhodolph Hackett and Mary his wife, b. 13 Nov 1763

Hackett, Mary Magdalene, d/o aboe, b. 6 Dec 1766

Sanson, William, s/o John Sanson and Mary his wife, b. 3 Oct 1767

Thomas, Robert, s/o James Thomas and Elizabeth his wife, b. 25 Jul 1756

Page 49

Thomas, Jemima, d/o above, b. 4 Mar 1761

Edwards, Elizabeth, d/o John Edwards and Henrietta his wife, b. 23 Feb 1762

Edwards, Ann Chloe, d/o above, b. 4 May 1763

Forrest, Richard, s/o Zachariah Forrest and Ann his wife, b. 15 Nov 1767

Beverley, Annastatia, d/o George Beverley and Mary his wife, b. 2 Feb 1756

Beverley, Jemima, d/o above, b. 2 Sep 1763

Gough, Jane, d/o James Gough and Susannah his wife, b. 9 Oct 1755

Gough, Elizabeth, d/o above, b. 18 May 1757

Gough, Annastatia, d/o above, b. 9 Apr 1760

Gough, John Baptist, s/o above, b. 18 Feb 1764

Gough, Matthew, s/o above, b. 30 Jun 1766

Browne, Jeroboam, s/o Peter Browne and Frances his wife, b. 16 Nov 1764

Browne, Anna, d/o above, b. 9 Apr 1768

Payne, Winifred, d/o Baptist Payne and Ann his wife, b. 14 Apr 1763

Payne, Mary Ann, d/o above, b. 22 Sep 1765

Payne, Elizabeth, d/o above, b. 17 Apr 1768

Howard, Sarah, d/o George Howard and Ann his wife, b. 19 Jan 1761

Howard, Ignatius, s/o George Howard and Annastatia Spink his wife, b. 2 Mar 1765

Howard, Francis, s/o above, b. 6 Mar 1767

Breeden, Elizabeth, d/o Enoch Breeden and Elizabeth his wife, b. 9 Mar 1768

Page 50

Bradburn, John Baptist, s/o Mark Bradburn and Susanna his wife, b. 27 Sep 1757

Bradburn, Elizabeth, d/o above, b. 7 Oct 1759

Booth, Elizabeth, s/o John Booth and Mary his wife, b. 14 Mar 1762

Booth, Jane, d/o above, b. 14 Aug 1763

Booth, Rhodolph, s/o above, b. 30 Nov 1765

Booth, John Baptist, s/o above, b. 10 Mar 1768

French, Rodolph, s/o William French and Rinah his wife, b. 1 Aug 1755

French, Jeremiah, s/o above, b. 13 Oct 1761

French, Susannah, s/o above, b. 14 Oct 1766
Norris, Philip, s/o John Norris and Mary his wife, b. 25 Dec 1754
Norris, Henry Elijah, s/o above, b. 14 Mar 1758
Norris, Arnold, s/o above, b. 26 Jun 1761
Norris, Bibrana, d/o above, b. 17 Mar 1766
Greenwell, Emma Ransean Anna, d/o Henry Greenwell and Frances his wife, b. 10 Jan 1754
Greenwell, Richard, s/o above, b. 9 Jan 1760
Greenwell, Joseph, s/o above, b. 17 Apr 1764
Jarboe, Frances, s/o Clement Jarboe and Ann his wife, b. 15 Jun 1762
Jarboe, Eleanor, d/o above, b. 30 Jul 1764
Jarboe, Monica, d/o above, b. 26 May 1767
Norris, Enoch, s/o Joseph Norris and Elizabeth his wife, b. 27 Feb 1765
Norris, Luke, s/o above, b. 3 Jan 1767
Norris, Susanna, d/o above, b. 27 Sep 1768

Page 51
Sewall, Element, s/o Henry Sewall and Mary his wife, b. 10 Jun 1757
Sewall, Mary Smith, s/o above, b. 7 Jul 1762
Sewall, Henry, s/o above, b. 3 Jun 1764
Sewall, Charles, s/o above, b. 20 Jul 1767
Abell, Jane, d/o Edward Abell and Susanna his wife, b. 6 Nov 1760
Abell, Benjamin, s/o above, b. 7 Apr 1764
Abell, Catharine, d/o above, b. 22 Apr 1766
Abell, Samuel, s/o above, b. 23 Apr 1768
Abell, Elizabeth, d/o John Abell and Jane his wife, b. 3 Dec 1759
Reshwick, Thomas, s/o John Reshwick and Appolonia his wife, b. 15 Oct 1752
Reshwick, Mary, d/o above, b. 23 Mar 1755
Reshwick, Joseph, d/o above, b. 15 Aug 1757
Reshwick, Francis, s/o above, b. 4 Nov 1763
Hall, Ann Mary, d/o Henry Hall and Catherine his wife, b. 11 Jun 1754
Hall, George, s/o above, b. 10 May 1756

Hall, John Basil, s/o above, b. 21 Oct 1762
Abell, George, s/o George and Elizabeth Abell, b. 27 Jul 1768
Harriss, Zacharias, s/o Samuel Harriss and Elizabeth his wife, b. 5 Nov 1763
Harriss, Austin, s/o above, b. 31 Oct 1766
Long, John Read, s/o John Long and Barbara his wife, b. 23 Jul 1754
Long, Reuben, s/o above, b. 22 Dec 1756

Page 52

Long, Nicholas, s/o above, b. 15 Dec 1759
Long, Hannah, d/o above, b. 10 Jan 1762
Long, Gabriel, s/o above, b. 1 Oct 1765
Long, William, s/o above, b. 28 Feb 1768
Wathen, Francis Hudson, s/o Henry Hudson Wathen and Ann his wife, b. 3 Nov 1764
Wathen, Henry Hudson, s/o above, b. 11 May 1766
Hammett, Richard, s/o McKelvie Hammett and Henrietta his wife, b. 21 Jan 1754
Hammett, Henny, d/o above, b. 10 Feb 1757
Hammett, Dolly, d/o above, b. 12 Aug 1739
Hammett, Mary, d/o above, b. 5 Feb 1762
Hammett, Francis, d/o above, b. 25 Nov 1764
Hammett, Sarah, d/o above, b. 1 Mar 1767
Abell, James, s/o John Abell (younger) and Ann his wife, b. 26 Jun 1766
Abell, John Standfill, s/o above, b. 16 Jan 1768
King, Adam, s/o Edward King and Eleanor his wife, b. 17 Oct 1757
Greenwell, John, s/o Charles Greenwell and Eleanor his wife, b. 2 Oct 1760
Greenwell, Jane, d/o above, b. 20 Mar 1763
Greenwell, Richard, s/o above, b. 7 Oct 1765
Greenwell, Edward, s/o above, b. 30 Jan 1768
Heard, Mary, d/o John Heard and Ann his wife, b. 9 Jul 1764
Heard, Ann, d/o above, b. 5 Apr 1766

Page 53

Heard, Hellen, d/o above, b. 29 Sep 1767

St. Andrew's Parish

Greenwell, Bennett, s/o James Greenwell and Hannah his wife, b. 28 Aug 1755
Greenwell, William, s/o above, b. 21 Jul 1757
Greenwell, Joseph, s/o above, b. 3 Aug 1759
Greenwell, Elizabeth, d/o aove, b. 23 Jul 1763
Gough, Charles, s/o Benjamin Gough and Susanna his wife, b. 25 May 1755
Gough, Mary, d/o above, b. 24 Jun 1762
Gough, Rebecca, d/o above, b. 3 Jun 1766
Wootton, Susanna, d/o Thomas Wootton and Susanna his wife, b. 7 Mar 1759
Wootton, Isaac, s/o above, b. 9 Jun 1761
Wootton, Bennett, s/o above, b. 10 Jul 1762
Wootton, Frances, d/o above, b. 9 May 1765
Pyke, Mary Ann, d/o James Pyke and Ann his wife, b. 14 May 1753
Pyke, Henry, s/o above, b. 3 Feb 1756
Pyke, James, s/o above, b. 18 Apr 1759
Hackett, Henrietta, d/o Rodolph Hackett and Mary his wife, b. 14 Aug 1757
Hackett, Ann, d/o above, b. 7 Nov 1758
Medley, Eleanor, d/o Clement Medley and Mary his wife, b. 27 Feb 1762
Medley, Joseph, s/o above, b. 3 Nov 1764
Medley, Matthew, s/o above, b. 16 Feb 1766

Page 54

Medley, Ann Elizabeth, d/o above, b. 1 Feb 1768
Nottingham, Mary Ann, d/o Athana Nottingham and Mary his wife, b. 18 Nov 1762
Nottingham, Ann, d/o above, b. 3 Sep 1763
Nottingham, Enoch, s/o above, b. 25 Dec 1766
Greenwell, William, s/o Ignatius Greenwell and Jane his wife, b. 26 Nov 1752
Manning, Ignatius, s/o Cornelius Manning and [?Jane] his wife, b. 23 Dec 1754; [microfilm shows ditto of above Jane under name for wife Cornelius Manning; some sources question that his wife was named Jane and list Ignatius as Ignatius Greenwell]

Manning, Monica, d/o above, b. 26 Oct 1759
Manning, Frances, d/o above, b. 10 Jan 1762
Smith, Ann, d/o John Smith and Elizabeth his wife, b. 3 May 1756
Greenwell, Thomas, s/o Philip Greenwell and Winifred his wife, b. 4 Sep 1754
Greenwell, Mary, s/o above, b. 17 Oct 1762
Greenwell, Ann, d/o above, b. 6 Jun 1767
Armsworthy, Aaron, s/o William Armswrothy and Mary his wife, b. 3 Sep 1765
Armsworthy, Eleanor, d/o above, b. 2 Sep 1767
Fish, William, s/o William Fish and Jennet his wife, b. 30 May 1765
Fish, Ann, d/o above, b. 11 May 1768
Mills, John, s/o Justinian Mills and Mary his wife, b. 5 Feb 1753
Mills, Elizabeth, s/o above, b. 9 May 1755

Page 55

Mills, Mary, wife of Justinian Mills, b. 1 Sep 1736
Mills, Winifred, d/o Justinian and Mary, b. 30 Oct 1757
Mills, Margaret, d/o above, b. 30 Jan 1760
Mills, Joseph, s/o above, b. 26 Feb 1762
Mills, Justinian and Mary, son and dau. of above, b. 7 Oct 1764
Mills, Ann, d/o above, b. 3 Dec 1767
Mills, Charles, s/o above, b. 24 Aug 1770
Bean, Bennet, s/o Robert and Margaret Bean, d. 5 Aug 1771
Silence, Edmund, s/o John Silence, Jr. and Elizabeth his wife, b. 9 Mar 1771
Reeves, Susanna, d/o George and Mary Reeves, b. 7 Aug 1771
Hammett, Margaret, d/o Cartwright Hammett and Elizabeth his wife, b. 17 Oct 1771
Brown, Monica, d/o Anthony and Mary Brown, b. 22 May 1771
Norris, Susanna, d/o John Norris and Mary his wife, b. 14 Mar 1771
Fish, Robert, s/o William and Janet Fish, b. 11 Oct 1771
Armsworthy, Bennet, s/o Abraham and Eleanor Armswrothy, b. 26 Dec 1771
Taylor, Ann, d/o Ignatius Taylor and Elizabeth his wife, b. 15 Dec 1770

Page 189
Mills, Ignatius, s/o Nicholas and Anastatia his wife, b. 16 Nov 1758 (4)
Mills, Bernard, s/o above, b. 27 Sep 1760
Mills, Ethelbert, s/o above, b. 12 Nov 1764
Mills, Stephen, s/o above, b. 2 Jan 1767
Mills, Nicholas, s/o above, b. 9 Mar 1769
Greenwell, John Basil, s/o John Baptist Greenwell and Susanna his wife, b. 17 Aug 1764
Greenwell, Mary Ann, d/o above, b. 17 Mar 1767
Cushman, John, s/o William Cushman and Eleanor nis wife, b. 6 Apr 1760
Cushman, James, s/o above, b. 6 Mar 1761
Cushman, Mary, d/o above, b. 23 Nov 1763
Cushman, Ann, d/o above, b. 5 Sep 1767
Cushman, Eleanor, b. 10 Feb 1769
Wheatley, Anastatia, d/o Ignatius Wheatley and Henrietta his wife, b. 20 Feb 1765
Wheatley, Eleanor, d/o above, b. 9 Apr 1768
Greenwell, Noah, s/o Justinian Greenwell and Mary his wife, b. 10 Nov 1760
Greenwell, Benedict, s/o above, b. 3 Feb 1763
Greenwell, Elizabeth, d/o above, b. 2 Sep 1765
Greenwell, Jeremiah, s/o above, b. 17 Jul 1767
Norris, Mary Ann, d/o Rhodolph Norris and Dorothy his wife, b. 22 Apr 1768
Langley, John Francis Xaviers, s/o Josias and Susanna Langley, b. 22 Jun 1768
Page 190
Norris, Elizabeth, d/o Thomas Norris and Mary Ann his wife, b. 26 Oct 1768
Hilton, John, s/o Stephen Hilton and Diana his wife, b. 11 Jan 1770
Thompson, Samuel, s/o John Thompson and Rebecca his wife, b. 28 Mar 1755
Abell, Mary, d/o Caleb Abell and Mary his wife, b. 20 Oct 1769
Buchanan, George, s/o George Buchanan and Elizabeth his wife, b. 22 Sep 1769

Redman, William, s/o William Redman and Ann his wife, b. 6 Aug 1767
Redman, Britannia, d/o above, b. 5 Feb 1769
Redman, Benjamin, s/o above, b. 8 Jun 1770
Brown, Mary, d/o Peter Brown and Frances his wife, b. 30 Sep 1770
Norris, Susanna, d/o Philip Norris and Monica his wife, b. 24 Dec 1761
Norris, Henrietta, d/o above, b. 13 Sep 1764
Norris, Eleanor, d/o above, b. 13 Nov 1767
Norris, Thomas, s/o Clement and Elizabeth Norris, b. 1 May 1753
Norris, Vincent, s/o above, b. 5 Apr 1755
McCave, John Bond, s/o Alice McCave, b. 23 Nov 1760
McCave, Eleanor Ann, d/o above, b. 5 Aug 1764
McCave, Margaret Ann, d/o above, b. 20 Nov 1767

Page 191

Sims, Elizabeth, d/o Anthony Sims and Mary his wife, b. 28 Oct 1768
Ford, Ignatius, s/o Peter Ford and Anastatia his wife, b. 26 Sep 1755
Ford, John Francis, s/o above, b. 8 Mar 1758
Newton, Rhodolph, s/o Joseph Newton and Mildred his wife, b. 13 May 1763
Newton, John Shadrach, s/o above, b. 1 Jan 1767
Newton, James, s/o above, b. 11 Feb 1769
Wootton, Thomas, s/o Thomas Wootton and Elizabeth his wife, b. 27 Apr 1769
Norris, Cuthbert, s/o Mark Norris and Elizabeth his wife, b. 26 Jun 1760
Norris, John, s/o above, b. 6 May 1762
Norris, Henrietta, d/o above, b. 9 Jul 1765
Norris, Mathias, s/o above, b. 1 Sep 1767
Norris, Mary, d/o above, b. 20 Jul 1769
Wise, John, s/o Adam Wise and Frances his wife, b. 28 Jan 1770
(5)
Mugg, Ann, d/o Walter Mugg and Priscilla his wife, b. 12 Dec 1766

Mugg, Elizabeth, d/o above, b. 10 Jan 1770
Kendrick, Elizabeth, d/o William Kendrick and Diana his wife, b. 23 Apr 1764
Cole, Mary Ann, d/o Francis Cole and Ann his wife, b. 2 Feb 1760
Vowles, Sarah, d/o Cyrus Vowles and Victoria his wife, b. 3 Feb 1770

Page 192

Gough, Britainnia, d/o Benjamin Gough and Susanna his wife, b. 19 Dec 1768
Gough, Ann, d/o James Gough and Susanna his wife, b. 3 Feb 1768
Booth, Ann, d/o John Booth and Mary his wife, b. 10 Feb 1770
Sanson, John, s/o John Sanson and Mary his wife, b. 5 Jul 1771
Jarboe, Stephen, s/o Mary Jarboe, b. 7 Jan 1765
Evans, Mary, d/o Philip Evans and Ann his wife, b. 10 Sep 1764
Evans, Elizabeth, d/o above, b. 12 Jul 1767
Hopewell, Mary, d/o Richard and Eleanor Hopewell, b. 12 Jan 1763
Combes, Raphael, s/o William Combes and Eleanor his wife, b. 6 Oct 1760
Combes, Eleanor, d/o above, b. 29 Aug 1762
Combes, Margaret, d/o above, b. 13 Apr 1764
Combes, William, s/o above, b. 12 Apr 1766
Combes, Mary Ann, d/o above, b. 18 Dec 1768
Medley, Ann, d/o Clement Medley and Mary Ann his wife, b. 28 Mar 1755
Medley, William, s/o above, b. 20 Apr 1757

Page 193

Medley, Catharine, d/o above, b. 20 Jan 1760
Medley, Sarah, d/o above, b. 29 Jul 1763
Medley, Charles, s/o above, b. 29 Jul 1763
Medley, Mary, d/o above, b. 14 Nov 1768
Connelly, Rhodolph, s/o Rhodolph Connelly and Ann Chloe his wife, b. 29 Mar 1767
Milburne, Eleanor, d/o Jeremiah Milburne and Elizabeth his wife, b. 10 Feb 1757
Peake, Eleanor, d/o Monica Peake, b. 5 Apr 1767

Wheatley, Henry, d/o George Wheatley and Elizabeth his wife, b. 10 Jan 17855
Wheatley, Ann, d/o above, b. 12 Aug 1756
Wheatley, William, s/o above, b. 18 Sep 1762
Wheatley, Ignatius, s/o above, b. 25 Feb 1765
Wheatley, Bernard, s/o above, b. 29 May 1768
Combes, Mary, d/o Bennet Combes and Elizabeth his wife, b. 28 Jun 1765
Combes, Barbara, d/o above, b. 9 Feb 1767
Taney, Eleanor, d/o John Taney and Eleanor his wife, b. 10 Mar 1756
Taney, Sarah, d/o above, b. 26 Dec 1764
Manning, Joseph, s/o John and Susanna Manning, b. 2 Oct 1767
Bould, William, s/o John Bould and Monica his wife, b. 7 Jan 1752
Bould, Susanna, d/o above, b. 1 Oct 1753
Page 194
Bould, Jane, d/o above, b. 25 Mar 1757
Bould, Henrietta, d/o above, b. 15 Sep 1760
Bould, John Baptist, s/o above, b. 15 Nov 1762
Bould, Mary, d/o above, b. 30 Jun 1767 **(6)**
Bould, Catharine, d/o above, b. 20 Oct 1769
Greenwell, Elizabeth, d/o Philip Greenwell and Winifred his wife, b. 23 Feb 1769
Layton, Joseph, s/o John Layton and Jane his wife, b. 13 Jun 1762
Layton, Zachariah, s/o above, b. 13 Jan 1765 (sic)
Layton, Ignatius, s/o above, b. 24 Aug 1768
Layton, Susanna, d/o above, b. 12 Mar 1765 (sic)
Hammond, Ann, d/o Uel Hammond and Susanna his wife, b. 11 May 1768
Pyke, Mary Ann, d/o John Pyke and Kezia his wife, b. 17 May 1757
Pyke, John, s/o above, b. 1 Jun 1759
Pyke, William, s/o above, b. 18 Sep 1761
Manning, William, s/o James Manning and Margaret his wife, b. 22 Jun 1762
Manning, Mary, d/o above, b. 17 Sep 1765

Manning, John, s/o above, b. 27 Mar 1767
Medley, Eleanor, d/o Joseph Medley and Anastatia his wife, b. 14 Dec 1764
Medley, Joseph, s/o above, b. 22 Mar 1766
Medley, Bernard, s/o above, b. 22 Dec 1768
Greenwell, Joseph, s/o George Greenwell and Elizabeth his wife, b. 2 Aug 1755

Page 195

Greenwell, Justinian, s/o above, b. 15 Oct 1757
Greenwell, Bennet, s/o above, b. 7 Dec 1761
Greenwell, Austin, s/o above, b. 14 Mar 1765
Latham, Jeremiah, s/o John Latham and Rebecca his wife, b. 25 May 1763
Fenwick, William, s/o John Fenwick and Monica his wife, b. 30 Dec 1759
Fenwick, Eleanor, d/o above, b. 17 Oct 1761
Fenwick, Catharine, d/o above, b. 27 Feb 1763
Edwards, John, s/o Jane Edwards, b. 17 Feb 1758
Wheatley, Ann, d/o Mary Wheatley, b. 17 Oct 1758
Harper, Elizabeth, d/o James Harper and Mary his wife, b. 15 May 1760
Harper, Henrietta, d/o above, b. 4 Mar 1763
Harper, Mary Ann, d/o above, b. 27 May 1766
Harper, Rebecca, d/o above, b. 25 Jul 1769
Peake, Ann, d/o William Peake and Henrietta his wife, b. 19 Nov 1761
Peake, Raphael, s/o above, b. 20 Feb 1765
Peake, Eleanor, d/o above, b. 5 Jun 1767
Peake, Joshua, s/o above, b. 28 Sep 1769
Peake, Mary, d/o Peter Peake and Mary his wife, b. 6 Nov 1755
Dillihay, Stephen, s/o John Dillihay and Winifred his wife, b. 19 Nov 1766
Dillihay, Joseph, s/o above, b. 22 Feb 1768
Norris, Winifred, d/o Bennet Norris and Frances his wife, b. 3 Apr 1768

Page 196

Grogan, Anastatia, d/o Catharine Grogan, b. 27 Apr 1766

Page 56

BIRTH OF BLACKS

Lucinda, d/o Sam & Beck, property of Robt. Hammett, b. 8 Oct 1813, bapt. May 1814

Lucy, belonging to Mrs. Rebecca Watts, b. 19 Jan 1814; bapt. May 1814

Jane, d/o Phil & Rose, belonging to Mrs. Billingsley, b. 12 Jul 1813; bapt. 16 Jul 1814

Stephen, s/o Bob & Fanny, property of Henry G. A. Key, b. 2 Oct 1814; bapt. 6 May 1815

Sarah, d/o Peter & Rachel, property of Bennett Hammett, b. 5 Mar 1815; bapt. 26 Mar 1815

Moses, s/o Moses & Jane, property of Francis Abell, b. 9 Apr 1815; bapt. 8 Jun 1815

Henry, property of same, b. 1811; bapt. 30 Jul 1815

Sarah, d/o Sam & Beck, property of Robt. Hammett, b. 19 Mar 1816; bapt. 19 May 1816

Walter, belonging to Gerard N. Causin, b. and bapt. 19 May 1816

Harriet, d/o Sam & Beck, property of Robt. Hammett, b. 7 Jan 1819; bapt. Jul 1819

Page 57

MARRIAGES (18)

Jenkins, Joseph and Mary _____	23 Jan 1742
Vowles, Thomas and Susanna Chunn	27 Dec 1747
James, Thomas and Mary Manning	25 Sep 1752
Abell, Caleb and Mary Williams	29 Dec 1763
Mills, Justinian and Mary Dant	26 Oct 1751
Bean, George and Anne Dillion	14 Oct 1778
Abell, Edward and Statia Taylor	7 Nov 1778
Wise, William and Elizabeth Clocker	19 Nov 1778
Norris, William and Dorothy White	22 Nov 1778
Wheeler, Moses and Henrietta Redman	28 Nov 1778
Jarboe, Peter and Nancy Jarboe	16 Jan 1779
Carter, Henry and Elizabeth Hogan	7 Feb 1779
Thomas, William and Henrietta Biscoe	14 Apr 1779
Brice, John and Elizabeth Harding	25 Apr 1779
Thomas, Tyler and Rachael Thomas	9 May 1779

Davis, Moses and Anne Evans | 18 May 1779
Allison, Henry and Margaret Dillman | 25 May 1779
Abell, Clarke and Catharine Hutchins | 3 Jun 1779
Aisquith, John and Mary Chesley | 3 Jun 1779
Somervel, William and Elizabeth Chesley | 7 Sep 1779
Smith, Walter and Mary Hendley | 19 Sep 1779
Emory, Thomas and Elizabeth Hopewell | 23 Sep 1779
Owens, John and Sarah Saunders | 3 Oct 1779
Price, William and Elizabeth Carter | 31 Oct 1779
Wise, Adam and Susannah Bryan | 2 Nov 1779
Cheseldine, Seneca and Elizabeth Biscoe | 4 Nov 1779
Hutchins, Bennett and Jane Stone | 7 Nov 1779

Page 58 | (18)

Watson, Edward and Anne Sanner | 26 Nov 1779
Kendrick, Benjamin and Mary Smith | 31 Dec 1779
Holton, William and Elizabeth Craghill | 31 Dec 1779
Jenkins, Thomas and Mary Mackall | 13 Jan 1780
Armsworthy, John and Mary Armsworthy | 16 Jan 1780
Otley, James and Elizabeth Richardson | 24 Jan 1780
Martin, William and Anne Thompson | 3 Feb 1780
Fielder, Nicholas and Anne Collosen | 16 Jan 1780
Cheverlin, Jesse and Catharine Gruther | 12 Feb 1780
Gibbons, Francis and Rebecca Eden | 20 Feb 1780
Lurty, John and Susannah Nugent | 30 Apr 1780
Thomas, William and Anne Allen | 2 May 1780
Taylor, Ignatius and Margaret Jordan | 13 May 1780
Abell, John and Elizabeth Abell | 4 Jun 1780
Hanning, Caleb and Susannah Kelly | 22 Jun 1780

(35)

Hall, Joseph and Mary McGill | 2 Jul 1780
Boney, Thomas and Jean Davidson | 20 Oct 1780
Graves, Jeremiah and Rachel Craig | 3 Oct 1780
Buchanan, Moses and Eleanor ____ (by publication) | 15 Oct 1780
Flower, Charles and Mary Hutchins (by publication) | 28 Oct 1780
Ross, Lazarus and Jane Cox (by license) | 28 Nov 1780
Stone, Joseph and Winifred Hutchins (by license) | 28 Nov 1780
Beal, Josias and Mary Hellen (by license) | 14 Dec 1780

Bailey, Basil and Dorothy Hutchins (by license)   28 Dec 1780
Page 59
Daffin, Robert and Elizabeth Simmonds (by license)   16 Jan 1781
Greaves, Absolom and Alathia Smith (by license)   16 Jan 1781
Leatherland, Wm. and Elizabeth Kirby (by license)   16 Jan 1781
Wootton, Thomas and Nancy Bentley (by publication)   5 Jun 1781
McKenzie, James and Casandra Magruder (by license) 1 Apr 1781
Thomas, Thomas and Jane Abell (by license)   27 Apr 1781
Bean, John and Ann Henning (by license)   26 Jun 1781
Henning, John and Mary Abell (by license)   5 Sep 1781
Read, Philip and Eleanor Tawney (by license)   1 Oct 1781
Haywood, Thomas and Mary Shermentine (by license) 16 Oct 1781
Clarke, William and Monica Woodward (by license) 18 Oct 1781
Ticklin, Jeremiah and Mary Raily (by license)   6 Nov 1781
McKenzie, Alexander and Sarah Anderson (by license)8 Nov 1781
Kirby, Francis and Millburn Hagar (by license)   1 Jan 1782
Baker, William and Jane Davis (by license)   1 Jan 1782
Page 60
McClain, John and Elizabeth Clarke (by license)   14 Jan 1782
Jenkins, George and Margaret Wise (by license)   31 Mar 1782
Wiseman, Robert and Eleanor King (by license)   5 Feb 1792
Flower, Thomas and Eleanor Bond (by license)   2 Dec 1781
Cox, John and Anne Shermintine (by license)   2 Sep 1782
Breedin, Robert Hammett and Ann Nuthall (by license)29 Sep 1782
Reeder, Benjamin and Susannah Bond (by license)   29 Sep 1782
Biscoe, Thomas and Margaret Bennet (by license)   27 Nov 1782
Sanner, Isaac and Eleanor Price (by license)   12 Dec 1782
Parran, Charles Somersett and Margaret Ireland
                              (by license) 17 Dec 1782
Goldsburry, James and Araminta Roberts (by license)   9 Jan 1783
Saxe, Henry and Rennis Denton (by license)   10 Jan 1783
Tybills, James Theobold and Mary Griffin (by license)13 Jan 1783
                                                    (36)
Hunter, Andrew and Ann Poole (by license)   2 Feb 1783
Page 61
Parran, Thomas and Jane Mackall (by license)   6 Feb 1783
Greenwell, Stephen and Henrietta Wise (by license) 18 Feb 1783

St. Andrew's Parish

Barrett, William and Margaret Malley (by license) 23 Feb 1783
Keech, Timothy and Araminta Uldra (by publication) 27 Feb 1783
Tarlton, Ignatius and Mary Adams (by publication) 9 Mar 1783
Burnet, Stephen and Anastatia Jones (by license) 12 Mar 1783
Taylor, John and Elizabeth Tarlton (by license) 13 May 1783
Wolstenholme, Daniel, Esq. and Deborah Beck
 (by license) 25 Aug 1783
Wise, Caleb and Catharine Wise (by license) 13 Nov 1783
Gray, John and Elizabeth Turner (by license) 27 Nov 1783
Sanner, Thomas and Mary Collason (by license) 23 Dec 1783
Vessels, Elijah and Ann Choram (by license) 5 Jan 1784
Abell, Arthur and Henrietta Raily (by license) 12 Jan 1784
Griffin, Thomas and Elizabeth Jarboe (by license) 29 Jan 1784

Page 62

Joy, William and Eleanor Armsworthy (by license) 24 Feb 1784
Aisquith, George and Elizabeth Gruder (by license) 3 Mar 1784
Sissel, William and Sarah Adams (by license) 27 Apr 1784
Biscoe, Basil and Mary Standworth (by license) 9 May 1784
McGil, Charles and Mary Bradford (by publication) 11 May 1784
Clocker, Benjamin and Lydia Baldwin (by license) 19 May 1784
King, Henry and Catharine Watts (by license) 17 Jun 1784
Ramsay, Charles and Anne Taylor (by license) 1 Aug 1784
Burnit, Henry and Eleanor Dougan (by publication) 3 Aug 1784
Edwards, John and Mary Morgan (by license) 8 Aug 1784
Adams, Abraham and Sabra Silance (by license) 14 Sep 1784
Silance, Enoch and Eleanor Rhodes (by license) 14 Sep 1784
Breedin, Mark and Darkas Baker (by license) 15 Sep 1784
Gardner, Isaac and Ann Hollyday (by license) 23 Sep 1784

Page 63

Sanner, John and Susannah Goodin (by license) 17 Oct 1784
Smoot, Alexander and Abigail H. Tabbs (by license) 4 Nov 1784
Richardson, Nicholas and Elizabeth Collison
 (by publication) 19 Dec 1784
Abell, Cuthbert and Mary Simmons (by license) 1 Feb 1785
Floyd, Jesse and Elizabeth Taylor (by license) 6 Feb 1785
Buchanan, Aron and Joanna Wells (by publication) 21 Feb 1785
Smith, Walter and ____ King (by publication) 31 Mar 1785

Watts, Henry and Susannah Watts (by license)   7 Apr 1785
Sanner, John and Elizabeth Abell (by license)   1 May 1785
Wildey, William and Sarah Aderton (by license)   3 May 1785
Oney, Nathaniel and Mary Smith (by license)   18 Jul 1785
Flower, Joseph and Patty Wise (by license)   19 Jul 1785

Page 64

Clarke, William and Elizabeth Abell (by license)   1 Nov 18[10]*
Clarke, George and Barbary Flower (by license)   17 Jan 18[11]*
Wise, George and Sophia Hammett (by license)   24 Nov 1813
Evans, Richard and Elizabeth Thomas (by license)   31 Jan 1814
Corum, James and Celia Simmonds (by license)   21 Feb 1814
Hutchins, Bennett and Ann Hutchins (by license)   13 Mar 1814
Armsworthy, Thomas and Elizabeth Hopewell (by license)
    23 Jun 1814
Abell, Francis and Ann Hebb (by license)   17 Jan 1815
Redman, Zachariah and Fanny Mattingly (by license)   7 Sep 1815
Biscoe, George Washington (of Prince George's)
    and Maria Hopewell (by license)   26 Sep 1815
Dent, Thomas Edward and Susanna Hammett (by license)
    20 Dec 1827

Page 65   Baptisms; Rev. George R. Warner, Rector

Dent, Charles Francis, s/o Charles and Sarah M., b. 3 Nov 1857; bapt. 10 Dec 1858

Hopewell, Antionette, d/o James R. and Maria A., b. 10 Aug 1855; bapt. 16 Jan

Ridgel, Frederick, s/o Thomas Ransell and Ann Maria Ridgel, b. 8 Sep 1757; bapt. 28 Feb

Abell, Ann Elizabeth Catharine, d/o William C. and Martha H. Abell, b. 3 Mar 1858; bapt. 7 Mar

Wible, Henry Cornelius, s/o Martin and Henrietta Wible, b. 20 Apr 1857; bapt. 4 May

Somerville, Margaret Alberta (col'd), d/o Francis and Louise, b. 9 Jan 1886; bapt. 30 Jun 1886 by Rev. M. H. Vaughn; the mother, Sarah Bowen, and Abram Hayden, sponsors

                     Married; George R. Warner, Rector

Barnes, Richard, Jr. and Mrs. Mary Elizabeth Key; both of Charles County; 24 Dec 1857

Ridgel, Richard, age between 70 & 75 years, burial 9 Nov
Dent, Mrs. Susan, age 54 years, burial 19 Dec
James, Mary, wife of Thomas, d. 25 Oct 1757
Wellman, Michael, d. 18 Oct 1773

Page 66

Hammitt, Dorcus, wife of Bennet, d. 31 Jan 1819 at 3 p.m.
Dent, Mary Ann, wife of Thomas, d. 30 May 1823 at 11 a.m., age 89 years

Found in *Chronicles of St. Mary's, Vols. V to VII*; not found on microfilm:
Clowe, Catharine, d/o James and Mary, b. 19 Feb 1767
Clowe, Susanna, d/o above, b 23 Sep 1759
Daley, Susanna, d/o Daniel and ____, b. 29 Jul 1752
Daley, Charles, s/o above, b. 25 Sep 1746
Henrick, Benjamin and Mary Smith; m. 3 Dec 1779
Henning, Caleb and Susanna Kelly; m. 22 Jun 1780
Thompson, Eleanor, d/o James and Ann, b. 16 Oct 1748

ALL FAITH'S PARISH, ST. MARY'S COUNTY

Volume 2, page 192:
Copsey, John L., s/o Enock (dec'd) and ____ Copsey (widow), 27 Aug 1805, student at Charlotte Hall

Volume 2, page 349:
[A note on this sheet states this is from King and Queen Parish, but the "present librarian, Mr. George Utley, says that Miss Whittingham always believed it to be of All Faith's Parish..]

Blackiston, Nehemiah Hubert, s/o John and Eleanor Blackiston, m. Mary Cheseldine, d/o Kenelm and Chloe Cheseldine on 30 Jan 1772
Blackiston, Thomas, s/o Nehemiah Blackiston and Mary his wife, b. 10 Apr 1773
Blackiston, Kenelm, s/o N. H. Blackiston and Mary Blackiston, b. 24 Dec 1776
Blackiston, Mary, d/o N. H. Blackiston and Mary his wife, b. 6 Dec 1778
Blackiston, George, d/o N. H. Blackiston and Mary his wife, b. 6 Dec 1778
Bond, Richard, s/o John & Elizabeth Bond, m. Susanna Gardiner Key, s/o Dr. John and Cecilia Key on Sunday, 18 Jul 1773 at 9 o'clock in the morning by Rev. George Goldie
Bond, John Key, s/o Richard and Susanna Bond, b. 14 May 1774
Bond, Ann, d/o above, b. 13 May 1775
Bond, Cecilia Brown, d/o above, b. 17 Mar 1778

Volume 2, page 350:
Bond, Elizabeth Allaway, d/o Richard and Susanna Bond, b. 17 Jun 1779
Bond, Susanna Key, d/o Richard and Susanna Bond b. 2 Mar 1781
Goldsmith, William, s/o J. and Ann Goldsmith, b. 30 Dec 1776
Goldsmith, William, s/o J. and Ann Goldsmith, b. 20 May 1778
Mort, John, s/o Jos. and Eleanor Mort, b. 20 Jan 1774
Mort, James, s/o Jos. & Eleanor Mort, b. 2 Oct 1776

Bond, Matilda, d/o Richard and Susanna G. Bond, b. Tuesday 7 Jul 1784 at 3 o'clock in the evening

Bond, Samuel, s/o Richardand Susanna G. Bond, b. 16 Oct 1778

Bond, Clarissa, d/o Richard and Susanna G. Bond, b. 2 Jun 1790

Bond, William, d/o Richard and Susanna G. Bond, b. 2 Oct 1792

INDEX

Abbott, Jane, 84
Abell, Abner, 117
  Allethea, 117
  Ann Elizabeth Catharine, 138
  Ann, 113, 117, 126
  Arthur, 137
  Barbara, 111
  Benjamin, 100, 125
  Caleb, 93, 104, 119, 129, 134
  Catharine, 100, 125
  Clarke, 135
  Cuthbert, 93, 137
  Edmund, 110
  Edward, 100, 111, 125, 134
  Eleanor, 111, 116, 117
  Elizabeth, 93, 99, 100, 108, 109, 110, 111, 112, 119, 125, 126, 135, 138
  Francis, 108, 113, 134, 138
  George, 100, 108, 109, 119 126
  James Crane, 112
  James, 126
  Jane, 99, 100, 125, 136
  Janet, 110
  Jean, 110
  Jeremiah Williams, 119
  John Standfill, 126
  John, 99, 110, 111, 125, 126, 135
  Jonathan, 110
  Lucy, 88
  Martha H., 138
  Mary Elizabeth, 113
  Mary, 93, 104, 111, 119, 129, 136
  Matthew, 112
  Peter, 88
  Pharmel, 111
  Pollard, 109
  Rachel, 104
  Richard, 117
  Robert, 116
  Samuel, 100, 111, 116, 117, 125
  Sarah, 88, 111
  Stasia, 111
  Susanna, 100, 111, 125
  William C., 138
Adams, Abraham, 93, 112, 137
  Ann, 93, 112
  Austin, 93
  Dorothy, 112
  Elizabeth, 93, 112
  Enoch, 93
  George, 112, 113
  Hatton George, 107
  James, 107
  John, 112
  Mary, 107, 137
  Sarah, 112, 113, 137
  Susan, 113
Aderton, Sarah, 138
Adkinson, Joshua, 117
  Mary Brent, 117
  Susanna, 117
Ailing, Elizabeth, 58
  James, 58
  Jane, 58
  Margaret, 58
Aisquith, George, 137
  John, 135
  Sarah, 86
Allen, Anne, 22, 135
  Bartholomew, 3
  Charles, 61, 84
  Eleanor, 22, 71, 84
  Elizabeth, 54, 71

Index

Ja's, 7
John, 22
Joseph Davis, 7
Joseph, 3, 7
Mary, 50, 71
Pentheceelia, 3
Susannah, 7
Thomasin, 50, 54
William, 24, 50, 54, 71
Allison, Henry, 135
Anderson, James, 117
  John Baptist, 117
  John, 117
  Sarah, 136
  Tabitha, 117
Armsworthy, Aaron, 128
Allanson, Thomas, 46
Allein, Richard, 86
  William, 85
Allnutt, Sarah, 85
Allsup, Mary, 60
  Prisela, 60
  Rachell, 60
  Richard, 60, 86
  Sarah, 60
Allward, Anne, 22
  John, 22
  Margarett, 22
  Mary, 22
Ambler, Thos., 84
Amery, Ann, 6
  Catherine, 20
  Eleanor, 7
  John, 1, 20
  Lydia, 7
  Margaret, 9
  Mary, 1, 7, 10, 20
  Mary, Sr., 20
  Samuel John, 20
  Samuel, 1, 7, 10, 20

Samuel, Sr., 20
Thomas, 20
William, 20
Anderson, Ann, 88
  Chloe, 88
  Edward, 22
  Elizabeth, 107
  George, 22
  Henrietta, 88
  John, 22, 88
  Margaret, 107
  Mary, 22, 88
  Thomas, 88
  William, 107
Andrew, Patrick, 83
Appelton, James, 63
  Appelton, John, 56, 63
  Appelton, Mary, 63
  Elizabeth, 56, 63
Armsworthy, Aaron, 102
  Abraham, 88, 103, 128
  Ann, 90, 93
  Barton, 90
  Bennet, 92, 103, 128
  Daniel, 92
  Eleanor, 88, 102, 103, 128, 137
  Elizabeth, 113
  Frances, 116
  George, 92
  Henrietta, 93
  James, 90
  John, 88, 116, 135
  Jonathan, 93
  Katey, 116
  Mack, 92
  Mary, 102, 109, 128, 135
  Rebecca, 92
  Sarah, 92
  Susanna, 90
  Thomas, 92, 138, 113

Index

William, 102, 109, 128
Asborough, Thomas, 22
Ashbrooke, John, 22
Ashcom, Mary, 61, 83
  Nathaniel, 83
Ashman, Allward Hardy, 22
  Anne, 22
  Elizabeth, 22
  Mary, 22
  Richard, 22
  Standidge, 22
Askew, Anne, 78, 81
  Dinah, 77, 81
  Henry, 77
  James, 77
  Joseph, 78
  Mary, 78
  Michael, 78
  Susannah, 78
Askey, Mary, 85
Aurkhutt, Alexander, 83
  see Urquahart
Austin, Eleanor, 108
  Elizabeth, 108
  George, 108
  John, 84
  Priscilla, 108
Avis, Ann, 49, 58
  Dorcas, 55
  Jane, 49
  Jarvis, 58
  John, 86
  Robert, 49, 55, 58

Bacome, James T., 80
Baden, Elisabeth, 81
  Jeremiah, 81
Bagnall, Rebecka, 54
  Samuel, 54
  Sarah, 54

Bailey, Basil, 136
Baker, Andrew, 22
  Darkas, 137
  Ellinor, 49
  Isaack, 49
  John, 22, 83
  Martha, 22
  Mary, 82
  Nathaniel, 85
  Rebecca, 85
  Thomas, 22
  Violetta, 49
  William, 136
Baldwin, Lydia, 137
Bannister, Benjamin, 86
Bardburn, Susanna, 124
Barker, Margarett, 43
  Mary, 3
Barnes, Elizabeth, 23
  Godshall, 23
  Jane, 23
  Matthew, 23
  Richard, Jr., 138
Baron, John, 23
  Martha, 23
  Mary, 23
  Richard, 23
Barrett, William, 137
Barrot, Ann, 51
  Ellinor, 51
  James, 51
Barrow, see Baron, 23
Barrs, Leonard, 86
Barton, Ann, 83
  Betty, 87
  Catherine, 51, 83
  David, 23
  Easther, 52, 55
  Elizabeth, 23
  Eve, 62

Grace, 23
John, 52, 55, 62, 82
Nathan, 23
Postena, 51
Sarah, 55
Thomas, 23
William, 23, 51, 52, 62, 83
William, Jr., 23
Barze, Mary, 81
Bateman, Elizabeth, 23
George, 23
Bates, Ann, 92
Grace, 62
James, 62
John, 92
Lowry, 92
Mary, 62
Richard, 62
Sarah, 62
Susanna, 92
Baxter, Francis, 106
Margaret, 106
Bayly, James, 23
John, 23
Mary, 23
Beade, Mary, 23
Nicholas, 23
Sarah, 23
Beal, Josias, 135
Beane, Anne, 110
Barton, 110
Bennet, 102, 128
George, 110, 134
John, 136
Margaret, 102, 128
Robert, 102, 128
Walter, 44
Beck, Deborah, 137
Elizabeth, 23
Margarett, 23

Mary, 23
Richard, 23
Beckett, Humphrey, 87
John, 59
Rebekah, 59
Susannah, 59
Belaine, Elizabeth, 24
Grace, 24
Jemima, 24
John, 24, 42
Mary, 24
Nicholas, 24
___, 42
Bellsom, Jona'n, 63
Sarah, 63
Belt, Mary Skinner, 81
Benden, Elizabeth, 95, 120
John, 95, 120
Monica, 95, 120
Benjamin, Anne, 65
Bennett, James Lewis, 113
Margaret, 136
Pheebe, 113
William, 113
Bentley, Nancy, 136
Beveridge, John, 86
Margaret, 69
Beverly, Anastatia, 98, 124
George, 98, 116, 124
Jemima, 98, 124
Mary, 98, 116, 124
William, 116
Bigger, Ann, Mrs., 83
Margret, 83
Biggs, Charity, 1
Elinor, 1
Elizabeth, 1
John, 1
Priscilla, 1
Ruth, 1

Sarah, 1
Billingsley, Mrs., 134
Binnion, Elizabeth, 52
  John, 52
  Paslo, 52
  Thomas, 52
Birchmore, Margaret
  Rebekah, 115
  William, 115
Birmingham, Ann, 82
Biscoe, Ann Clarke, 112
  Basil, 137
  Eleanor, 111, 112
  Elizabeth, 135
  George Washington, 138
  Henrietta, 134
  James Lewis, 111
  Richard, 111, 112
  Thomas, 136
Blackburn, Barbara, 75
  Benjamin, 75
  Lydia, 85
  Sarah, 75
Blackett, Elizabeth, 83
Blackiston, Eleanor, 140
  George, 140
  John, 140
  Kenelm, 140
  Mary, 140
  Mary, 140
  Nehemiah Hubert, 140
  Thomas, 140
Blinkhorne, Martha, 52
  Mary, 52
  Robert, 52
Boarman, Batris, 94, 119
  Francis Ignatius, 94, 119
  Francis, 94, 119
  John, 94, 119
  Sarah, 94 120

Boguet, James, 86
Bohanan, Elizabeth, 91
  George, 91
  Jonathan, 91
Bond, Ann, 140
  Basil Duke, 80
  Benjamin Young Hance 80
  Benson, 80
  Cecilia Brown, 140
  Clarissa, 141
  Eleanor, 136
  Elizabeth Allaway, 140
  Elizabeth Masiah, 80
  Elizabeth, 86, 140
  James Alexander Chesley, 80
  James Alexander, 80
  James, 80
  Jas. A., 80
  John Key, 140
  John L., 80
  John Thos, 80
  John, 80, 140
  Juliet Ann, 80
  Mary Rebecca, 80
  Matilda, 141
  Rebecca, 86
  Richard, 140, 141
  Samuel, 141
  Sarah Howe, 80
  Sarah, 80, 82
  Susanna G., 141
  Susanna Key, 140
  Susanna, 136, 140
  Thos. H., 80
  Thos. Holdsworth, Dr., 80
  William, 141
Boney, Jane, 75
  Mary Dale Davidson, 75
  Thomas, 75, 86, 135
Bonner, Henry, 24, 43

Boon, Grace, 83
Booth, Ann, 131
  Eleanor, 96, 122
  Elizabeth, 99, 124
  George, 96, 122
  Ignatius, 96, 122
  Jane, 99, 124
  John Baptist, 99, 124
  John, 99, 124, 131
  Justinian, 122
  Leonard, 96, 122
  Mary, 96, 99, 122, 124, 131
  Rebecca, 96, 122
  Rodolph, 99, 124
  Sarah, 96, 122
  Thomas, 96, 122
Boswell, Elizabeth, 13
Bould, Catharine, 132
  Elizabeth, 108
  Henrietta, 132
  Jane, 132
  John Baptist, 132
  John, 132
  Mary Ann, 110
  Mary, 108, 110
  Mary, 132
  Monica, 132
  Susanna, 132
  William, 108, 110, 132
Bourne, Ann, 79
  Eleanor, 65
  Elizabeth, 57, 65
  George, 81
  James E., 79
  Jesse Jacob, 79
  Jesse, 65, 66, 67
  Rebecca, 66, 67
  Sarah, 66, 67
  Thomas, 57
Bowen, Anne, 85
  Barbara, 77
  Basil, 77
  Benj'm G., 82
  Benjamin, 77
  Cassandra, 85
  Charles, 77, 86
  David, 81
  Dinah, 77
  Elenor, 77
  Elisabeth Godsgrace, 81
  Elisabeth, 81, 82
  Isaac Godsgrace, 81
  Isaac, 81
  James G., 82
  John, 77, 85
  Martha, 77, 81
  Mary, 77
  Parker, 77
  Rebecca, 77, 81
  Sarah, 81, 138
  Susannah, 82
Bowes, Eleanor, 97, 122
  Joseph, 88
  Mary, 88, 96, 122
  Timothy, 88, 96, 122
Bowld, Elizabeth, 24
  Jane, 24
  Mary Anne, 24
Bowling, James, 44
Boyle, Barbara, 52
  Catherine, 52
  David, 52, 55
  Sarah, 52, 55
Boyse, Elenor, 24
  John, 24
  William, 24
Brabant, Wm., 83
Bradburn, Anastatia, 89
  Ann, 89, 103
  Benjamin, 89, 103

Catherine, 103
Eleanor, 103
Elizabeth, 99, 124
James, 103
John Baptist, 99, 124
Margaret, 103
Mark, 99, 124
Mary Ann, 103
Mary, 89
Matthew, 89
Notley, 103
Sarah, 103
Susanna, 99
Bradford, Mary, 137
Brady, Rebecca, 69
Brawner, Henry, 24
John, 24
Mary, 24
Brayne, Jane, 24
Breeden, Aaron, 92
Elizabeth, 98, 118, 124
Enoch, 98, 118, 124
James, 92
Joseph, 86
Mark, 137
Robert Hammett, 118, 136
Sarah, 92, 118
Brent, Elizabeth, 1
George, 1
Jane, 1
Mary, 1, 117
Nicholas, 1
Robert, 1
Susanna, 1
William, 117
Brice, John, 134
Briscoe, Anne, 7
Casandra, 7
Eleanor Wilson, 8
Elizabeth, 14

Hezekiah, 8, 9, 14
John, 7
Margaret, 8
Mary, 9
Philip, 2, 7
Ralph, 7
Susanna, 7, 8, 9, 14
Walter, 14
Britton, William, 44
Broady, Elisabeth, 19
Brook, Anne, 81
Broome, Ann, 49, 51, 52, 58, 85
Betty Heighe, 74
Henry, 49
James Mackall, 74
John, 49, 51, 52, 58, 74
Mary, 51, 61
Thomas, 58
Brown, Allusia, 109
Ann, 98, 108
Anna, 124
Anthony, 97, 103, 123, 128
Benedict, 97, 123
Chloe, 108
Dorothy, 97, 123
Dryden, 108
Eleanor, 106, 109
Elizabeth, 24, 41
Frances, 97, 98, 106, 110, 123, 124, 130
Gerrard, 24
Heneretta, 109
Jereboam, 98, 124
John Baptist, 109
John Barton, 109
John, 24
Leander, 109
Leonard, 108
Lucy, 109
Martin, 108

Mary, 97, 103, 123, 128, 130
Monica, 103, 128
Nicholas, 109
Peter, 98, 106, 108, 110, 124, 130
Raphael, 109
Rebecca, 109, 97, 108, 123
Thomas, 24
William, 85
Winifred, 109
Bruce, Elizabeth, 6, 17
Bryan, Mary, 2
  Susannah, 135
  William, 2
Buchanan, Aaron, 117
  Aron, 137
  Eleanor, 110
  Elizabeth, 105, 129
  George, 105, 117, 129
  Margaret, 117
  Moses, 110, 135
  Rebecca, 105
  William Thompson, 110
Buckingham, Anne, 76
  John, 76, 79, 84
  Katharine, 76
  Martha, 76, 79
  Mary, 76
  Rebeccah, 76
  Sarah, 76, 79
  Thomas, 76
Bulkley, Olcott, Rev., 80
Bullott, Benjamin, 24
  Elizabeth, 24
  Joseph, 24
Bumnalley, Andrew, 83
Burch, Benjamin, 15
  John, 6
  Justinian, 12
  Martha, 18

Mary, 6
Orpah, 6
Burdit, Elizabeth, 24
  Francis, 24
  Parthenia, 24
  Sarah, 24, 29
  Thomas, 24, 29
  Verlinda, 24
Burnet, Stephen, 137
  Henry, 137
Bussey, Edward, 82
Button, Roger, 86
Byrn, Eleanor, 69

Cable, John, 28
Cage, John, 41
Caine, John, 24
Cammell, Bridgitt, 56
  James, 56
  William, 56
Campbell, Frances, 10
  Gustavus Brown, 8
  Isaac, 8, 11
  Isaac, Rev., 8, 9, 10, 11, 19, 20
  Jane, 8, 9, 10
  Jean, 11
  William, 9
  __mes, 11
Canter, Truman, 15
Carico, Abel, 4
  Elisabeth, 4
  Mary Ann, 4
Carpenter, Elizabeth, 115
  George, 115
  William, 115
Carr, Grace, 24, 36
Carrico, Katherine, 17
Carter, Elizabeth, 135
  Henry, 134
Cartwright, Hezekiah, 10

Jesse, 9, 10
Judith, 10
Margaret, 9, 10
Mary, 9
Causens, Eleanor, 112
Gerard N., 112, 134
Ignatius, 25
Jane Pope Row, 112
Jane, 25
William, 25
Cawood, Mary, 14
Cay, Jonathan, Rev, 61, 52, 59, 60, 62, 63 84
Madam, 52
Chandler, Jane, 25
Mary, 25, 29
William, 25, 35
Wm., Col, 29
Chapman, Elizabeth, 25
Lucretia, 4
Mary, 25
Thomas, 25
Chapple, Elizabeth, 83
Charleson, Charles, 25
Charlton, Jean, 86
Cherrybub, Elizabeth, 25
John, 25
Mary, 25
Walter, 25
William, 25
Cheseldine, Chloe, 140
Kenelm, 140
Mary, 140
Seneca, 135
Chesley, Elizabeth, 135
John, 86
Mary E., 114
Mary, 135
Cheverlin, Jesse, 135
Chew, Samuel, 48

Chilton, Cuthbert, 82, 54
John, 54
Mary, 54
Ching, Elinor, 5
John, 5
Mary, 5
Chittam, Charles, 52
Dorothy, 83
John, 52
Mary, 52
Choram, Ann, 137
Chrisman, Elisabeth, 93
John, 93
Luke, 93
Chunn, Andrew, 9, 13
Aquila, 5, 16
Benjamin, 1, 2
Cassandra, 2, 5
Charity, 11
Charles Courts, 11, 20
Chloe, 1
Deborah, 13 14
Elizabeth W__n, 16
Elizabeth, 5, 10
Heneritta, 11
John Thomas, 12
Jonathan, 10
Judith, 10
Lancelot, 10
Levi, 2
Mary, 5, 16
Mersilva, 5
Rebekah, 1, 2
Sam'l, Capt., 6
Samuel, 5, 14, 16
Susanna, 5, 6, 134
Thomas, 10
Virlinder, 13
Walter, 5
Winifred, 12, 13

Zachariah, 11, 13, 14
Cissell, Anastatia, 115
  Ann, 95, 107, 108, 119, 120
  Baptist, 95, 120
  Bernard, 117
  Catharine, 111
  Delbert, 94, 119
  Dorothy, 96, 122
  Edmund Barton, 117
  Elizabeth, 95, 104, 117, 120, 121
  Henrietta, 94
  Henrietta, 115
  Ignatius, 95, 104, 117, 120
  James Rodolph, 95, 120
  James, 95, 104, , 117, 121
  Jeremiah, 105
  John Baptist, 104, 105, 107, 108
  John, 94, 96, 107, 115, 119, 121
  Joseph, 95, 107, 120
  Margaret, 96, 121
  Mary, 104, 107, 111, 115
  Matthew, 107, 108
  Peter, 95, 121
  Rebecca, 95, 104, 105, 120
  Shedrick, 96, 121
  Susanna, 117
  Thomas, 104
  Wilford, 104
  William, 95, 111, 120, 137
Clagett, Elizabeth, 67
  Rev. Dr., 81
  Richard Dorsey, 67
  Samuel, 67
  Thomas John, Rev., 86, 87
Clare, Ann, 69
  Elizabeth, 69, 84
  Isaac, 84
  John, 69, 84
  Rebecca, 69

William, 69
Clarke, Ambros, 25
  Ann, 89, 108
  Eleanor, 89, 97, 105, 123
  Elizabeth, 108, 136
  George, 138
  John, 25, 89, 97, 123
  Joshua, 105, 108
  Mary, 89, 105, 108
  Richard Langhorn, 97, 123
  Robert, 89
  Susanna, 108
  Thomas, 108
  William, 136, 138
Clarkson, Henry, 14
Clash, John, 25
  Mary, 25
  Nicholas, 25
Clocker, Benjamin, 137
  Elizabeth, 134
Clouder, Elizabeth, 27
  Temperance, 27
Clowe, Catharine, 139
  James, 117, 139
  John, 117
  Mary, 117, 139
  Susanna, 139
Cobb, James, 55
  Paul, 55
  CSarah, 55
Cobbart, Ann, 86
Cockram, Edward, 4
  Nathan, Jr., 4
  Sarah, 4
Cockshett, Thomas, Rev., 48, 83
Coe, Ann, 73
  Elizabeth, 73
  Samuel, 73
  William, 73
Cofer, Elizabeth, 25

John, 25
Mary, 25
Sarah, 25
Thomas, 25
Coghill, Christian, 25
James, 25
William, 25
Cogwell, Anne, 26
Christian, 26
James, 26
William, 26
Cole, Ann, 90, 115, 131
Francis, 90, 115, 131
James, 1
John, 26
Mary Ann, 131
Mary, 26
Philip, 26
Susanna, 115
Winifred, 90
Collason, Mary, 137
Collenbr, Alice, 60
Elizabeth
John, 60
Rebaca, 60
Thomas, 60
Colley, James, 21
Mary, 21
William, 21
Collings, Mary, 51
Robert, 51, 83
Thomas, 51
Collison, Elizabeth, 137
Collosen, Anne, 135
Combes, Barbara, 132
Bennet, 132
Eleanor, 131
Elizabeth, 132
Margaret, 131
Mary Ann, 131

Mary, 132
Raphael, 131
William, 131
Compton, Alexander, 9
Barton, 9
Elinor, 31
Elizabeth, 9, 14
John, 9, 31
Marget, 13
Matthew, 9
Rachel, 9
Susanna, 9, 14
William, 14, 20
Connelly, Ann Chloe, 131
Rhodolph, 131
Constable, Grace, 83
Cooke, Benjamin, 91
Catharine, 91
Elizabeth Lander, 73
George, Rev., 69
Jane, 90, 91
Joanna, 91
Susannah, 90
Thomas, 90
Cooksey, Christian, 4
Elinor, 5
Elizabeth, 4, 12, 13
Henry, 8
Jane, 13
John, 4
Justinian, 4, 5
Mary, 4
Samuel, 4
Sarah, 4, 5, 12, 20
Susanna, 4
Thomas Reed, 8, 12, 13
___tny, 8
_____, 8
Cooper, Anne, 26
Henrietta, 115

Henry, 114
John, 26
Mary, 114
Nicholas, 26
Penelope, 26
Prudence, 26
Susanna, 114
William, 115
Copsey, Enock, 140
John L., 140
Corner, Gilbert, 26
_____, 26
Cornish, Edward, 26
Elizabeth, 26
John, 26
Margarett, 26
Martha, 26
Richard, 26
Corum, Barbara, 111
Isaac, 111
James and, 138
John Rollins, 111
Cosleton, Marie, 26
Robert, 26
Cotterell, Elizabeth, 26
James, 26
Jane, 26
Cotton, Sarah, 85
Courts, Anne, 26
Charity, 11, 26, 27
Elizabeth, 27
John, 26, 27
Margarett, 27
Covene, Mary, 83
Cowen, Elizabeth, 85
Mary, 85
Cox, Anne, 27
James, 27
Jane, 135
John, 136

Margarett, 27
Thomasine, 27
Crafford, Addam, 58
Mary, 58
Richard, 83
Susanna, 58
Craghill, Elizabeth, 135
Craigg, Eleanor, 116
Elizabeth, 116
Jesse, 116
Peter, 116
Rachel, 116, 135
Reuben, 116
Sarah, 116
Crane, Elizabeth, 64, 65
James A., 111, 112
James, 111
Jane, 64, 65
Mary, 65, 111, 112
William Samuel, 112
Creed, Easther, 83
Crichard, John, 60
Tommison, 60
Crompton, Catherine, 65
Mary, 65
Thomas, 65
Croson, Charles, 51, 57
John, 51
Lydia, 11
Martha, 51, 57
Mary, 51
Thomas, 11
Zepheniah, 11
Cullember, Casse, 81
Mary, 84
Nathaniel, 85
Sarah, 84
Thomas, 84
Culpepper, Ellinor, 48, 51
John, 51

Mary, 48
Michael, 48, 51, 83
Currant, Grace, 84
Cushman, Ann, 129
  Eleanor, 129
  James, 129
  John, 129
  Mary, 129
  William, 129

Daffin, Robert, 136
Daft, Elizabeth, 97, 117, 123
  John Baptist, 117
  Mary, 97, 123
  William, 97, 117, 123
Daley, Charles, 114, 139
  Daniel, 114, 139
  Eleanor, 114
  Susanna, 114, 139
Dant, Mary, 134
Dare, Elizabeth, 72
  Mary, 86
  Nathaniel, 85
  Sarah, 86
  Susanna, 67
Davidson, Jean, 135
Davis, Alexander, 15
  Ann, 5, 6, 13, 17, 18, 19
  Barton, 5
  Benjamin, 14, 17, 19, 20
  Catherine, 15
  Charity, 6, 10, 12, 13, 17, 18, 19
  Chloe, 6, 15, 20
  Cornelious, 5
  Eleanor, 17
  Elizabeth Reeder, 16
  Elizabeth, 5, 9, 15, 27
  Essac Young, 14
  Francis, 14
  George, 10, 15

  Henrietta, 12
  Hope, 10
  Isaac, 13
  James, 9
  Jane, 15, 136
  John, 27, 56
  Joseph, 3, 86
  Joshua, 10, 13
  Luke, 5, 6
  Lydia, 13, 14
  Margaret, 12, 13, 14, 16
  Martha, 56
  Mary R__my, 15
  Mary, 3, 5, 14, 20, 27
  Moses, 12, 135
  Notley, 3
  Pamela, 20
  Peter, 6, 10, 19
  Philip, 15, 20
  Priscilla, 5
  Rachel, 12
  Randolph, 6, 15
  Rebecca, 14, 15
  Rhoda, 14
  Sarah, 12, 13, 82
  Solome, 3
  Susanna, 3, 6
  Thomas Blackman, 18
  Thomas, 9, 27, 56
  Violetta, 13
  William, 14, 15, 56
  William, Jr., 14
  Winifred, 14
  Zacchius, 12, 13, 14, 16
Dawkins, Anne, 50, 63, 75
  Barbara, 73, 74
  Benet, 50
  Benjamin, 64
  Charles, 64, 75
  Dorcas, 64, 69, 75

Index

Elizabeth, 50, 64
James, 50, 51, 64
James, Jr., 64
Jesse, 65
Joseph, 49, 51, 64
Mary, 63, 64, 65
Rebecca, 50, 64, 69, 75
Sarah, 49, 51, 64
William, 50, 63, 64, 65, 69, 75, 84
Dawson, Elizabeth, 27
  John, 27
  Mary, 27
Day, Benjamin, 66
  Daniel, 66
  Eleanor, 66, 81
  Elizabeth, 70
  Jane, 70
  Rebecca, 70
  Sarah, 81
  William, 70
Delaine, Margrett, 83
Delamere, David, 82
  Sarah, 62
Dement, Anne, 2, 10, 17
  Benajah, 2
  Dorcus, 2
  Eleanor, 17
  Elizabeth, 2, 9, 17
  George, 2
  Jesse, 2
  John Fenley, 17
  John, 17
  Lydia, 6
  Mary, 2, 6, 10, 17
  Susannah, 2, 18
  Walter, 10
  William, 2, 6, 10, 17, 18
Demilliane, Ann, 51, 52
  Elizabeth, 51

Gabriel, 48, 52, 82
Gabril, Rev., 51, 52, 84
Dent, Alexander, 15
Anne, 3, 10, 12, 27
Benjamin, 114
Catherine, 3, 15
Charles Francis, 138
Charles, 138
Choloe, 17
Drusilla, 18
Elizabeth, 11, 27, 28
Esther, 3, 13, 15
George, 27
Hatch, 3, 16, 18
Hatch, Rev., 19
Hezekiah, 3, 15, 16, 18, 113
James Hammett, 114
James Thomas, 113
James, 12
John Baptist, 15
John Chapman, 18
John Shelton, 20
John, 3, 12, 15, 20
Joseph Chappelear, 114
Jutith, 18
Lucinda, 18
Lydia, 3, 14
Margaret, 12, 15
Martha Ann, 114
Martha Matilda, 113
Martha, 16, 18
Mary Ann
Mary, 3, 18, 20
Peter, 27
Rebeckah, 12
Rhoda, 3, 12
Sarah M.
Sarah Matilda, 113
Susan, 139
Susanna, 113

Thomas E., 113
Thomas Edward, 138
Thomas Hatch, 12
Thomas, 28, 114, 139
William, 27, 28, 29
_____, 18
Denton, Edward, 85
  Jno., 82
  Priscilla, 82
  Rennis, 136
Dever, Elizabeth, 52
  Gilbert, 52
  Grace, 52
Deverell, Anne, 28
  Elizabeth, 28
  Thomas, 28
Dickason, Jeremy, 28
  Thomas, 28
Diggs, Wm., 29
Dillihay, John, 133
  Joseph, 133
  Stephen, 133
  Winifred, 133
Dillion, Anne, 134
Dillman, Margaret, 135
Dilworth, William, 87
Dixon, Benjamin, 50, 67
  Lydia, 81
  Mary, 50, 67
  Obed, 57, 67
  Phebe, 86
  Robert, 50, 57, 67, 82
  Ruth, 50, 57, 67
  Sarah, 67
  Thomas, 28
Dod, Anne, 28
  John, 28
  Mary, 28
  Richard, 28
Dogan, Ann, 93

  Eleanor, 93
  James, 93
  Jeremiah, 92
  John, 93
  Monica, 92
  Thomas, 92
  William, 93
Donaldson, John, Rev., 6
Dooley, Elinor, 2
  Elizabeth, 2
  James, 2
  John, 2
  Thomas Read, 2
Dorans, John, 114
Dorman, John, 52
  Mary, 52
Dorrumple, Betty, 63
  Grace, 63
  John, 63, 83, 84
  Rebecca, 63
  William, 63
Dorsey, Anne, 65
  Elizabeth, 65
  James, 65
  Phillip, 65
  Rebecca, 65
Dossey, Martha, 69
  Philip, 69
Dotron, Elenor, 81
Dougan, Eleanor, 137
Douglas, Ann, 57
  James, 57
  Sarah, 57
Downes, Ann, 89
  Elizabeth, 89
  Ignatius, 89
  John, 89
  Joseph, 89
  Mary, 89
  Robert, 28

Index

Downing, Abednago, 17, 18
  Anne, 18
  Eleanor, 17
  Lydia, 18
  Milicent, 18
Duffey, Anne, 1
  Cassandra, 1
  Elizabeth, 1
  Leonard, 1
  Martha, 1
  Patrick, 1
Duglas, Catherine, 28
  Elizabeth, 28
  John, 28
  Mary, 28
Duke, Ann P., 78
  Basil, 79
  Elizabeth, 48
  James, 48, 79, 80
  James, Dr., 80
  Martha, 48, 83
  Mary, 80, 81
  Nathaniel, 80
  Rebecca, 79, 80
  Sarah Broome, 80
  Sarah, 80
Dungerman, Christopher, 58
  Elizabeth, 58, 59
  Lothea Renard, 59
  Rennis Rennar, 58
  Stephen, 59
Durkhurt, Alexander, 49
  Ann, 49
  Margaret, 49
Dusheel, Benjamin, 87
Dutton, Elizabeth, 28
  Matthew, 28
  Notley, 28
  Thomas, 28
Dyson, Abigail, 6, 7

Adeline, 21
Amelia, 13
Andrew, 14
Ann, 5
Anna, 12, 13
Anne E., 21
Barton, 7
Bennet, 5, 12, 13, 14
Dorcas, 11, 12, 14
Elisabeth, 10
Esther, 13, 18
James, 6, 11
John Baptist, 5, 12
John, 12, 13
Joseph, 10, 12, 13
Maddox, 5
Margaret, 12
Mary, 5, 6, 11
Philip, 5
Richard, 21
Samuel Turner, 12
Thomas Andrew, 10
Thomas, 5, 6, 13, 18
Thomas, Jr., 5
Walter, 13
William, 18
Winifred, 10, 12, 13, 14
Zepheniah, 6
Rebekah, 6
Sarah, 6

Easterling, Elizabeth, 50
  Henritta, 49
  Henry William, 49
  Henry, 50
  John, 49
  Martha, 50
  Mary, 50
Eden, Rebecca, 135
Edgar, Elizabeth, 28

Index

Joanna, 28
John, 28
Richard, 28
Sarah, 8, 11, 28
William, 28
Edmonds, Dolly, 81
Easorn, 81
Edwards, Ann Chloe, 98, 123
Elizabeth, 98, 123
Henrietta, 98, 123
Jane, 133
John, 98, 123, 133, 137
Egan, Barnaby, 71, 72
Henrietta Reeder, 71
Henrietta, 71, 72
Susanna, 72
Thomas Henry, 71
Elliott, Joan, 29
William, 29
Ellsom, Elizabeth, 63
Ellt, Benjamin, 62, 65
Elizabeth, 52, 56, 62, 84
Ellinor, 56, 59, 62, 65
Henry, 52, 56, 62, 83
Margrit, 83
Mary, 59, 63
Rebekah, 62, 86
Thomas, 52
William, 59, 62
Emerson, Nicholas, 29
William, 29
Emmatt, Alce, 51
John, 51
William, 51
Emory, Thomas, 135
Emson, James, 52
Rebeckah, 52
Ettye, Arthur, 29
Elizabeth, 29
Rachell, 29

Evans, Alice, 85
Ann, 111 131, 135
Daniel, 111
Elizabeth, 131
Jane Abell, 113
Jane Elizabeth, 113
Jane, 111
John B., 113
Martha, 82
Mary, 131
Patty, 113
Philip, 131
Richard, 111, 113, 138
Sarah, 113
Everist, Mary, 81

Farlor, see Farlowe, 29
Farlowe, Ambros, 29
William, 29
Farr, Henrietta, 20
Mary, 5
Farrand, Catherine, 5, 19
Elisabeth, 17, 19
Hezekiah, 8
John, 5, 8, 9, 10, 12, 19
Marget, 19
Mark, 9
Mary, 5, 8, 9, 10, 12, 19
Susannah, 19
Thomas, 5, 19
William, 19
Zephaniah, 12
Fendall, Josias, 29, 44
Samuel, 29
Fenwick, Catharine, 133
Eleanor, 133
John, 133
Monica, 133
William, 133
Fidgarrill, Elliner, 83

Index

Fielder, Nicholas, 135
Files, Ann, 92
  John, 92
  Sarah, 92
  Thomas, 92
  William, 92
Finnacy, Ann, 96, 109, 122
  John Archibald, 96, 122
  Joseph Normand Mack, 96, 122
  Mary Ann, 96, 122
  Rosanna, 109
  Stephen, 96, 109, 122
Fish, Ann, 102, 128
  Bennet, 91
  Elizabeth, 91
  James, 91
  Jennet, 102, 103, 128
  Priscilla, 118
  Robert, 103, 118, 128
  Thomas, 91
  William, 102, 103, 128
Fitzhugh, Mary E. Chesley, 114
  William, 114
Fleet, Sarah, 86
Flower, Barbary, 138
  Charles, 135
  Joseph, 138
  Thomas, 136
Floyd, Jesse, 137
Ford, Anastatia, 130
  Charles, 107
  Clare, 107
  Edward, 29, 46
  Eleanor, 107
  Elizabeth, 29, 46
  Ignatius, 130
  John Francis, 130
  Peter, 130
  Philip, 107
  Posthuma, 29
Fordinandoe, Agatha, 29
  Elinor, 29
  Peter, 29
Forgisson, Christian, 55
  Elizabeth, 52, 55
  Ellinor, 56
  John, 52, 55, 56
  Mary, 52
Forrest, Ann, 98, 124
  Nancy, 110
  Richard, 98, 124
  Uriah, 110
  Zachariah, 98, 110, 124
Fowke, Anne, 28, 29
  Elizabeth, 28, 29
  Frances, 29
  Gerard, 29
  Katherine, 29
  Mary, 29
  Sarah, 29
Fowler, Agnis, 58
  Catherine, 64
  Dorothy, 58
  George, 64
  Joseph, 64
  Margaret, 110
  Parker, 64
  Peter, 58, 82
  Sarah, 110
Fraizer, Anne, 70
  Betty H., 81
  Catherine, 70
  Chaney, 70
  Charles, 70
  China, 85
  Elizabeth, 70
  James Hasletine, 70
  James, 70
  Margaret, 70, 72

160 Index

Mary, 70
Franklin, Elizabeth, 57
  Grace, 57
  Henry, 29
  Jane, 29
  Mary, 29
  Thomas, 57, 84
Freeland, Martha, 86
Freeman, Abraham, 58
  Cassander, 56
  Elizabeth, 68
  George, 56, 57, 58
  Isaac, 56
  Israel, 81
  John, 68
  Mary, 52
  Rachel, 56, 57, 58
  Richard, 52
French, Anastatia, 116
  Ann, 96, 121
  Bennet, 96, 121
  Bernadine, 96, 121
  Elizabeth, 96, 107, 108, 121
  Ignatius, 107, 108, 116
  Jane, 108
  Jeremiah, 99, 124
  John, 96, 108, 121
  John, Jr., 116
  Joseph, 107
  Mary, 107, 116
  Monica, 96, 116, 121
  Peter, 108
  Philip, 108
  Rinah, 99, 124
  Rodolph, 99, 124
  Susanna, 99, 116, 125
  William, 99, 124
Fryar, John Edward Henry, 71
  Mary, 71
  William, 71

Zachariah, 71

Gabril, Elizabeth, 49
  Richard, 49
Galimore, Ellinor, 51
  George, 51
  Jane, 51
Games, Martha, 85
  Mary, 85
Gantt, Betty Heighe, 74
  Mary, 81
Gardiner, Elizabeth, 84
  Isaac, 85, 137
  John, 52, 82
  Kinsey, 85
  Rebeckah, 52
  Robert, 52
  William, 86
Garlick, John, 52
Garner, Anne, 59
  Dorcas, 59
  Elizabeth, 58, 59
  Jacob, 59
  James, 58
  Mary, 59
  Matthew, 58, 59
  Rachel, 59
  Sarah, 59
Garrett, Charles, 29
  Joyce, 29
Geer, Anne, 30
  George, 30
  Mary, 30
  Sarah, 30
Gibbons, Francis, 135
Gibson, Elizabeth, 30, 80, 82
  James Richard, 80
  Peter, 79, 80
  Sarah, 85
  Thomas, 30

Index

Gill, Barton, 17
  Charles, 17
  Druscilla, 20
  Elizabeth, 13, 19, 20, 21
  George, 20
  John, 13, 14, 17, 18, 19, 20, 21
  Joseph Allen, 14
  Lydia, 17
  Mary Anne, 19
  Robert, Jr., 6
  Susanah, 13, 14, 17, 18, 19
  Ursilla, 20
  _____, 21
Glasgow, Elizabeth, 16
  Hezekiah, 16
Glover, Richard, 83
Godfrey, George, 30, 39
  Mary, 30
  Thomas, 30
  William, 30
Godgrace, John, 84
Goldie, George, Rev., 140
Goldsbury, Athanatius, 113
  Charles, 90
  Christian, 90
  Diann, 58
  James, 136
  Jonathan, 90
  Mary, 113
  Robert, 58
  Thomas Maynard, 58
Goldsmith, Ann, 140
  J., 140
  William, 140
Good, Ann, 15
  Catherine, 15
  Cloe, 15
  Elizabeth, 15
  Thomas, 15
  William, 15

Goodin, Susannah, 137
Goodrick, Mary, 30
  Robert, 30
Goodrum, James, 7, 9
  Mary, 9
  Susannah, 7
  William, 7
Goos, Anne, 30
  George, 30
  Mary, 30
  Sarah, 30
Gough, Anastatia, 98, 124
  Ann, 131
  Benjamin, 101, 127, 131
  Britainnia, 131
  Charles, 101, 127
  Elizabeth, 98, 124
  James, 98, 124
  Jane, 98, 124
  John Baptist, 98, 124
  Margaret, 70
  Mary, 101, 127
  Matthew, 98, 124
  Rebecca, 101, 127
  Salathael, 85
  Susanna, 98, 101, 124, 127, 131
  Thomas, 85
Goureley, Barbary, 30
  Elizabeth, 30
  John, 30
  Thomas, 30
Gowndril, George, 105
  George, Rev., 105
  Hannah, 105
  Katherine, 105
Graves, Alice, 30
  George, 30
  Jeremiah, 135
  John, 30
Gray, Agnes, 82

Ann, 7, 8, 9, 10
Eleanor, 10, 19
Elizabeth Sheredine, 85
Elizabeth, 65, 66, 74
George, 7
James, 7, 66
Jane, 65, 66
Jean, 85
John, 65, 66, 74, 84, 137
Joseph, 9
Katharine, 8
Margaret, 65, 85
Martha, 51, 86
Mary, 74, 86
Rebecca, 65, 66, 74, 85
Samuel, 65
Sarah, 74
Thomas, 51, 74, 85
William, 7, 8, 9, 10, 51, 74, 83
Greene, Elizabeth, 30
Francis, 30
Leonard, 30
Mary, 30
Robert, 30
Verlinda, 30
William, 30
Greenfield, Kisia, 87
Greenwell, Ann, 102
Ann, 128
Austin, 133
Benedict, 129
Bennet, 101, 127, 133
Charles, 101, 126
Edward, 101, 126
Eleanor, 97, 101, 123, 126
Elizabeth, 101, 127, 129, 132, 133
Emma Ransean Anna, 99, 125
Frances, 99, 125
George, 133

Hannah, 101, 127
Henry, 99, 125
Ignatius, 102, 127
James, 97, 101, 123, 127
Jane, 101, 102, 126, 127
Jeremiah, 129
John Basil, 97, 123, 129
John, 101, 126
Joseph, 99, 101, 125, 127, 133
Joshua Leonard, 97, 123
Justinian, 129, 133
Mary Ann, 129
Mary, 102, 128, 129
Noah, 129
Philip, 102, 128, 132
Richard, 99, 101, 125, 126
Stephen, 136
Susanna, 129
Thomas, 102, 128
William, 101, 102, 127
Winifred, 102, 128, 132
Greves, Absolom, 136
Ann, 116
Elizabeth, 57
James, 83
Jeremiah Adkey, 116
Margaret, 57
Robert, 57, 83
Thomas, 116
Griffin, Mary, 81, 86, 136
Thomas, 137
Grogan, Anastatia, 133
Catharine, 133
Grover, Anne, 85
Mary, 84
Priscilla, 81
Groves, Alice, 30, 31
Elizabeth, 30
George, 30, 31
William, 31

Index   163

Gruder, Elizabeth, 137
Gruther, Catharine, 135
Guy, Charles, 31
　Elizabeth, 31
Gwynn, Anne, 31
　Christopher, 31
　Susanna, 31
Gyatt, Mary, 83

Hackett, Ann, 101, 127
　Henrietta, 101, 127
　Joshua, 98, 123
　Mary Magdalene, 98, 123
　Mary, 98, 101, 127
　Rhode, 101
　Rhodolph, 98, 123, 127
Haddert, Elizabeth, 18
Hagar, Millburn, 136
Hall, Ann Mary, 125
　Ann, 91
　Arthur, 110
　Benjamin, 91
　Bennet, 91
　Catharine, 110, 118, 125
　Dorothy, 88
　Elinor, 3
　Elizabeth, 91
　Frances, 118
　George, 125
　Henry, 118, 125
　Ignatious, 3
　John Basil, 126
　John, 31
　Joseph, 88, 91, 135
　Mary, 3, 31, 36, 88, 91
　Priscilla, 91
　Rebecca, 3, 110
　Richard, 31, 36
　Thomas Lant, 3
　Thomas, 88

　William, 31
Hamilton, Jonathan, 106
　Margaret Abell, 106
　Philemon, 106
Hammet, Ann, 103, 104, 105, 107
　Bennet, 105, 134, 139
　Cartwright, 103, 128
　Catharine Hebb, 113
　Catharine, 110, 112, 113
　Dolly, 100, 126
　Dorcus, 139
　Elizabeth, 103
　Elizabeth
　Frances, 100, 103, 105
　Francis, 126
　George Alexander, 112
　Henny, 126
　Henrietta, 100, 126
　Henry, 100
　James, 109
　John, 103, 104, 107, 109
　John, Jr., 105, 110
　Johnson, 92
　Luther, 113
　Margaret, 103, 128
　Margery, 103, 105, 109
　Mary, 100, 126
　McKelvie, 100, 104, 105, 107, 126
　Rebecca, 92
　Richard, 100, 126
　Robert, 92, 112, 113, 134
　Sarah, 100, 113, 126
　Sophia, 138
　Susanna, 138
　William, 103
Hammond, Ann, 132
　Susanna, 132
　Uel, 132

Hance, Ann, 77
  Benjamin, 86
  Francis, 77
  Harriet, 77
  John, 77
  Margaret, 86
  Mary Ann, 77
  Samuel, Jr., 85
  Sarah Elizabeth Chesley, 80
Hanning, Caleb, 135
Hanson, Anne, 31
  John, 31
  Mary, 31
Harbutt, Jno., 83
Hardesty, Mary, 86
Harding, Elizabeth, 134
Hardy, Henry, 31
Harper, Elizabeth, 133
  Henrietta, 133
  James, 133
  Mary Ann, 133
  Mary, 133
  Rebecca, 133
Harris, Austin, 100, 126
  Betty, 81
  Elisabeth, 81, 100, 126
  Jane, 112
  John, 31
  Joseph, 81, 112
  Martha, 112
  Mary, 31
  Richard, 31, 86
  Samuel, 100, 126
  Susanna, 31, 112
  Thomas, 31, 40
  William, 81
  Zachariah, 100
  Zacharias, 126
  _____, 31
Harrisson, Catherine, 31

  Elizabeth, 31
  Jane, 31, 32
  Joseph, 31
  Mary, 31
  Richard, 31, 32
  Tabitha, 32
Haseltine, Ann, 59
  Charles, 59, 60, 84
  Catherine, 60
  Eleanor, 59, 60
Hasler, Elizabeth, 114
  Henrietta, 114
  Richard, 114
  William, 114
Haw, Mary, 7
Hawkings, Mary, 32
  Sarah, 32
  William, 32
Hawkins, Alexander Smith, 32
  Henry, 32
  Henry, Jr., 32
  John, 8
Hayden, Abram, 138
Haywood, Thomas, 136
Hazell, John, 50, 52, 82
  Mary, 50, 52
Headlow, Edith, 32
Hearben, Allen, 1
  Elisah, 1
  Elizabeth, 1
  Rachel, 1
Heard, Ann, 101, 126
  Hellen, 101, 126
  John, 101, 126
  Mary, 101, 126
Heath, Ann Elizabeth, 112
  Kitty, 112
  Thomas, 112
Hebb, Ann, 138
Hebedine, Thomas, 83

Index

Hechky, Elizabeth, 15
Hellen, Alexd'r, 61
  Ann Parran, 88
  Ann, 71, 72, 75, 81
  Barbara, 72
  Benjamin, 72, 74
  David, 49, 52, 53, 64, 88
  Dorcas, 85
  Elizabeth, 67, 85
  George Aisquith, 88
  James, 53, 71, 72, 75, 85
  Jane, 61, 62, 63, 64, 75, 88
  John, 53
  Joseph Johnson, 79
  Maria, 79
  Mary, 63, 67, 71, 72, 75, 81, 85, 135
  Penelope, 52, 71, 72
  Peter, 52, 61, 62, 63, 64, 71, 72
  Rebeker, 79
  Richard, 49, 67, 72
  Susan, 62
  Susanna Aisquith, 88
  Susanna, 49, 52, 53, 88
  Thomas, 79, 88
  Thos. John, 79
  Walter, 79
  William, 71, 86
Henley, Edward, 57
  Ezabell, 57
  James, 57
  Mary, 135
Henning, Ann, 109, 136
  Caleb, 139
  Jeremiah, 109
  John, 17, 136
  Rhoda, 17
  Sarah, 109
Henrick, Benjamin, 139
Henry, James, 106
  Martin, 106, 110
  Mary, 106, 110
  Philip, 110
Herbert, Catherine, 32
  Elizabeth, 32
  John, 32
  Mary, 32
  William, 32
Herman, Jediah, 15
  John, 15
  Rhoda, 15
Hernley, Ann, 48, 49, 52, 57
  Darbey, 48, 49, 52, 57
  Edmond, 49
  John, 49
  Mary, 57
  Priscilla, 48
Higdon, Benedict Leonard, 2
  Benjamin, 2
  Clair, 2
  Ignatious, 2
  Jane, 2
  Martha, 2
  Susanna, 2
  William, 2
Hill, Margit, 12
  Mary, 32
  Onsley, 32
  Thomas, 32
  William, 32
Hilton, Anne, 110
  Diana, 129
  Elizabeth, 110
  John, 129
  Stephen, 129
  Thomas, 110
Hinsey, William, 43
Hobs, John, 82
Hodges, Elisabeth, 82
Hogan, Elizabeth, 134

Holdsworth, Ann, 63
  Barbara, 51, 52, 63
  Betty, 51
  Mary, 51
  Rebakah, 52
  Thomas, 51, 52, 63, 83, 84
Holland, Grace, 86
Hollandshead, Mary, 86
Hollyday, Ann, 137
  Eleanor, 81
  Elisabeth, 76
Holmes, Hester, 82
  Rachel, 84
Holshot, Jno., 82
Holt, Ann, 9
  James, 32
  Jane, 32
  John, 9
  Margarett, 32
  Mary, 9
  Milicent, 9
  Robert, 32
  William, 9, 32
Holton, William, 135
Hooper, Abraham, 67, 72, 73, 77
  Anne, 76
  Benjamin, 77
  Betty, 67
  Elisabeth, 77
  Elizabeth Downs, 73
  Isaac, 72, 76, 77
  Jacob, 67, 72
  James, 76
  John, 76
  Mary, 72, 73
  Priscilla, 76
  Rachael, 77
  William, 77
Hopewell, Angelica, 112
  Antionette, 138

Bennet, 104
Dorcas, 91
Eleanor, 131
Elizabeth, 135, 138
Francis, 104
George, 91
James R., 138
James Robert, 112
James, 112
Jane, 104
John, 91
Joseph, 91
Joshua, 104
Maria A., 138
Maria, 138
Mary Ann, 104
Mary, 131
Richard, 91, 104, 131
Teresia, 104
Horton, Alise, 24
Hoskins, Benedistal, 32
  Elizabeth, 32, 33
  Jane, 32
  Margarett, 32
  Mary, 33
  Philip, 32, 33
  William, 33
How, Elizabeth, 57
  Mary, 57
  Mauldin, 57
  Rebecka, 57
  Sarah, 57
  Thomas, 52, 57, 67
Howard, Anastatia Spink, 104
  Ann, 98, 124
  Annastatia Spink, 124
  Austin, 116
  Charles, 95, 121
  Elizabeth, 104
  Francis, 99, 124

George, 64, 98, 104, 124
Henrietta, 116
Henry, 95, 121
Ignatius, 99, 124
John, 64
Joseph, 95, 121
Joshua, 116
Margaret, 64
Mary Ann, 95, 121
Mary, 95, 116, 121
Sarah, 98, 124
Howe, Elizabeth, 52
  Margrett, 83
  Rebeckah, 52
  Sarah, 84
  Thomas, 52
Howerton, Elizabeth, 55
  John, 55
  Martha, 55
Howling, see Hawking
Howse, Keziah, 86
Hudson, Richard, 85
Hungerford, Ann, 73
  Benjamin, 66, 67, 73
  Edmund, 65, 73
  Elizabeth, 33, 65
  James, 65, 66, 73
  Jane, 65, 66
  Jean, 67
  John, 67, 85
  Margarett, 33
  Mary, 73
  William, 33
Hunt, Alice, 33, 42
  Ann, 5
  Mary, 33
Hunter, Andrew, 136
Huntington, Mary, 3
Hus, Robert, 33
Hussey, Thomas, 33, 39

Hutchens, Alathea, 119
  Ann, 91, 138
  Bennett, 135, 138
  Catharine, 135
  Dorothy, 136
  Elisabeth, 16, 82
  Frances, 119
  James, 91
  Jane, 91
  John, 109
  Joseph, 86
  Mary, 135
  Rachel, 109
  Robert, 91
  Susannah, 16, 119
  Thomas, 16, 85
  Winifred, 135

Inge, Ambrose, 97, 123
  Ann Maria, 97, 123
  Ann, 116
  John, 97, 123
  Mary, 116
  Susanna, 97, 123
  Vincent, 97, 116, 123
Ireland, Dorothy, 82
  George, 86
  Margaret, 136
Ivey, Abigail, 66
  Eleanor, 66, 67
  Elizabeth, 66
  James, 67
  John, 66, 67, 86
  Mary, 66
Izall, 33

Jackson, Joseph, Rev., 111
James, Champion, 116
  Chloe, 115
  George, 115

Hannah, 57
Jane, 85
John, 57
Mary, 115, 116, 139
Thomas, 115, 116, 134, 139
Jameson, Benjamin, 11
Sarah, 11
Jarboe, Abner, 105
Ann, 99, 125
Bennet, 105
Charles, 105
Clement, 99, 125
Eleanor, 99, 105, 125
Elizabeth, 137
Frances, 99, 125
Jean, 105
Joshua, 105
Mary, 131
Monica, 99, 125
Nancy, 134
Peter, 134
Stephen, 131
Jefferson, John, 86
Rebecca, 86
Jenifer, Daniel of St. Thomas, 51
Elizabeth, 51
Mary, 51
Michael, 83
Jenkins, Agusutine, 114
Daniel, 33
Edmund Courtney, 114
Elizabeth, 33
Enock, 33
George, 136
John, 114
Joseph, 114, 134
Mary, 81, 114
Thomas, 81, 114, 135
Jenkinson, Ignatius, 33
Mary, 33

Jerrcons, Edward, 84
Johnson, Ann, 49
Dorcas, 86
Dradon, 15
Eleanor, 15
Elizabeth, 49, 57
Frances, 49
Francis, 56
Jane, 69
Jemima, 15
John, 49, 56, 69
Joseph, 49, 53
Mary, 53
Sarah, 49, 53, 57
Thomas, 53, 56
Thomas, Jr., 74
William, 49, 53, 57
Jones, Anastatia, 137
Anne, 33
Benjamin, 85
Elizabeth, 33, 86, 92
Jane, 33
Johnson, 92
Margarett, 33
Mary, 33, 83
Moses, 33
Richard, 33
Thomas, 33, 83
Uel, 92
William, 54
Jordan, Margaret, 135
Joy, Benedict, 93
Eleanor, 88, 92
Elizabeth, 91
Henrietta, 88
John, 91, 92
John, Jr., 88
Joseph, 91
Mary, 91
Sarah, 91

Index

Thomas Tarlton, 91
William, 92, 137
Winifred, 91

Karnes, Henry, 33
  Mary, 33
  Robert, 33
  William, 33
Keech, Timothy, 137
Kelley, Elizabeth, 53, 57
  John, 53
  Patrick, 53, 57, 82
  Randall, 57
  Rebecka, 57
  Sarah, 53
  Susanna, 135, 139
Kelshew, Elizabeth, 105
  James, 105
  Mary Ann, 105
Kemp, William, 84
Kendrick, Benjamin, 135
  Diana, 131
  Elizabeth, 131
  William, 131
Kent, Elizabeth, 72, 73
  Gideon Dare, 73
  Isaac, 63, 72
  Jane, 60
  Jannett, 60, 63, 73
  John, 53, 60, 63, 72, 73
  Joseph, 73
  Kessah, 72
  Mary, 53
  Rebackh, 63
  Richard, 73
  Thomasin, 53, 60, 63
Kersahw, James, 81
  Cortinia Ann, 78
  Francis, 76, 78
  James L., 78

  John, 76
  Mary, 85
  Rebecca, 76
Key, Cecilia, 140
  John, Dr., 140
  Mary Elizabeth, 138
  Susanna Gardiner, 140
Kidd, Ann, 60
  Gidian, 60
  William, 60
King, Adam, 101
  Adam, 126
  Ann, 16
  Anna, 20
  Aquilla, 16
  Barton, 10
  Basil, 16, 19, 20
  Benjamin, 7, 10, 80
  Bennet, 106, 117
  Chloe, 7
  Cornelius, 10, 16
  Deborah, 19
  Dorcas, 10
  Draden, 18
  Edward, 101, 126
  Eleanor, 101, 103, 126, 136
  Elias, 16
  Elizabeth, 7, 10, 20
  Henry, 137
  James Carrol, 16
  James, 110
  Jane, 103
  Joseph, 15, 16
  Margaret, 106, 117
  Mary, 85
  Millicent, 16
  Orpha, 19
  Richard, 85
  Sarah, 20
  Susanna, 80

Thomas B., 80
Thomas, 103
Vinson, 16
Walter, 16
William, 110
Zephaniah, 16
Kingersley, Elizabeth, 34
  George, 34
  Mary, 34
Kirby, Elizabeth, 92, 117, 136
  Francis, 136
  Henrietta, 91, 119
  Hopewell, 92
  Mary, 117, 119
  Peter, 91
  Rebecca, 91
  Richard, 91
  Thomas, 117, 119
  William, 92
Kirkley, Catherine, 34
  Christopher, 34
  Susanna, 34
Kirshaw, Ann, 78, 79
  Armeneco, 78
  Benjamin D., 78
  Benjamin Wrigh, 77
  Cavey R., 78
  Cortiana, 78
  Dinah, 69
  Francis, 60, 69, 78, 79, 84
  James D., 79
  James, 60, 78, 84
  John, 78, 79
  Joseph S., 78
  Joshua, 69, 78
  Kesya, 78, 81
  Margaret, 60, 69, 77, 84
  Osburn, 78
  Patsey, 78
  Pricale, 78

Priscilla, 78
Rebecca, 69, 78, 82, 84
Sarah A., 78, 79
William, 79
Knight, Anne, 34
  Jennett, 34
  John, 34
  Mary, 34
Knott, Bennett, 117
  Eleanor, 117
  Ignatius, 117
  James, 117
Kylborne, Eliza, 34
  Francis, 34

Lake, Elizabeth, 91
  John, 91
  Susanna, 91
Lambert, Elinor, 34
  Elizabet, 34
  John, 34
  Samuel, 34
  William, 34
Lampton, Anne, 34
  Elizabeth, 34, 35
  Isable, 34
  John, 34
  Marke, 34, 35
  Mary, 34
  Victoria, 35
  William, 35
Land, Elizabeth, 35
  John, 35
  Penelope, 35
  Richard, 35
  Susanna, 35
Lander, Francis, Rev., 74
Lane, Elizabeth, 35
  Mary, 82
  N. W., Rev., 79

William, 35
Langley, John Francis Xaviers, 129
  Josias, 129
  Mary, 35
  Susann, 129
Latham, James, 93, 119
  Jeremiah, 133
  John, 133
  Margaret Ann, 88
  Mary, 89
  Matthew, 88, 93, 119
  Rebecca, 133
  Susanna, 88, 93, 119
  William, 88
Laveille, John L., 80
  Uriah, 80
Layton, Ignatius, 132
  Jane, 132
  John, 132
  Joseph, 132
  Susanna, 132
  Zachariah, 132
Leach, Effnis, 53
  Elizabeth, 53
  Jane, 53
  John, 53
  Mary, 87
  Preserv, 53
  William, 53
Leatherland, Wm., 136
Lee, Charles, 87
  Robert, 82
Leech, Elizabeth, 3
  Nefel, 3
  Rebekah, 3
Leete, Elinor, 35
  George, 35
  Leete, John, 35
  Lewis, Ann, 53

  Charles, 117
  David, 35
  George Rogers Williams, 3
  Griffin, 53
  Henrietta Lewis Williams, 3
  Henry, 35
  Isable, 35
  James, 117
  Jane, 35, 117
  Joseph, 5
  Mary, 3, 5, 35, 53
  Thomas, 3, 5
Lindsey, Edmond, 35
  James, 35, 39
Ling, Francis, 35
  Mary, 35
  Michaell, 35
  William, 35, 36
Lomax, Blanch, 36
  Catherine, 36
  Cleborne, 36
  John, 36
  Katherine, 36
  Ralph, 36
  Susanna, 36
  Thomas, 36
Long, Barbara, 88, 100
  Barbara, 126
  Gabriel, 100, 126
  Hannah, 100, 126
  Jemima, 36
  John Read, 100, 126
  John, 88, 100
  John, 126
  Margaret, 88
  Nicholas, 100, 126
  Reuben, 100, 126
  Robert, 36
  William, 100, 126
Louder, Francis, Rev., 85

Love, Ann, 3, 8
  Charles, 7, 8
  Elinor, 7
  Elizabeth, 3, 36
  Jane, 7
  Martha, 7, 8
  Mary, 7, 8
  Pamela, 7
  Pentheselia, 7
  Sam'l, Jr., 7
  Samuel Abbot William Augustine, 8
  Samuel, 7
  Susanna, 5
  Thomas, 7
  William, 3, 36
Lucas, Joshua, 114
  Rachel, 114
  William, 114
Luckett, Elizabeth, 36
  Ignatius, 36
  Samuell, 36
  Thomas, 36
Lumbrozo, John, 36
Lurty, John, 135

Mackabe, Abraham, 56
  Ann, 53
  Elizabeth, 53, 56
  James, 53, 56
  Lacey, 56
  Rachel, 53
  Thomas, 53
Mackall, Ann, 66, 68, 70
  Barbara, 60, 68
  Benjamin, 60, 65, 68, 71, 72
  Dorcas, 73
  Elizabeth, 68
  James John, 52, 67, 68, 69
  James, 62, 63, 65, 66, 68, 71
  Jane, 136
  John, 52, 63, 67, 70, 71, 72, 73
  Margaret, 68, 70 72, 73
  Mary, 62, 63, 65, 66, 67, 68, 69, 70, 71, 84, 135
  Prissilla, 69
  Rebecca, 70
  Richard, 68
  Sarah, 68, 73
  Susanah, 52, 67
  Thomas Howe, 70
  Thomas, 68
Mackcon, Ann, 10
  Robert, 10
Mackeath, Barbara, 59
  Benjamin, 59
  Sarah, 59
Mackenney, Alexander, 77, 83, 84
  John, 77, 85
  Margaret, 77
  Priscilla, 77
Mackey, ___ck, 11
Mackhon, Ann, 7, 9
  Dorcas, 7
  Mary, 7
  Robert, 6, 7, 9
  Walter, 9
Mackmelon, Compton, 10
  Hugh, 10
  Tabith, 10
  Zechariah, 10
Mackmillion, George, 24, 36
  Grace, 36
  Peter, 36
Macknew, Cathrine, 59
  David, 59
  Elliner, 59
Mackon, Ann, 9
  Elizabeth, 9

Robert, 9
Maddox, Elizabeth, 3
　James, 3
　John, 3
Magitee, James, 36
　Patrick, 36
　Rose, 36
Magowan, Walter, 75
Magruder, Casandra, 136
Makenny, Dorcas, 77
Makgill, David, 83
Malden, Margett, 84
Malley, Margaret, 137
Mankin, Elizabeth, 36
　Hope, 36
　James, 36
　John, 37
　Josiah, 37
　Margarett, 37
　Mary, 36, 37
　Stephen, 36, 37
　Tubbman, 37
Manning, Anne, 62
　Cornelius, 102, 127
　Frances, 102, 128
　Grace, 62, 83
　Ignatius, 127
　James, 132
　Jane, 102, 127
　Jochan, 62
　John, 62, 132, 133
　Joseph, 132
　Margaret, 132
　Mary, 62, 132, 134
　Monica, 102, 128
　Ruth, 82
　Sarah, 62
　Susanna, 132
　Thomas, 62
　William, 132

Mannister, Jno., 37
Mareman, Ann, 107, 108
　Ann, 115
　Elizabeth, 95, 107, 108, 121
　James, 105
　John Baptist, 105
　John, 115
　Joseph, 95, 107, 108, 115, 121
　Joshua, 105, 108, 115
　Lydda, 105
　Mary Attaway, 105
　Mary, 105, 108
　Richard, 95, 121
　Susanna, 105, 108
　William, 105, 108
　Zachariah, 108, 115
Maris, Sarah, 37
　Thomas, 37
Marshall, Barbary, 37
　Elizabeth, 37
　Thomas, 37
　William, 33, 37, 44
Martin, Anne, 37, 38, 93
　Catherine, 37
　Damaris, 37, 38
　Elizabeth, 37, 38, 113
　George, 93
　James, 37, 38
　Jane Dorothy, 93
　Jane, 93
　Jillian, 37
　John Curry, 93
　John, 37, 38
　Joseph, 37
　Katherine, 37
　Laura Sophia, 113
　Mary Ann, 93
　Mary, 37
　Penelope, 38
　Stephen, 113

Thomas, 93
William, 38, 83, 93, 135
Mason, Elizabeth, 38
  John, 38
  Mary, 38
  Philip, 38
  Samuell, 38
  William, 38
Mastin, Ann, 10
  John, 38
  Mary, 10, 38
  Richard, 10, 38
Mathena, Elizabeth, 38
  George, 38
Matheny, Elizabeth, 111
  Thomas, 111
Mathes, Mary, 15
Matthews, Alexander, 21
  Ann, 18, 21
  Billy, 18, 21
  Catherine, 8, 20, 21
  Elias Poston, 21
  Elisabeth, 8
  Elizabeth Barnes, 21
  Henry Cooksey, 21
  Jane, 44
  John, 21
  Mary, 8
  Thomas, 8, 18, 21, 44
  Victoria, 44
  William, 8
Mattingly, Ann, 115
  Catharine, 109
  Clement, 115
  Elisabeth, 115
  Fanny, 138
  John Baptist, 115
  Mary Ann, 109, 115
  Robert, 109
  Ruth, 115

Thomas, 115
Mauldin, Elizabeth, 53, 82
  Frances, 59
  Francis, 53
  James, 53
  Ludah, 59
  Margrett, 53
  Sarah, 53
  Thomas, 59
  William, 53
Maycocke, Seabright, 38
Maynard, Ann, 56
  Diana, 56
  Thomas, 56, 83
McBride, John Duncan, 3
  Lazerus, 3
  Mary, 3
McCartney, Ann, 110
  Edward, 110, 111
  Fanny, 110
  Mary, 110, 111
  Sarah, 110
  Susanna, 111
McCave, Alice, 130
  Eleanor Ann, 130
  John Bond, 130
  Margaret Ann, 130
McClane, Arthur, 118
  Enoch, 118
  John Vowles, 93, 119
  John, 136
  Mary, 93, 118, 119
  Richard, 118
  William, 93, 118, 119
McDowell, John, 86
McGill, Abell, 119
  Charles, 137
  Jannett, 119
  Marianne, 119
  Mary, 135

McHon, Chloe, 3
  Elizabeth, 2
  Lorana, 2
  Martha, 1
  Priscilla, 2, 3
  Robert, 3
  Virlinda, 2
  William, 2, 3
  James, 136
McPherson, Alexander
  Wilkinson, 11
  Ann, 11
  Charles, 12
  Eliner, 11, 12
  Elizabeth, 11
  Helen, 11
  John, 11
  Kerenhappuck, 11
  Mary, 11
  Theophilus, 11
  William, 11, 12
McWherter, Andrew, 110
  Elizabeth, 110
  Mary, 110
Medcalf, Ignatius, 93, 119
  John Kenelin, 93, 119
  Sarah, 93, 119
Medley, Anastatia, 133
  Ann Elizabeth, 102, 127
  Ann, 95, 120, 131
  Augustine, 95, 120
  Bernard, 133
  Catharine, 131
  Charles, 131
  Clement, 101, 106, 127, 131
  Eleanor, 101, 127, 133
  George, 95
  George, 120
  Joseph, 101, 127, 133
  Mary Ann, 131
  Mary, 101, 106, 127, 131
  Matthew, 102, 127
  Sarah, 131
  William, 131
Meken, Augustine, 94, 120
  Margaret, 94, 120
  Susanna, 94, 120
Merrell, Joshua, 107, 108
  Mary Ann, 107, 108
  Mary, 107
  Mills Eleanor, 108
  Philip, 107
Messenger, John Feron, 110
  Joseph, Rev., 110
  Mary, 110
  William, 110
Milburne, Eleanor, 131
  Elizabeth, 131
  Jeremiah, 131
Miller, Ellinor, 54
  Grace, 38, 54, 57
  John, 38
  Peter, 38
  Sarah, 86
  Susannah, 79
  William, 54, 57, 83
Mills, Anastatia, 129
  Ann, 102, 128
  Bernard, 129
  Chaney, 81
  Charles, 102, 128
  Elizabeth, 58, 102, 128
  Ethelbert, 129
  Ignatius, 129
  John, 58, 102, 128
  Joseph, 102, 128
  Justinian, 102, 128, 134
  Leonard, 85
  Margaret, 102, 128
  Mary, 102, 128

Index

Nicholas, 129, 102
Stephen, 129
Winifred, 102, 128
Millsteade, Edward, 38
Susanna, 38
William, 38
Mingoe, Charles, 38
Elizabeth, 38
Joseph, 38
Lewis, 38
Thomas, 38
Mitchell, Sarah, 86
Monett, Abraham, 73, 81
Ann, 72, 73
Isaac, 72, 73
Penelope, 72
Money, Abraham, 56
Ann, 56
Elizabeth, 56
Isaac, 56
William, 56
Montgomery, Margaret, 20
Moody, Anne, 38
Jane, 38
Sarah, 81
William, 38
Moore, Elizabeth, 9, 38, 39
Henry, 38, 39
James, 9
John, 39
Sarah, 9
Thomas, 39, 81
Moreland, Sarah, 12
Moreton, Anne, 14
Marget, 14
William, 14
Morgan, Mary, 137
Thomas, 83
Morris, Anne, 39
Mary, 39

Penelope, 39
Richard, 39, 43
Thomas, 39
Mort, Eleanor, 140
James, 140
John, 140
Joseph, 140
Mugg, Ann, 130
Elizabeth, 131
Peter, 106
Priscilla, 106, 130
Walter, 106, 130
Mulgraves, Dorothy, 25
Munday, Elizabeth, 82
Murphey, Abraham, 13
Ann, 11
Anne, 17, 19
Dan'l, Jr., 14
Daniel, 3, 11, 13, 14, 17, 19
Dennis, 39
Dorithy, 13
Edward Hill, 13
Eleanor, 19, 20
Elizabeth Moreton, 14, 19
Elizabeth, 13
Hezakiah, 13
Jane, 19
John Boswell, 13
Joseph, 17
Josias, 20
Kenelm, 14
Margaret, 13, 14, 19
Marget Hill, 19
Martha, 13
Mary, 3, 13, 14
Nathaniel, 14
Rebekah, 13
Samuel, 14
Sarah, 13
Susannah, 19

… Index … 177

Thomas, 19
Townley, 19
Walter, 14
William, 11, 14, 20
Zephaniah, 3, 12, 13, 14, 19, 20
Musgrave, Lydia, 6
Myles, Elizabeth, 50
Mary, 50
Tobias, 50

Nalley, Anne, 8
Elisabeth, 8
Rodolphea Gustavus, 8
Tho's, 8
Thomas Cooksey, 8
_ary, 8
Negro
Beck, 134
Bob, 134
Fanny, 134
Harriet, 134
Henry, 134
Jane, 134
Key, Henry G. A., 134
Lucinda, 134
Lucy, 134
Moses, 134
Peter, 134
Phil, 134
Rachel, 134
Rose, 134
Sam, 134
Sarah, 134
Stephen, 134
Walter, 134
Nevill, Joan, 39
John, 33
Nevitt, Mary, 82
Newen, Owen, 29
Newton, Bernard, 107

Elizabeth, 107
Grace, 66
James, 130
Jane, 39
John Shadrach, 130
Joseph, 130
Mary Ann, 107
Mildred, 130
Rhodolph, 130
Richard, 39
Thomas, 66
Ward, 66
Norris, Ann, 97
Ann, 122
Arnold, 99, 125
Barbara, 99
Bennet, 133
Bibrana, 125
Clement, 130
Cuthbert, 130
Dorothy, 106, 129
Eleanor, 130
Elizabeth, 99, 125, 129, 130
Enoch, 99
Enoch, 125
Frances, 133
Henrietta, 130
Henry Elijah, 99, 125
John, 99, 103, 125, 128, 130
Joseph, 97, 99, 122, 125
Luke, 99, 125
Mark, 130
Mary Ann, 97, 122, 129
Mary, 97, 99, 103, 106, 122, 125, 128, 130
Mathias, 130
Monica, 130
Philip, 97, 99, 122, 125, 130
Rebecca, 106
Rhodolph, 129

Susanna, 99, 103, 125, 128, 130
Thomas, 97, 106, 122, 129, 130
Vincent, 130
William, 97, 122, 134
Winifred, 133
Nottingham, Ann, 102, 127
　Athana, 102, 127
　Elizabeth, 96, 121
　Enoch, 102, 127
　Ignatius, 96, 121
　Mary Ann, 96, 102, 121, 127
　Mary, 96, 102, 121, 127
　Mathias, 121, 96
　Raphael Ignatius, 96, 121
Nugent, Susannah, 135
Nuthall, Ann Roach, 94, 121
　Ann, 136
　Brent, 117
　Margaret, 94, 121

OBryan, Elinor, 39
　Elizabeth, 39
　Magdalen, 39
　Matthias, 39
　William, 39
Ogg, Alexander, 75
Oney, Nathaniel, 138
Ord, Anne, 39
　James, 39
　Mary, 39
　Peter, 39
　Thomas, 39
Oswell, Jennit, 54
Otley, James, 135
Owens, Charles, 87
　John, 135

Page, Daniel, 87
Paine, John, 39, 46
Pardoe, Ann, 72, 75

　Catherine Hesletine, 72
　James, 73
　John, 72, 73, 75
　Margaret, 72, 73, 75
　Peter, 72, 75
Parker, Ann, 60, 61
　Eliza, 59
　Elizabeth, 15, 48, 53
　Fealder, 53
　Gabriel, 48, 59, 60, 61
　George, 48, 59, 83
　Hutchinson, 61
　Lansdown, 48
　Mary, 48, 53, 61, 83
　Sarah, 60
　Susannah, 48, 60, 83
　William Henry, 53
　William, 48, 53
Parran, Alexander, 55, 61, 83, 85
　Alexander, Jr., 55
　Ann, 61
　Benjamin, 61, 85
　Charles Somersett, 136
　Elizabeth, 61
　Jane, 55, 61
　John, 55, 61
　Mary Aschum, 86
　Mary, 55, 61
　Moses, 61
　Phillip, 61
　Samuell, 61
　Sarah, 61
　Thomas, 136
　Young, 61
Parrott, Elizabeth, 48
　Gabrill, 48
Parsons, James, 114
Pasture, Rebecca, 81
Pattison, James, 71
　Penelope, 71

Payne, Allelusia, 98, 123
  Anastatia, 109
  Ann, 94, 98, 104, 106, 120, 124
  Baptist, 98, 124
  Bernard, 98, 123
  Charles, 94, 120
  Eleanor, 104
  Elizabeth, 95, 98, 106, 121, 124
  Frances, 103
  Francis Exhuerus, 94, 120
  Henry Berryman, 95, 121
  Henry, 98, 123
  James, 94, 120
  Jane, 98, 123
  Jeremiah, 117
  John Baptist, 104, 106
  John Barton, 115
  John, 39
  Joseph, 103
  Leonard, 95, 103, 115, 117, 121
  Mary Ann, 124
  Mary, 98, 103
  Monica, 94, 95, 115, 117, 120, 121
  Priscilla, 94, 115, 120
  Raphael, 106, 109
  Richard, 94, 115, 120
  Rosa Ann, 106
  Sarah, 106
  Tabith, 106, 109
  Teresia, 103
  Vincent, 103
  Winifred, 98, 124
Peacock, Ann, 106
  Elizabeth, 63
  Ignatius, 106
  John Barton, 106
  Joseph, 63
  Samuel, 63, 84
Peake, Ann, 97, 103, 122, 133
  Augustine, 94, 120
  Charles, 97, 122
  Edward, 97, 103, 122
  Eleanor, 131, 133
  Elizabeth, 20
  Francis, 97, 122
  Henrietta, 97, 122, 133
  Henry Barton, 97, 122
  John, 94, 103, 104, 120
  Joseph, 104, 133
  Kenelm, 97, 122
  Mary, 97, 122, 133
  Monica, 131
  Peter, 133
  Raphael, 133
  Robert, 94, 120
  Susanna, 94, 104, 120
  William, 20, 133
Peircy, Thomas, 39
Penn, Elizabeth, 40
  Marke, 40
  Mary, 40
  William, 40
Perry, Elizabeth, 11
  Francis, 11
  _arity, 11
Phillips, Catherine, 2, 14
  Elizabeth, 2
  Hezakiah, 14
  Zephaniah, 2, 14
Philpott, Charles, 40
  Edward, 40
  John, 40
  Susanna, 40
Pierreviell, Ann Elizabeth, 59
  Jas. Gideon, 59
  John, 59
Piles, Leonara, 87
Piscood, Elizabeth, 84
Pitcher, Rebecca, 81

Place, Catherine, 83
Plater, Edward, 113
   Elizabeth, 113
   John R., 113
Platford, David, 85
Plunkitt, Catherine, 83
Poole, Ann, 136
Pope, Francis, 40
   John, 40
   Thomas, 35
Posey, Benjamin, 40
   Humphrey, 40
   John, 24, 40
   Mary, 40
   Susanna, 40
Poston, Alexander, 15, 17
   Anne, 15, 16, 18
   Catherine, 15
   Chloe, 15
   Elias, 15
   Jeremiah, 15
   Judith, 15, 18
   Leonard, 16
   Priscilla, 15
   Richard, 15
   William, 15, 17
Powell, Elizabeth, 86
   Robert, 40
   William, 85
Price, Anne, 40
   Eleanor, 136
   Mary, 40
   Robert, 40
   William, 135
Pye, Susanna, 9
Pyke, Ann, 101, 127
   Henry, 101, 127
   James, 101, 127
   John, 132
   Kezia, 132

   Mary Ann, 101, 127, 132
   William, 132

Raily, Henrietta, 137
   Mary, 136
Raines, Elizabeth, 40
   Henry, 40
   John, 40
   Lucy, 40
Ramsay, Charles, 137
   John, 86
   Sarah, 7
   William, 86
Randall, Richard, 40, 41
Ratclife, Bathsheba, 40
   John, 40
   Richard, 40
Rawlings, Elizabeth, 76
   Sarah, 85
   Thomas, 80
Raymie, Elizabeth, 83
Read, Philip, 136
Reason, Elizabeth, 40
Redferne, Faith, 40
   James, 40
   Mary, 40
Redman, Ann, 118, 130
   Benjamin, 130
   Britannia, 130
   Fanny, 113
   George, 118
   Henrietta, 134
   John, 118
   Rosanna, 113
   William, 118, 130
   Zachariah, 113, 138
Reeder, Benjamin, 136
Reeves, Ann, 8
   Bennett, 13
   Dorcas, 13

Elizabeth, 10
George, 103, 128
Josias, 8
Lydia, 10
Mary Ann, 7
Mary, 5, 7, 8, 10, 13, 103, 128
Samuel, 5
Susanna, 103, 128
Thomas, 5, 7, 8, 10, 13
William, 13
Regon, Charles, 41
  James, 41
  Joan, 41
  John, 41
  Margarett, 41
  Mary, 41
  Matthew, 41
  William, 41
Reshwick, Ann, 116
  Appolonia, 100, 125
  Francis, 100, 125
  George, 100
  John Basil, 100
  John, 100, 125
  Joseph, 100, 107, 125
  Mary, 100, 107, 125
  Monica, 116
  Thomas, 100, 107, 116, 125
  Wilford, 116
Reynolds, Elizabeth, 49
  James, 49
  Ros, 49
Rhodes, Eleanor, 137
  Susanna, 86
Rhodin, Elizabeth, 58
  John, 58
  Sarah, 58
  William, 58
Richards, Tho., 83
Richardson, Elizabeth, 135
  John, 62
  Nicholas, 137
  Thomas, 62
Ridgel, Ann Maria, 138
  Frederick, 138
  Richard, 139
  Thomas Ransell, 138
Rigby, Anne, 85
Rigden, Ann, 53
  Elizabeth, 53
  John, 53
Rights, Ellino, 41
  George, 41
Rigill, Mary, 110
  Rigill, Statia, 110
  Rigill, Thomas, 110
Rishwick, see Reshwick
Roberson, Deborah, 82
Roberts, Anne, 81
  Araminta, 136
  Benjamin, 49
  Elizabeth, 49, 50, 55
  Jacob, 55
  James, 49, 50, 55
  John, 50, 82, 83
  Mary Howe, 81
Robinson, Elizabeth, 62
  John, 24, 41
  Joyce, 41
  Margaret, 65
  Mary, 41, 65
  Richard, 41
  Samuel, 65
  Susanna, 41
Roby, Aquilla, 18
  Charles, 18
  Cornelius, 18
  Deborah, 19
  Elisabeth, 18
  George Dement, 18

Hezekiah, 19
Katherine, 18
Mary, 19
Richard, 18
Susannah, 18, 19
Townley, 18
Truman, 18
William, 18, 19
Rolle, Robert, 86
Rookwood, Edward, 41
　Mary, 41
Roolants, see Ruelants
Ross, Lazarus, 135
Rouland, Ann, 53
　Thomas, 53
Rouse, John, 41
Royston, Abel, 62
　Alce, 62
　Elizabeth, 62
Rozer, Benjamin, 32, 41
　Mary, 41
　Notley, 41
Ruelants, Dinah, 41
　Margery, 41
　Robert, 41
Rurk, Mary, 83
Russell, Allusia, 110
　Ann, 114, 115, 117
　Catharine, 96, 122
　Charles, 117
　Dryden, 108
　Eleanor, 105
　Ignatius, 105, 109, 110, 114
　James, 114
　John Baptist, 108
　John, 96, 122
　Mary Ann, 115
　Mildred, 105, 109, 110
　Philip, 109
　Susanna, 96, 122

　William, 108, 114, 115, 117

Saintclair, Thomas, 3
Sanner, Anne, 135
　Isaac, 136
　John, 137, 138
　Thomas, 137
Sanson, John, 98, 123, 131
　Mary, 98, 123, 131
　William, 98, 123
Sapcoate, Abram, 41
　Elizabeth, 41
　Rachell, 41
Saunders, Ann, 92
　Charles, 41
　Edward, 41, 42
　Elizabeth, 92
　Jane, 41, 42
　Mary, 41
　Sarah, 41, 135
　Sinnot, 92
　Thomas, 42
Saxe, Elizabeth, 86
　Henry, 136
Scarf, James, 86
　John, 42
Scott, Catherine, 2
　Christian, 8, 11, 13
　Elisa. Edgar, 11
　Elizabeth, 3
　Gustavus, 11
　John, 8
　John, 11
　Richard, 8
　Robert, Rev., 84
　Samuel, 13
　Sarah, 8, 11, 13
　Thomas, 8
　William, 8, 11, 13
Scroggin, Elizabeth, 42

George, 42
John, 42
Mary, 42
Susanna, 42
Seavern, James, 66
John Dewick, 66
Sarah, 66
Sebree, Ally, 86
Sedwick, Ann, 74, 81
  Benjamin, 66, 75
  Caroline Elisabeth, 76
  Daniel Rawlings, 76
  Elisabeth, 74, 76, 81
  Elizabeth Lander, 74, 75
  Eloisa Mary, 76
  Isabella, 74, 81
  James Cook, 75
  John, 73, 74, 75, 81
  John, Jr., 76
  Joshua, 74
  Mary, 66, 75
  Rebecker Prisciller, 76
  Thomas, 85
Seems, Chloe, 4
  Elizabeth, 4
  Francis, 4
  Ignatius, 4
  Jane, 4
  Joseph, 4
  Lucretia, 4
  Marmaduke, 4
Semmes, see Seems
  Sewall, Charles, 99, 125
  Clement, 99, 125
  Henry, 99, 125
  Mary Smith, 99, 125
  Mary, 99, 125
Shackerley, Edward, 42
  Francis, 42
  John, 42

Shair, Mary Burton, 84
Shekon, Elizabeth, 57
  Jane, 57
  John, 57
Shermintine, Anne, 136
  Mary, 136
Shrive, Martha, 82
Silence, Ann, 90
  Austin, 90
  Edmund, 103, 128
  Elizabeth, 90, 103, 128
  Enoch, 90, 137
  Jeremiah, 90
  John, 90, 103
  John, Jr., 90, 128
  John, Sr., 90
  Mary, 90
  Sabra, 137
Simmons, Celia, 138
  Elizabeth, 82, 136
  Mary, 137
Simpson, Alexander, 22
  Andrew, 8
  Ann, 51
  Hannah, 105
  Jeremiah, 51, 54
  John Francis Royes, 8
  John, 54
  Mary, 8, 51, 54, 83
  William, 105
Sims, Anthony, 130
  Elizabeth, 130
  Joseph, 11
  Mary, 130
Sinnett, Garrett, 33, 42
  Margaret, 42
Sissel, see Csissell
Skinner, Catharine, 79
  Christiana, 81
  Elisabeth, 81

Lethe, 81
Orphap, 81
Rebecca, 86
Slater, David, 63
  Ellis, 62, 63
  Jonathan, 62
  Sarah, 62, 63
Slye, Ann, 79
  Eleanor, 9
  Elisabeth, 18
  John, 9, 18, 79
  Robert, 9, 18
  Samuel, 79
  Susanna, 9
  Thomas Gerrard, 18
Smallpage, Robert, 33
Smallwood, Esther, 42
  James, 42
  John, 42
  Mary, 42
  Matthew, 42
Smart, Frances, 89
  Susanna, 89
  William, 89
Smith, Alethea, 67, 136
  Alexander, 42
  Ann, 42, 43, 54, 83, 102, 128
  Arthur, 42
  Barbara, 83, 84
  Elizabeth, 42, 102, 128
  Henry, 42, 43
  Humpry, 54
  James, 42, 87
  Jane, 43
  Joan, 43
  John, 43, 56, 83, 102, 128
  Margery, 42, 43
  Mary, 56, 135, 138, 139
  Patrick Sim, 75
  Richard, 42, 43
  Sarah, 54, 67
  Thomas, 43
  Walter, 67, 135, 137
  William, 43, 84, 85
Smoote, Abigal, 3
  Alexander, 137
  Arthur, 3
  Edward, 43
  Elizabeth, 43
  Grace, 43
  John, 43
  Lydia, 43
  Margarite, 3
  Mary, 3
  Richard, 43
  Thomas, 3
  William, 43
Snoggin, see Scoggin, 42
Sollers, James Mackall, 74
  James Marshall, 86
Somerset, Martha, 10, 16
  Mary, 10
  William, 10
Somervell, Alexander, 66, 69, 70
  Francis, 114, 138
  Howe, 68
  James, 60, 66, 67, 68, 84
  James, Dr., 84
  John, 66, 68
  Louisa, 114
  Louise, 138
  Margaret Alverta, 114
  Rebecca, 60, 69, 70
  Sarah Howe, 84
  Sarah, 60, 66, 67, 68
  Susanna, 68
  Thomas, 69
  William, 69, 135
Sparks, Jane, 84
Spellman, Ann, 58

Index

Elizabeth, 55, 58
Mary, 58
Richard, 55, 58
William, 55
Spencer, Francis, 54, 82
James, 54
Martha, 82
Mary, 54
Spink, Edward, 94, 116, 120
Joseph, 94, 120
Mary, 94, 116, 120
Monica, 94, 116, 120
Spong, Elizabeth, 117
Francis, 117
James, 117
Stallings, Alice, 85
Stallions, Susanna, 86
Standworth, Mary, 137
Sticklin, Jeremiah, 92
Joanna, 92
Josias, 92
Stigeleer, James, 43
Jane, 43
Mary, 43
Stinnet, Elizabeth, 54
William, 54
Stirmey, Katherine, 54
Mary, 54
Priscilla, 54
William, 54
Stirney, Priscilla, 82
Stone, Dorothy, 106
Francis, 110
Ignatius, 89
Jane, 135
John, 106
Joseph, 106, 110, 135
Marget, 12
Matthew, 89
Monica, 89

Winifred, 110
Stonestreet, Butler, 6, 9
Edward, 6, 9
Elisabeth, 6, 10
Mary, 5, 12
Richard, 10
Susanna Pye, 7
Thomas, 5
Thomasen, 5
Story, Elizabeth, 24, 43
Walter, 24
Sunderland, Lydia, 87
Swann, Abigale, 6
Ann Chapman, 12
Ann, 11, 12, 16
Asa, 12
Edward, 54
Eliner, 14
Elizabeth, 54
Esther, 16
Ezra, 16
George, 54
Hatch, 12
Jonathan, 14
Martha, 11
Mary Amery, 14
Samuel Amery, 14
Thomas, 10, 11, 12, 16
Zedakiah, 12
Swillaven, Daniel, 49, 58, 82
Priscilla, 58, 49
Synett, see Sinett

Tabbs, Abigail H., 137
Barton, 86
Talbot, Thomas, 86
Taney, Eleanor, 132, 136
John, 132
Sarah, 132
Tanner, Henry, 85

Mary, 81
Tarlton, Elijah, 118
  Elizabeth, 137
  Ignatius, 118, 137
  James, 105, 118
  Jane, 91
  Jeremiah, 91
  John, 105
  Mary Ann, 105, 118
  William, 91
Taylor, Ann, 43, 59, 103, 104, 128, 137
  Barbara, 73, 74
  Brian, 67, 73, 74
  Elizabeth Spink, 96, 121
  Elizabeth, 59, 88, 103, 104, 128, 137
  Everard, 67, 74
  George, 44
  Henrietta, 88
  Ignatius, 88, 96, 103, 104, 121, 128, 135
  James Mackall, 74
  John, 43, 59, 84, 137
  Mary, 59, 67, 96, 121
  Sarah, 67, 73
  Statia, 134
  Susannah, 44
  Thomas, 43
  William Dawkins, 73
Tells, Edward, 33
Tennison, Absolom, 90
  Ann, 90
  Eleanor, 90
  Jesse, 90
  John, 90
  Margaret, 90
  Susanna, 90
Theobald, John, 43
  Mary, 43

Thirst, Elizabeth, 27
Thomas, Abell, 90, 91
  Ann, 93
  Dorothy, 93
  Edward, 111
  Elizabeth, 88, 90, 98, 123, 138
  James, 98, 111, 123
  Jane, 111
  Jemima, 98, 123
  John, 93
  Luke, 91
  Mark, 88
  Mary, 92, 111
  Rachael, 134
  Robert, 98, 123
  Samuel, 88
  Sarah, 90, 91, 92
  Stanhope Rule, 92
  Thomas, 111, 136
  Tyler, 134
  William, 134, 135
Thompkins, Giles, 43
  Sarah, 43
Thompson, Anastatia, 106
  Ann, 90, 95, 106, 116, 120, 135
  Athanasius, 115
  Benjamin, 112
  Bennet, 94t, 119
  Charles James, 94, 119
  Charles, 106
  Cuthbert, 43
  Eleanor, 94, 119, 120, 139
  Elijah, 109, 112
  Elizabeth, 89, 94, 109, 112, 115, 119
  George Matthews, 93, 119
  Ignatius, 94, 120
  James Aloisus, 106
  James, 89, 94, 95, 109, 119, 120, 139

Index

Jane, 44
Janet, 89
John Baptist, 106
John Barton, 106, 116
John Gerard, 116
John, 44, 106, 129
Johnson, 89
Joseph Edmund, 120
Joseph Edward, 94
Joseph, 90, 106
Margaret, 94, 104, 116, 120
Mark, 94, 104, 116, 120
Mary Ann, 95, 106, 116, 120
Mary, 44, 94, 104, 106, 109, 115, 116, 119, 120
Monica, 94
Raphael, 106
Rebecca, 129
Robert, 94, 95, 115, 119, 120
Samuel, 129
Sarah, 106
Susanna, 93, 106, 115, 119
Thomas Alexius, 94, 120
Thomas, 44, 86, 90, 94, 106, 116, 120
Victoria, 43, 44
William, 43, 44, 93, 106, 119
Zachariah, 90
Thornton, Harriet, 111
  Priscilla, 111
  Vincent, 111
Ticklin, Jeremiah, 136
Tierce, Andrew, 104
  Catharine, 104
  Eleanor, 104
Tomkins, Aletha, 107
  John, 104, 107
  Mary Attaway, 104
  Mary, 104, 107
Topin, Elizabeth, 83

Trinity, Providence, 15
Truman, Thomas, 86
Tub, Martha, 16
  Mary Anne, 16
  William, 16
Tucker, Grace, 59
  James, 64
  John, 64, 86
  Priscilla, 58
  Rebekah, 58, 59
  Sarah, 64, 85
  Susannah, 81
  Thomas, 58, 59
Turling, John, 27, 28
Turlon, Catherine, 6
  John, 6
  Mary Ann, 6
  William, 6
Turnbull, James, 117
  John, 117
  Margaret, 117
Turner, Alexander, 21
  Ann, 9, 44
  Anna, 9
  Anne Mary, 21
  Arthur, 44
  Charles, 4, 21
  Deborah, 2, 11, 13, 21
  Dorcas, 2
  Edward, 4, 44
  Eleanor, 4, 21
  Elizabeth, 4, 12, 21, 54, 62, 137
  Heneritta, 12
  Hezekiah, 2, 12
  James, 44
  Johanna, 49, 54
  John, 4, 12, 49, 54, 82
  Joseph, 4
  Joshua, 4
  Lydia, 4

Margaret, 20, 21
Martha, 2, 12
Mary, 4, 9
Randal, 4
Rhoda, 12
Richard, 62
Samuel, 2, 4, 9, 12, 20, 21
Sarah, 62
Sophia, 62
Thomas, 49
Verlinda, 2, 9
William, 4, 12, 20
Zephaniah, 2
____, 11
Tybills, James Theobold, 136
Tymothy, Mabella, 44
William, 44

Uldra, Araminta, 137
Urquahart, Alexander, 55
Ann, 55
James, 55
see Aukhutt
Utley, George, 140

Vanreshwick, see Reshwick
Vanswaringgen, Eleanor, 70
Joseph, 69, 70, 72
Kezia, 72, 84
Margaret, 72
Martha, 70
Vassall, Elizabeth, 44
Levy, 44
Thomas, 44
Vaughn, M. H., Rebv., 138
W. H., Rev, 114
Veatch, Eunis, 54
Jane, 49, 56
Jane, 51, 54
Mary, 49

Virlinnea, 56
William, 49, 52, 54, 56
Venables, Dorcas Wright, 15
Margaret, 15
Mary, 15
Theodore, 15
Vessels, Elijah, 137
Vowles, Ann, 111, 114, 118
Cyrus, 104, 109, 115, 118, 119, 131
Elizabeth, 109
Henry, 111, 114
James, 103, 107
Jane, 115
John, 118
Mary, 104
Matthew, 111, 118
Priscilla, 103, 107
Richard, 107
Sarah, 131
Susanna, 103, 114
Thomas, 114, 119, 134
Victoria, 104, 109, 115, 118, 119, 131
Walter, 114

Wade, Ann, 56
Catherine, 56
Edward, 44
Elizabeth, 56
George, 56
John, 56
Mary, 44
Rachel, 56
Sarah, 44
William, 44
Zachary, 44
Walker, Bowen, 118
Elizabeth, 109, 118
John, 118

Index

Margaret, 109
Mary, 118
Nathaniel, 118
Roger, 109
Ward, Anne, 44, 45
  Damaris, 44, 45
  Hannah, 85
  John, 44, 45
  Mary, 45
Warner, Christopher, 45
  George R., 138
  George R., Rev., 138
  Margaret, 45
Warren, Benjamin, 45
  Britanina, 92
  Charles, 45
  Edward, 92
  Elinor, 45
  Elizabeth, 92
  Hannah, 84
  Humphrey, 23, 45
  John, 45
  Margery, 45
  Mary, 45, 92
  Notley, 45
  Thomas, 45
  William, 92
Waters, Ann, 4, 6, 10, 12, 16, 17, 18
  Anna, 11
  Asenath, 10
  Benjamin, 17
  Bennett, 13
  Deborah, 19
  Dent, 17
  Draden, 18
  Drusilla, 18
  Eda, 17
  Edward, 16
  Elisabeth, 7, 19
  Enos, 16
  George Dement, 17
  Hanson, 16
  Helin, 12
  James, 4, 6, 7, 11, 16, 17, 18, 19
  James, Jr., 10, 12
  James, Sr., 16
  Jane, 17, 19
  Jedidiah, 17
  John, 6
  John, Sr., 16
  Jonathan, 16
  Joseph Manning Dent, 17
  Joseph, 16, 17
  Josias, 16
  Katherine, 17
  Kezia, 17
  Kitty, 18
  Lydia, 17
  Mary, 6, 7
  Milicent, 10, 17
  Orpha, 12
  Phebe, 17
  Priscilla, 17
  Rezin, 16, 18
  Sarah, 6, 16
  Shelah, 13
  Susanna, 4, 16, 17, 19
  Thomas, 7
  William, 4, 16
  Winifred, 13
  Zephaniah, 17, 19
Wathen, Ann, 7, 100, 126
  Bennet, 6
  Elinor, 6
  Francis Hudson, 100, 126
  Henry Hudson, 100, 126
  Hudson, 6, 7
  Martin, 6
  Sarah, 6, 7

Watson, Anne, 82
  Benjamin, 116, 117
  Catherine, 117
  Edward, 135
  Elinor, 115
  Elizabeth, 115
  John, 115
  Mary, 83
  Sarah, 117
  Susanna, 116, 117
  William, 116
Watts, Ann, 107
  Catharine, 137
  Eleanor Delilah, 113
  Eleanor, 112, 113
  George Nelson, 112
  Henry, 138
  Jemima, 107
  Joshua, 112, 113
  Rebecca, 134
  Susannah,, 138
  William, 107
  Willoughby, 107
Webb, Eleanor, 84
Webster, Ann, 59
  John, 59
  Mary, 59
Welch, Elisabeth, 16
Wellman, Elijah, 118
  Elizabeth, 116, 118, 119
  James, 119
  Jared, 116
  Jemima, 118
  Joshua, 116
  Michael, 116, 118, 119, 139
  Rhoda, 118
Wells, Joanna, 137
West, George William, 103
  Susanna, 103
  William, Rev., 103

Wharton, Elizabeth, 45
  Margaret, 45
  Mary, 1
Wheatley, Anastatia, 129
  Ann, 132, 133
  Benedict, 97, 123
  Bernard, 132
  Edmund, 122
  Edward, 96
  Eleanor, 97, 123, 129
  Elizabeth, 132
  George, 132
  Henrietta, 96, 122, 129
  Henry, 132
  Ignatius, 129, 132
  James, 96, 97, 122, 123
  Joseph, 96, 122
  Mary, 133
  Rebecca, 96, 122
  William, 97, 123, 132
Wheeler, Ann, 108
  Francis, 45, 108
  Ignatius, 45
  James, 45
  John, 45
  Luke, 45
  Mary, 45
  Moses, 134
  Roger, 82
  Thomas, 45
  William, 108
  Winifrid, 45
Whichaley, Jane, 45
  Thomas, 45, 46
White, Ann, 11
  Barbara, 87
  Dorothy, 134
  Elizabeth, 50
  Jesse, 110
  Marie, 39, 46

Richard, 50
Thomas, 50, 82
Veache, 110
William, 110
Whittingham, Miss, 140
Whittymore, Anne, 46
  Christopher, 46
  Richard, 46
Wible, Francis, 138
  Henrietta, 138
  Henry Cornelius, 138
Wilde, Mary, 82
Wilder, Edward, 13, 14, 46
  Elizabeth, 14
  Ever Elday, 46
  John, 46
  Margaret, 14
  Mary, 14
  Susannah, 14
Wildey, William, 138
Wilkinson, Ann, 118
  Eliner, 11
  James, 89
  Lancelot, 46
  Mark Thomas, 118
  Mary Thomas, 89
  Mary, 46, 54, 118
  Nancy, 89, 118
  Rebecca, 54
  Richard, 85
  Sarah, 82
  William, 46, 54, 89, 118
  Winifred, 89
Williams, Ann, 6, 54
  Elizabeth, 6
  Esther, 5
  Francis, 54
  Hannah, 83
  James, 5
  John, 46, 55, 79, 81

  Joseph, 83
  Justinian, 5
  Mary, 134
  Rebecca, 83, 86
  Sarah, 46, 54, 55, 79
  Thomas, 6
  William, 46, 54, 55
Williamson, James, Rev., 60
  John, 83
Willin, Keziah, 86
  Mary, 86
  Thomas, 86
Willis, John, 54
  Martha, 54
  Mary, 54
  Richard, 54
  Samuel, 54
Wilson, Elisabeth, 81
  James, 86
  John, 76
  Mary, 76, 81
  Nathaniel, 85
  Sarah, 82
Wimsatt, Ann, 95, 121
  Elizabeth, 95, 121
  Frances, 107
  Henrietta, 90, 95, 121
  John, 90, 95, 121
  Joseph Zachariah, 107
  Mary, 107
  Ralph, 95, 121
  Robert Henry, 95, 121
  William, 95, 121
Winnul, Elizabeth, 59
  John, 59, 81
  Sarah, 59
  William, 59
Winter, Eleanor, 9
  Elisabeth Bruce, 7
  Elizabeth, 6, 7, 8, 9

Ignatius, 8
John, 6, 7, 8, 9
Judith Townley, 6
Walter, 6
___lish?, 6
Wise, Adam, 90, 110, 112, 130, 135
   Allethea, 111
   Caleb, 89, 137
   Catharine, 137
   Charles, 112
   Clarke, 90
   Cuthbert, 88
   Dorcas, 92
   Dorothy, 89
   Edward Swann, 92
   Eleanah, 112
   Eleanor, 90
   Frances, 90, 110, 130
   George, 110, 112, 113, 138
   Henrietta, 118, 136
   James Clinton, 113
   James Manning, 90
   James, 90, 111
   Jane, 89
   Jemima, 92
   Jeremiah, 117
   John Clinton, 113
   John, 88, 90, 113, 130
   Joseph Adam, 112
   Joseph, 118
   Margaret, 88, 90, 136
   Mary, 89, 112, 113, 117, 119
   Nancy, 118
   Patty, 138
   Ransean, 119
   Rhode, 90
   Richard, 89
   Sarah, 118
   Sophia, 112, 113
   Thomas, 117, 119
   William Cornelius Francis, 111
   William Robert, 112
   William, 134
Wiseman, Robert, 136
Witter, Buckley, 46
   George, 46
   Mary, 46
   Thomas, 46
   William, 46
Wollcock, Christian, 46
Wolstenholme, Daniel, 137
Wood, Anne, 7
   Dorothy, 8
   Edward, 85
   Elisabeth, 19, 81, 86
   James, 12
   Jesse, 85
   Mary, 19
   Peter, 19
   Rebeccah Miles, 77
   Sabret, 77
   Sarah, 12, 77
   Susanna, 86
   Walter, 12
Woodward, Dorcas, 85
   Monica, 136
Woolcock, Christopher, 46
   Mary, 46
Woolingham, Ann, 95, 121
   Appolonia, 95, 121
   John Baptist, 95, 121
   John, 95, 121
Wootton, Bennet, 101, 127
   Elizabeth, 89, 130
   Frances, 101, 127
   Isaac, 101, 127
   John, 89
   Joseph, 89
   Mary, 89

Susanna, 101, 127
Thomas, 89, 101, 127, 130, 136
Worrell, Margaret, 46
Robert, 46
Wright, Anne, 46
Elinor, 46
George, 46
Wynne, Elizabeth, 46
Thomas, 46

Yates, Charles, 46
Rebeckah, 46
Robert, 46
Yoe, Ann, 79, 87
Benjamin Skinner, 79
Benjamin, 79
Catharine, 79
Hariet, 79
James, 79
John, 79, 79
Mary, 79
Robert, 79
Susannah, 79
Walter, 79
William, 79
Young, Ann, 58, 82, 100
Eleanor, 60
Elizabeth, 50, 58
Francis, 67
George Parker, 68
George, 58, 85
George, Jr., 50, 54, 59
Grace, 58, 83
Henry, 58
James, 100
Jane, 67
John Abell, 100
John Standfill, 101
John, 47, 60, 61
Lawrence, 47

Mary Grace, 58
Mary, 50, 54, 59, 60, 61, 68
Miles, 73
Parker, 59, 67, 68
Parker, 73
Phillemon, 58
Rebekah, 58
Richard, 60, 61
Samuel, 58
Sarah, 47, 59, 67, 68, 73
Susanna, 81
Thomas, 47, 73
William Miles, 68
William, 58
Younger, Joseph, 86

www.ingramcontent.com/pod-product-compliance
Lightning Source LLC
Chambersburg PA
CBHW051055160426
43193CB00010B/1187